EVALUATING METHODOLOGY
IN INTERNATIONAL STUDIES

MILLENNIAL REFLECTIONS ON INTERNATIONAL STUDIES

EVALUATING METHODOLOGY IN INTERNATIONAL STUDIES

Edited by

Frank P. Harvey and Michael Brecher

Ann Arbor

THE UNIVERSITY OF MICHIGAN PRESS

Published in the United States of America by
The University of Michigan Press
Printed and bound by CPI Group (UK) Ltd, Croydon, CR0 4YY

2005 2004 2003 2002   4 3 2 1

*A CIP catalog record for this book is available from
the British Library.*

Library of Congress Cataloging-in-Publication Data applied for
ISBN 978-0-472-08861-4

ISBN13 978-0-472-08861-4 (paperback)
ISBN13 978-0-472-02366-0 (electronic)

ACKNOWLEDGMENTS

The editors would like to thank the distinguished scholars who contributed to this project for their gracious response to our demands over an extended period. We are very grateful to Jeremy Shine, political science editor of the University of Michigan Press, for his encouragement and support; to the International Studies Association for the opportunity to organize the millennial reflections panels at the Los Angeles conference in March 2000; to Ann Griffiths and Graham Walker for their excellent editorial assistance; to Kevin Rennells, of the University of Michigan Press, and to Impressions Book and Journal Services, for steering this multivolume project to publication with skill and empathy; and to Sarah Lemann for valuable word-processing assistance in the preparation of the typescript.

Frank Harvey would like to thank Michael Brecher for the privilege of serving as ISA program chair in 1999–2000 and for his truly outstanding contribution to the intellectual quality of the final manuscript, the Social Sciences and Humanities Research Council of Canada, the Centre for Foreign Policy Studies (Dalhousie University), and the Security and Defence Forum (Directorate of Public Policy, Department of National Defence, Canada) for supporting various stages of the project. Michael Brecher wishes to thank Frank Harvey for his selfless and invaluable role as coeditor of the Millennial Reflections Project. He also appreciates the reduced teaching load accorded by McGill University for the autumn term of 1999, which facilitated the organization of the millennial reflections panels and, more generally, the ISA's Los Angeles conference in March 2000.

CONTENTS

The Essence of Millennial Reflections on International Studies

Methodology

Michael Brecher and Frank P. Harvey

When Michael Brecher was introduced to international relations (IR) at Yale in 1946, the field comprised international politics, international law and organization, international economics, international (diplomatic) history, and a regional specialization. The hegemonic paradigm was realism, as expressed in the work of E. H. Carr, Arnold Wolfers, Nicholas Spykman, W. T. R. Fox, Hans Morgenthau, Bernard Brodie, and others.[1] The unquestioned focus of attention was interstate war and peace.

By the time the other editor of this collection, Frank Harvey, was initiated into international relations at McGill in the late 1980s, the preeminent paradigm was neorealism,[2] but there were several competing claimants to the "true path": institutional theory,[3] cognitive psychology,[4] and postmodernism.[5] And by the time he received his doctoral degree, other competitors had emerged, notably, critical theory,[6] constructivism,[7] and feminism.[8]

The consequence, at the dawn of the new millennium, was a vigorous, still inconclusive, debate about the optimal path to knowledge about international studies (IS), most clearly expressed in the views that it is a discipline—international relations (IR) or world politics—like economics, sociology, anthropology, history, or that it is a multidisciplinary field of study; the "big tent" conception of the premier organization, the International Studies Association (ISA).

It was in this context that the Millennial Reflections Project was conceived. The origin and rationale of the idea may be found in the central theme of Michael Brecher's presidential address to the ISA conference in Washington in February 1999: "International Studies in the Twentieth Century and Beyond: Flawed Dichotomies, Synthesis, Cumulation." The next stage was the creation of a set of ten millennial reflections theme-panels by Michael Brecher, then ISA president, and Frank Harvey, the program chair for ISA 2000: these panels served as the highly successful centerpiece of the Los Angeles conference in March 2000. Soon after, we enlisted the enthusiastic support of the University of Michigan Press for the idea of publishing revised and enlarged versions of these conference papers. Most of the participants in the Los Angeles panels readily agreed to revise and enlarge their papers. A few other papers were invited. The result is this volume and the accompanying set of four shorter, segment-focused volumes, prepared for the benefit of teachers and students of IS in colleges and universities everywhere.

Whether a discipline or a multidisciplinary field of study, IS has developed over the last half century with diverse philosophical underpinnings, frameworks of analysis, methodologies, and foci of attention. This diversity is evident in the papers that were presented at the panels at the 2000 Los Angeles conference and revised for publication in this state-of-the-art collection of essays on international studies at the dawn of the new millennium.

In an attempt to capture the range, diversity, and complexity of IS, we decided to organize the forty-four "think piece" essays into eight clusters. The mainstream paradigms of realism and institutionalism constitute the first two concentrations; critical perspectives (including critical theory, postmodernism, and constructivism); feminism and gender perspectives; methodology (including quantitative, formal modeling, and qualitative); foreign policy analysis; international security, peace, and war; and international political economy make up the remaining six.

The raison d'être of the Millennial Reflections Project was set out in the theme statement of the Los Angeles conference, titled "Reflection, Integration, Cumulation: International Studies Past and Future." As we noted in that statement, the number and size of subfields and sections has grown steadily since the founding of the International Studies Association in 1959. This diversity, while enriching, has made increasingly difficult the crucial task of identifying intrasubfield, let alone intersubfield, consensus about important theoretical and empirical insights. Aside from focusing on a cluster of shared research questions related, for example, to globalization, gender and international relations, critical theory, political economy, international institutions, global development, democracy and peace, foreign and security policy, and so on, there are still few clear signs of cumulation.

If the maturity of an academic discipline is based not only on its capacity to expand but also on its capacity to select, the lack of agreement *within* these communities is particularly disquieting. Realists, for instance, cannot fully agree on their paradigm's core assumptions, central postulates, or the lessons learned from empirical research. Similarly, feminist epistemologies encompass an array of research programs and findings that are not easily grouped into a common set of beliefs, theories, or conclusions. If those who share common interests and perspectives have difficulty agreeing on what they have accomplished to date or do not concern themselves with the question of what has been achieved so far, how can they establish clear targets to facilitate creative dialogue across these diverse perspectives and subfields?

With this in mind, our objective was to challenge proponents of specific paradigms, theories, approaches, and substantive issue areas to confront their own limitations by engaging in self-critical reflection within epistemologies and perspectives. The objective was to stimulate debates about successes and failures but to do so by avoiding the tendency to define accomplishments with reference to the failures and weaknesses of other perspectives.

It is important to note that our call to assess the state of the art of international studies was not meant as a reaffirmation of the standard proposition that a rigorous process of theoretical cumulation is both possible and necessary. Not all perspectives and subfields of IS are directed to accomplishing cumulation in this sense. Some participants found the use of such words as *synthesis* and *progress* suspect, declaring in their original papers that they could not, or were not prepared to, address these social science–type questions. We nevertheless encouraged these individuals to define what they considered to be fair measures of success and failure in regard to their subfield, and we asked them to assess the extent to which core objectives (whatever they may be) have or have not been met, and why.

Our intention obviously was not to tie individuals to a particular set of methodological tenets, standards, assumptions, or constraints.

We simply wanted to encourage self-reflective discussion and debate about significant achievements and failures. Even where critiques of mainstream theory and methodology are part of a subfield's raison d'être, the lack of consensus is still apparent and relevant.

As a community of scholars, we are rarely challenged to address the larger question of *success* and *progress* (however one chooses to define these terms), perhaps because there is so little agreement on the methods and standards we should use to identify and integrate important observations, arguments, and findings.

To prevent intellectual diversity descending into intellectual anarchy, the editors set out "guidelines" for the contributors, in the form of six theme questions, or tasks. The panelists were requested to address one or more of these tasks in their essays:

1. Engage in self-critical, state-of-the-art reflection on accomplishments and failures, especially since the creation of the ISA more than forty years ago.
2. Assess where we stand on unresolved debates and why we have failed to resolve them.
3. Evaluate the intrasubfield standards we should use to assess the significance of theoretical insights.
4. Explore ways to achieve fruitful synthesis of approaches, both in terms of core research questions and appropriate methodologies.
5. Address the broader question of progress in international studies.
6. Select an agenda of topics and research questions that should guide the subfield during the coming decades.

The result, as is evident in the pages to follow, is an array of thought-provoking think pieces that indicate shortcomings as well as achievements and specify the unfinished business of IS as a scholarly field in the next decade or more, with wide-ranging policy implications in the shared quest for world order. Readers will no doubt derive different conclusions from the various contributions. Some will observe that divisions within and across subfields of international studies are so entrenched that constructive dialogue is virtually impossible. Others will conclude that there is much more consensus than might have been imagined. In either case, the need for self-critical assessment among IS scholars is imperative as we enter the new millennium.

Methodology

The reflections on methodology comprise nine papers on formal modeling (Michael Nicholson, Harvey Starr, Bruce Bueno de Mesquita, Steven Brams), quantitative methods (Dina Zinnes, James Lee Ray, Russell Leng), and qualitative methods (Jack Levy, Zeev Maoz).

Nicholson

The purpose of Michael Nicholson's overview of "Formal Methods in International Relations" is "to discuss the principles behind formalization . . . [and] to justify its extensive use mainly by conceptual argument and by referring very briefly to some of the achievements . . . [which] are genuine," as well as to spell out future directions. The tone is modest throughout: Nicholson does not claim that all aspects of IR, only "some very important problems in the discipline," must be formalized to achieve progress.

The core of his argument is stated concisely: natural languages are good at description but "awkward and clumsy" for deductive argument; formal languages, notably mathematics, are the reverse. Moreover, theories involve deductive arguments, ergo, they need mathematical methods. In that context, he defines formal modeling as "the use of mathematical, diagrammatic, and symbolic methods in the study of problems in international relations." He adds that because the ultimate purpose of theory is to describe the real world, formal and statistical methods are closely related.

Nicholson surveys some notable applications of game theory to IR in the area of decisions and choice. He cites the pioneering contributions of Schelling, Boulding, and Rapoport, followed by a relative drought until the hostility models of Zinnes and her associates and Brams's theory of moves. He pays special tribute to the innovative role of Richardson in both formal modeling—notably models of arms races and hostility—and statistical methods from 1919 until the early 1950s.

His rationale for using mathematical methods in IR is that they have proved very successful in other disciplines—notably physics, but also in economics—within the social sciences. And these methods became central in social scientific inquiry with Hempel's covering law of explanation. He rejects the counterargument that IR is different and is better served by natural languages, claiming that stating a problem formally may uncover important findings that would otherwise be concealed.

As for the future of formal methods, Nicholson remains refreshingly modest: "All we can do is suggest some plausible lines of progress that may be shown in the future to have been good or bad guesses. . . . As theory advances, it is more likely to become more deductively complex than less. . . . simulation methods will be used more frequently, and . . . these will generate a whole set of quasi-experimental worlds."

Because this is so, he urges formal modelers to make a special effort to communicate their findings effectively to readers who lack the training or interest in these methods. He also reiterates the limited use of formal analysis. And he concludes with an important cautionary note to his colleagues: "We must, at all cost, avoid becoming a mathematical priesthood purporting to dispense knowledge from behind a secure barrier of incomprehensibility."

Starr

There are two recurring themes in Harvey Starr's reflections on "Cumulation, Synthesis, and Research Design for the Post–Fourth Wave." One is the importance of the "research triad"—theory, logic, and method—and the centrality of theory: it "must be at the forefront of our endeavors, whatever the subfield or . . . the methodology employed." The second is his emphasis on "an agent-structure theoretical framework. . . . I continue to see that approach as the most useful way to synthesize across levels of analysis, disciplines, and different forms of causal relationships."

Starr also reaffirms the importance and relevance of his "opportunity-willingness" concept, based on the work of Harold and Margaret Sprout: he terms it "simply one version of a more general agent-structure approach." That approach and concept leads him to renew the view that "the current treatment of the agent-structure problem in the international relations literature is problematic . . . [and to criticize] the confusion among ontological, epistemological, and methodological issues and analyses." He also cites their "methodological individualist model," which is congenial to models of choice, such as expected utility and prospect theory.

In this context, he discusses three challenges. One is "due to the lack of variance within the opportunity structure," that is, insufficient cases. To cope with this problem he urges the wider use of simulations because they "permit the control and experimentation necessary to look for causal relationships . . . [, to assess] a model for its internal consistency, and to examine the plausibility of its assumptions."

The second challenge is "how [to] construct research designs to deal with the logical differences between models of necessity and sufficiency." The controversy over deterrence illustrates for Starr the problem in studying necessity: there is nothing to observe if deterrence is successful, but failed deterrence can be observed. Thus critics focus on deterrence failures and conclude they are solving the *not-y* problem; they also conclude that rational deterrence theory does not predict to successful deterrence—but their logic is flawed.

The third challenge is how to investigate "substitutability," which is closely related to opportunity and willingness: it "indicates that any single cause may have multiple effects, and that any single effect may have multiple causes. Different problems may lead to similar responses . . . [and] a given problem may be dealt with in multiple ways. . . . Substitutability . . . thus lies at the heart of . . . agent-structure frameworks."

Starr concludes that "cumulation and 'progress' [in IR] will depend on the quality and rigor of our theories and our methods." The latter must facilitate our entry into "the continuous feedback loops between agent and structure . . . [, enable us to] design studies of necessity . . . [and of] phenomena that do not occur . . . [and of] substitutability. . . . Formal models . . . will most certainly constitute the main analytical approach of the post-fourth wave [following Deutsch's four waves—international law, then diplomatic history and international organization, behavioral sciences, and analytic and quantitative research], as a natural means to synthesize agency and structure, and choice (willingness) given constraints (opportunity)."

Bueno de Mesquita

Bruce Bueno de Mesquita's "Accomplishments and Limitations of a Game-Theoretic Approach to International Relations" provides "one person's views . . . focusing . . . on broad patterns and generalizations."

The bulk of his paper is devoted to five contributions of game theory: "(1) the provision of a motivational foundation for action; (2) an explanation of strategic behavior; (3) an ability to integrate other theories and approaches; (4) cumulative knowledge; and (5) insights into methodological issues influencing analyses of decision making."

The merit of illuminating a motive for action is "that the link between correlation and causation is readily discerned." As for "problems involving strategic choice—and this surely includes most interesting problems in international relations—game theory is significantly advantaged over other approaches." In particular, "psychological theories lack an equivalent to game theory's notion of equilibrium . . . and are unable at this time to achieve the subtlety of game theoretic accounts when choices involve strategy or the transmission of private information."

At the same time, game theoretic models can incorporate "the concerns and assumptions of structural, behavioral, constructivist, and psychological theories . . . while retaining the logical rigor imposed by [game theory's] axiomatic foundations." Bueno de Mesquita acknowledges that no methodology has a monopoly over cumulating knowledge about IR. At the same time, he claims an advantage for game theory: "explicit assumptions make it easy to determine what the logical consequences are of relaxing one or another condition, substituting alternative assumptions, or . . . adding new assumptions. . . . In this way, anomalous cases can be carefully explored, modified theories constructed . . . while also uncovering new facts."

The fifth contribution relates to methodological insights: "endogeneity, selection effects, independence between argument and evidence, and prediction represent areas where rational choice models are especially helpful in clarifying empirical problems that frequently arise in other modes of analysis." In substantive terms, Bueno de Mesquita notes a game theory contribution to understanding many important topics in IR: alliance formation, reliability, and termination; the democratic peace; deterrence; economic sanctions; and paths to cooperation.

He acknowledges that "game theory endures significant limitations": some may be overcome with improved knowledge; others are "inherent to the approach." However, his discussion of shortcomings is limited to two aspects—information and multiple equilibria. As for the first, "games assume that everyone knows what the prior beliefs held by others are, whether they agree with them or not"; but this information assumption is a constraint that may undermine the analysis of expected behavior. The multiple equilibria problem is more serious: "game theory can predict a probability distribution over actions but cannot say definitively when one action or another will be taken provided each such action is part of an equilibrium strategy."

On the whole, however, Bueno de Mesquita's assessment is markedly positive about the contribution of this methodology to IR.

Brams

"Game Theory in Practice: Problems and Prospects in Applying It to International Relations" comprises three sections: a brief discussion of shortcomings in classical game theory; a presentation of Steven Brams's alternative approach, the theory of moves (TOM); and its application to President Sadat's peace initiative to Israel in 1977.

The first of four "major pitfalls . . . [is] misspecifying the rules." Using as a "reality check" the idea that "any game-theoretic models . . . should propose rules of play that reflect how players think and act in the strategic situation being modeled," Brams asserts: "Players do not usually . . . choose strategies simultaneously, or independently of each other, as assumed in the normal or strategic form of a game that can be represented by a payoff matrix; [or] adhere to a specified sequence of choices, as assumed in the extensive form of a game that can be represented by a game tree."

The second problem is "confusing goals with rational choice. . . . Rationality does not concern the ends themselves, which are neither rational nor irrational." The third is "arbitrarily reducing the multiplicity of equilibria . . . [for] many games have multiple Nash equilibria . . . [and] a game-theoretic model may not be helpful in narrowing down a plethora of stable outcomes to a few precise predictions." And finally, he criticizes "forsaking backward induction," noting that "real players do not painstakingly work backward from the endpoints of a game tree. . . . Rather, players develop heuristics and use rules of thumb that simplify this process."

The merits of his corrective approach, which is briefly summarized, are clearly stated by Brams: "In my view, the rules of TOM, which allow players to move and countermove within a payoff matrix, capture the changing strategic nature of situations that evolve over time. TOM's ability, as well, to incorporate differences in power—moving, order, or threat—reflects an asymmetry of player capabilities in many IR games."

In his application of TOM to Sadat's 1977 peace initiative, Brams argues that what led Sadat to so act was not merely the "psychological barrier" between Arabs and Israelis, which the Egyptian leader emphasized in his memoirs, but also a rational calculus of choice for both adversaries: to initiate or not to initiate, for Sadat, to cooperate or not to cooperate, for Begin.

He spells out the four possible outcomes: (1) Israel cooperates by offering concessions before Egypt commits to a permanent end to the conflict (the worst payoff for Israel and the best for Egypt); (2) no peace initiative is offered, which means continued Israeli occupation of Sinai (the next worst payoff for Egypt and the next best for Israel because it gets continued security but at a high price); (3) Israel doesn't cooperate with Sadat's initiative (the worst outcome for Egypt and not very satisfactory for Israel because of the likely loss of U.S. support and the likelihood of another war); and (4) Israel responds positively to Sadat's initiative (the best outcome for Israel, that is, the likelihood of permanent peace with the most powerful Arab state, and the next best for Egypt, that is, peace and the end of the drain on Egypt's resources, but alienation of the Arab world). As became evident soon after the peace treaty was signed in 1979 and since then, Sadat's initiative and Begin's response were rational and beneficial acts by the two adversaries.

Brams concludes: "What TOM offers that classical game theory does not is a simple and dynamic rationale for the players' making their moves and countermoves. . . . In specific games, it provides detailed prescriptions for optimal play . . . that could aid foreign policy decision makers, especially in crises." But, Brams writes, "TOM is no panacea." It works best in two-person games, but many IR situations, such as alliance behavior, require modeling as n-person games, that is, a more general dynamic theory.

Zinnes

In "Reflections on Quantitative International Politics," Dina Zinnes is skeptical about the relevance of the millennial reflections theme questions to this methodological strand of IR. Instead, she presents "more of a personal statement about where we have been, where we seem to be going, and what we need to consider in the decades ahead." To answer her first two questions she initiated a survey of six academic journals from 1990 to 1999 to discover whether there were differences in the use of statistics and mathematical modeling.

The findings, presented in table 1, are instructive: first, except for the *Journal of Peace Research*, especially from 1990 to 1994, most of the published work in IR uses statistics, mathematical modeling, or both; second, quantitative research increased or, in the *Interna-*

tional Studies Quarterly, remained unchanged; third, quantitative work took the form mostly of statistical analysis; fourth, game theory was the dominant form of mathematical modeling; and finally, few quantitative articles contained both strands.

As for the future, quantitative international politics seems likely to move increasingly to statistical analysis, and modeling is expected to remain primarily game theoretic. The first anticipated trend Zinnes finds "disturbing" because she questions the adequacy of generating theory through a statistical analysis of data: "We have reduced what may have been a rich interpretation of the international world to an often uninteresting if-then statement. . . . we are replacing possible explanation with far less interesting statements about what is associated with what. . . . in actual fact it might reasonably be argued that we have become less theoretical."

This view leads her to make a strong plea for greater use of mathematical models in the years ahead. And, to that end, she maps out a precise three-step program: first, "move statistics courses out of the limelight of graduate programs" and get incoming students to think in terms of puzzles "and teach the student how to 'tell stories' that fit these anomalies into what we know about the way the world works"; second, teach students how to translate stories into a mathematical language; and only then turn to statistics to test the story (theory).

Similarly, Zinnes questions the overwhelming reliance on game theory: while it "is an excellent modeling language for capturing conflictual decision-theoretic situations . . . not all stories involve rational actors." Moreover, even if her view of theorizing, that is, "telling stories about puzzles," and translating the stories into a mathematical language were achieved, this would not be sufficient. To close the circle, the mathematical model must be tested—that is, "story and data must meet." Thus, even after decades in the forefront of quantitative international politics, Zinnes concludes, "we have a long way to go in making our ideas, our theories explicit and an even longer way before we understand how to test our models."

Ray

James Lee Ray's "Reflections on Millennia, Old and New: The Evolution and Role of Quantitative Approaches to the Study of International Politics" focuses on two questions: "Where have we been?" and "Where are we (and where should we be) going?" His survey of

the past draws on evidence from Rosenau's two important editions
of *International Politics and Foreign Policy*, published in 1961 and
1969, to make several pertinent observations: first, the 1950s were
dominated by the idealist-realist debate, while the 1960s shifted
attention to the "behavioralist revolution"; second, this change has
deeper roots—it is evident in IR works during the 1950s by Richard
Snyder, North and his associates, Deutsch, Benson, and Rapoport advocating, respectively, game theory, content analysis, quantitative
studies, computer simulations, and formal modeling; third, the theme
of continuity is emphasized, that is, "the more things change, the
more they remain the same," notably the persistence of idealism versus realism, in a different garb, and the enduring debate over the merits of formal/quantitative and qualitative methods of analysis; and
fourth, Ray notes the attention to economic issues and variables in
IR from the 1970s onward, which he regards as "real, tangible progress."

Ray also discerns "important insights" into quantitative IR from
research on the democratic peace since the 1960s, which he surveys
briefly. He quotes, approvingly, Vasquez's view that it is a "source of
inspiration for a 'rebirth' of . . . quantitative approaches." Moreover,
he attributes the enormous growth of this literature in the 1990s not
only to the spread of democracy after the cold war but also to vast
improvements in the quality of evidence, the coherence of its theoretical structure, and the availability of large computerized data sets.

His most novel "insight" relates to the theoretical impact of research on the democratic peace, likely to be as important as the evidence on the absence of war between democratic adversaries. Specifically, he cites the view of Bueno de Mesquita and associates that
state behavior in conflict is motivated more by the wish of leaders
to stay in power than the search for power or security per se; and
this, in turn, facilitates the integration of domestic and international
factors in explaining foreign policy and international politics, as pos-
tulated in Putnam's "two-level games" concept.

Turning to the future, Ray welcomes the broadening of the IR
agenda in the last two decades to include class, ethnicity, gender,
and the Third World. At the same time, he is critical of their "miscommunication, misperceptions, and misunderstandings."

Quantitative IR, he contends, is not free from these flaws. Moreover, he confesses to being "confused about the ideal model or theory
or product toward which large-N analysts are striving": "[an] extra-
large multivariate equation? A set of simultaneous equations? A com-

puter simulation? What?" And he is critical of the claim to total objectivity by quantitative IR specialists, calling on them to state clearly the aim of their research. At the same time, he is skeptical of postmodernist attacks on the statecentric model of mainstream IR and democracy: he cites Booth's remark, "The enemy is us. Western consumerist [capitalist] democracy . . . is the problem," and urges advocates of critical perspectives to clarify what they propose in its place.

Leng

Much of Russell Leng's "Quantitative International Politics and Its Critics: Then and Now" takes the form of a debate with one of the earliest and most visible IR antiscience classicists. In a celebrated critique thirty-five years ago, Hedley Bull dismissed quantitative IR and its findings as marginal and its challenge to the classical—historical and philosophical—approach as "positively harmful." Leng notes that regrettably during the first two decades of what Karl Deutsch termed the "fourth wave" of IR research—that is, the application of quantitative methods—"the only cross-fertilization between the two fields was in the form of mudslinging."

Bull's criticism was threefold: quantitative international politics research questions are—and are destined to remain—trivial because they are confined to aspects of IR that are measurable; it fails to cumulate knowledge; and methodological training of students is at the expense of access to the insights of classical scholarship. Leng responds to each of these points.

Citing the self-doubt expressed by Thucydides about the reliability of his sources on the Peloponnesian Wars, Leng comments, "Issues of descriptive validity and reliability continue to be a problem in classical historical research. . . . A major advantage of the scientific approach is its methodological explicitness, its replicability."

He acknowledges that scientific research on world politics (quantitative international politics) has been unduly influenced by data availability and, further, that some aspects, normative and legal issues, are not accessible to scientific research. However, he claims that qualitative judgments are aided by empirical findings. Similarly, while accepting the postmodernist claim that research can never be entirely free from preconceptions, the effort to narrow the gap "distinguishes scientific research from pamphleteering." And he invokes Weber's view that "the first presupposition of science is that the scientific method is valid."

As for Bull's second criticism, Leng responds vigorously, "We now know a great deal about war per se": when it has occurred; its magnitude, intensity, severity, evolution over time, and relationship to structural changes in the international system; the fact that democracies do not go to war against each other; that a few states account for a large proportion of wars; that disputes over territory are a very frequent cause of war; and so on. And these findings, argues Leng, are not trivial. Yet they are only "islands of findings," in Guetzkow's language, still in quest of an explanatory theory of war.

Leng finds "some validity" in Bull's third criticism—"the scientific study of world politics could lead to an emphasis on methods over content" and the danger that students will not acquire the "feel" for the political and historical content of the subject matter of world politics; and, he adds, there is "the danger of dogmatism regarding what qualifies as acceptable knowledge." Leng makes an intriguing comparison between quantitative international politics findings on war and research findings on coronary artery disease, and he views the former as no less persuasive than the latter. However, its policy relevance, unlike medical findings, depends on the political agenda of states.

Like Ray, he discusses the democratic peace thesis and notes the criticisms of the alleged spurious correlation—that democracies often do not share borders, are wealthy and thus satisfied with the status quo, and are more likely to be members of international organizations. Acknowledging that definitive proof of the validity of either major explanation, cultural or structural, is not yet possible, he cites the quest for indirect indicators. And on this point he concludes: "The scientific frontier is a contentious place. . . . [In the Darwinian tradition] no new finding is accepted without challenge, and only the most robust survive."

His concluding remarks are optimistic: "over the past decade some of the competitiveness has lost its edge, and there is a growing tendency to combine classical and scientific approaches"; he anticipates an end to their cold war through "an unconscious integrative solution."

Levy

Jack S. Levy's wide-ranging assessment of "Qualitative Methods in International Relations" begins by noting a marked change—for the better—during the last three decades. In 1970 qualitative analysis was "historically specific rather than theoretically driven"; and its "ideographic nature" created an image as "highly subjective, pliable in fitting facts to theoretical arguments, nonreplicable, and essentially nonfalsifiable. . . . By the early 1990s, the [new, scientific] methodology of comparative and case study analysis had a well-defined place in the fields of comparative and international politics."

The closely interrelated foci of Levy's paper are "the meaning of the case concept, the different kinds and purposes of case studies, the different types of case study designs for testing theories, and the distinctive contributions and limitations of case study methods." A "case" for Levy and, in his view, for most scholars is "an *instance* of something else, of a theoretically defined class of events. . . . [Moreover, cases] are made, not found; invented, not discovered." He discusses several typologies of case studies, notably Lijphart's atheoretical, interpretive, hypothesis-generating, theory-confirming, theory-infirming, and deviant case studies and Eckstein's configurative-ideographic, disciplined configurative, heuristic, and crucial case studies, as well as the additional category of plausibility probe.

Levy aligns himself with Achen and Snidal's view that dependable theory requires a more deductive orientation than case studies can provide. However, he notes several ways in which case studies can contribute to theory: hypothesis-generating case studies help to refine existing hypotheses; plausibility probes link hypothesis construction and hypothesis testing; deviant case studies "can help to identify omitted variables, interaction effects, or causal paths," as can the analysis of the dependent variable. In sum, case studies play "an essential role in the explanation of individual historical episodes and a contributory role in the generation of hypotheses . . . [as well as] to test hypotheses and theories."

Levy evaluates several varieties of case selection strategies: "most different" and "most similar" systems designs, which he considers comparable to John Stuart Mill's "method of agreement" and "method of difference," respectively (like most analysts, he favors "a careful selection of nonrandom cases" for the analysis of a limited number of cases); "no variance" designs, which are especially limiting; the crucial case strategy advocated by Eckstein, which is linked to "most likely" or "least likely" research designs; and the "process-tracing" method advocated by George, which he regards as fruitful, but he notes the problem raised by Hume, that is, "the logical impossibility of establishing causality from empirical observation."

Along with his overall positive evaluation of case study methods, Levy notes "rather serious limitations. . . . One is the large number of variables relative to the small number of cases. . . . A related problem is that case study methods cannot easily get at 'probabilistic' theories . . . a major strength of statistical analysis and a serious limitation of small-n research. . . . Case study methods also have difficulty in assessing the relative causal weights of the various factors influencing a particular outcome."

Levy is also aware that "statistical methods have their own limitations" and notes that many advocates of case study and statistical methods call for combining the two methods of analysis, though he deplores the few efforts to elaborate how this can be accomplished effectively. Beyond this technical task, he concludes that the most important challenge for qualitative researchers is to develop strong theory and "to think more carefully about the testable implications of existing theories, in terms of quality as well as quantity . . . at the juncture of theory and research design."

Maoz

In an in-depth critique, "Case Study Methodology in International Studies: From Storytelling to Hypothesis Testing," Zeev Maoz focuses "on three aspects . . . that are symptomatic of the misuse of this methodology . . . case selection, case design, and cross-case comparison" and offers suggestions for improving the case study approach.

He begins by noting some advantages of case study as a research method. It is "cost-effective"—that is, it enables "exploratory analyses at relatively low cost of resources." Moreover, "the actual ability to match a hypothetical story that contains an explicit process derived from the theory with an actual story [process tracing] is a unique feature of the case study method." It also has "the ability to uncover nonevents and their characteristics." And "systematic comparison of processes may reveal unspecified features of the theory, even theories that were supported by quantitative evidence." At the same time, Maoz deplores the paucity of cumulation in case studies of politics generally.

Maoz's discussion of case selection contains an unconcealed criticism of many case studies "for freeform research where everything goes": authors do not specify their research method; the criteria for selection of a case or several cases; their choice, processing, and analysis of data; and how their sweeping generalizations and lessons were derived from the case study, what he terms "heroic inferences." In sum, "case selection entails the risk of selection bias and thus of resultant inferential bias." To correct this shortcoming, he offers some principles of a "rational case selection strategy in case study design": "Understand your theory. Lay out the hypotheses and spell out their status"—x as a necessary or sufficient condition of y, or both. "Define what kind of variability is required to test your theory. . . . Identify potentially confounding variables. . . . Explicitly define your population. . . . Attempt, as far as possible, to determine how the population is distributed on the confounding variables."

Maoz cites case design as "the key difference between exploratory and confirmatory case studies." He defines "the art of case study design [as]—to a large extent—the art of reconstruction." And he emphasizes that in confirmatory research, where "the design of the case is theory driven . . . the design . . . must be based on both a priori specification of evidence *for* the theory and evidence *against* the theory," as well as identify the areas of competing and converging expectations.

Using deterrence as an illustration, his guide to "a good case study" requires specifying evidence that a challenger intended to alter the status quo by force; "identifying the deterrence effort and its operational manifestations"; identifying evidence that the challenger has received and absorbed the threat; identifying evidence that the threat was considered in the challenger's decision-making process; identifying evidence that the deterrent threat altered the calculus of decision; identifying that the challenger decided not to violate the status quo, thereby making this a "'candidate' case for deterrence success." But he emphasizes "the significance of testing evidence for a theory against competing explanations."

In his methodological critique, he also attaches importance to cross-case comparison, noting as "a necessary condition for generalization . . . a systematic design of individual cases and the execution of case studies in a manner that allows a fair comparison." To that end he specifies several "basic principles" or guidelines of comparative case design: recognize that all cases have common and unique elements that need to be sorted out; maintain transparency; devise a cross-comparative design; "define standards of inference from multiple cases in light of possible variability in results across cases"; and indicate the possibly confounding factors revealed by case studies. Maoz concludes his paper with a call for pluralism: "we must be open to using multiple and varied methodologies to test our theories."

Notes

1. E. H. Carr, *The Twenty Years' Crisis, 1919–1939: An Introduction to the Study of International Relations* (London: Macmillan, 1939); E. H. Carr, *Conditions of Peace* (London: Macmillan, 1942); Arnold Wolfers, *Britain and France between Two Wars: Conflicting Strategies of Peace since Versailles* (New York: Harcourt, Brace, 1940); Arnold Wolfers, *Discord and Collaboration: Essays on International Politics* (Baltimore: Johns Hopkins University Press, 1962); Nicholas J. Spykman, *America's Strategy in World Politics: The United States and the Balance of Power* (New York: Harcourt, Brace, 1941); W. T. R. Fox, *The Super-Powers: The United States, Britain, and the Soviet Union — Their Responsibility for Peace* (New York: Harcourt, Brace, 1944); Hans Morgenthau, *Scientific Man versus Power Politics* (Chicago: University of Chicago Press, 1946); Hans Morgenthau, *Politics among Nations: The Struggle for Power and Peace* (New York: Knopf, 1948); Bernard Brodie, ed., *The Absolute Weapon: Atomic Power and World Order* (New York: Harcourt, Brace, 1946).
2. Kenneth N. Waltz, *Theory of International Politics* (Reading, Mass.: Addison-Wesley, 1979); Robert Gilpin, *War and Change in World Politics* (Cambridge: Cambridge University Press, 1981).
3. E. B. Haas, *The Uniting of Europe* (Stanford, Calif.: Stanford University Press, 1958); E. B. Haas, *Beyond the Nation-State: Functionalism and International Organization* (Stanford, Calif.: Stanford University Press, 1964); Robert O. Keohane and Joseph S. Nye Jr., *Power and Interdependence: World Politics in Transition* (Boston: Little, Brown, 1977).
4. Robert Jervis, *Perception and Misperception in International Politics* (Princeton, N.J.: Princeton University Press, 1976); Robert Jervis, Richard Ned Lebow, and Janice Gross Stein, *Psychology and Deterrence* (Baltimore: Johns Hopkins University Press, 1985).
5. Richard K. Ashley, "The Poverty of Neorealism," *International Organization* 38, no. 2 (1984): 225–86.
6. Robert W. Cox, "Social Forces, States, and World Orders: Beyond International Relations Theory," *Millennium* 10, no. 2 (1981): 126–55; Robert W. Cox, *Production, Power, and World Order: Social Forces in the Making of History* (New York: Columbia University Press, 1987).
7. Alexander Wendt, "The Agent-Structure Problem in International Relations Theory," *International Organization* 41, no. 3 (1987): 335–70; F. V. Kratochwil, *Rules, Norms, and Decisions: On the Conditions of Practical and Legal Reasoning in International Relations and Domestic Affairs* (Cambridge: Cambridge University Press, 1989).
8. Jean B. Elshtain, *Women and War* (New York: Basic Books, 1987); Cynthia Enloe, *Bananas, Beaches, and Bases: Making Feminist Sense of In-*

ternational Politics (Berkeley: University of California Press, 1990); V. Spike Peterson, ed., *Gendered States: (Re)Visions of International Relations Theory* (Boulder, Colo.: Lynne Rienner, 1992); J. Ann Tickner, *Gender in International Relations: Feminist Perspectives on Achieving Global Security* (Minneapolis: University of Minnesota Press, 1992).

METHODOLOGY

FORMAL METHODS
IN INTERNATIONAL RELATIONS

Michael Nicholson

Introduction

Approaches to the analysis of international relations using formal methods are now well established. Models of international relations problems appear frequently in many of the leading journals. While there are still those who hold that formal methods only manage to render obscure what had hitherto been clear, the achievements of such methods, commonplace in all the other social sciences, make such positions hard to justify. The purpose of this paper is to discuss the principles behind formalization. I also wish to justify its extensive use, mainly by conceptual argument and by referring very briefly to some of the achievements. These achievements are genuine and require attention from those outside the formal tradition as well as those within it. Ultimately the aim of formal modeling is the same as that of any other tradition in international relations—to understand better the international system and point in the direction of making the world a pleasanter place in which to live. Has formal modeling contributed to this, and, if so, what are the directions in which it might continue to move?

Scholars have tried to model almost every area of empirical international relations with some attempts to look at the normative also. Thus issues of cooperation, conflict, deterrence, alliances, arms races decision structures, hostility patterns, and so on have passed under the formal modelers' eyes with varying success. They search for the nature of the logic of various situations such as conflict situations; they try to investigate the consequences of various sorts of assumptions being true; they also try to structure theories to make them amenable to empirical test by statistical means, something that is difficult unless some minimum degree of formality is allowed. Such analyses are necessary if many of the problems central to international relations are not to be vague and indeterminate. I am not claiming that all aspects of international relations have to be formalized in order to make progress, or even that they can be. However, I do argue that some very important problems in the discipline require formal approaches to make progress. In this we are no different from the rest of the social sciences. The same broad conceptual problems face them all.

The underlying basis of my argument is as follows. Natural languages, by which I mean the languages we speak, such as French, English, Chinese, and so on, are good at description but quickly become awkward and clumsy when faced with significant chains of deductive argument. By contrast, formal languages, and I mean particularly mathematics as it is normally understood, are very good at deductive arguments though rather weaker in fine description. Theories involve deductive structures, at least within the conventional empiricist tradition of the philosophy of science. Hence, if they are to be of any complexity they are going to require complex deductive arguments. In their turn these require mathematical methods. Further, we aim to explain events in international relations. An explanation shows how the events to be explained follow from certain initial conditions and a theory. Again we require deductive arguments that quickly become complex. Thus, for those issues of which complex deductive arguments are a part, we require formal methods. I assert there are many such issues.

We can restate this argument by looking briefly at the concepts of syntax and semantics. We use *syntax* to mean the internal structure of a language. Thus, "the king of France is a hobgoblin" is a perfectly syntactically correct sentence in the English language irrespective of its external truth claims. Using the word *language* in a slightly extended though perfectly conventional sense to include mathematics, we can also assert that if ">" is a transitive relationship and $A > B > C$, then $A > C$ irrespective of the interpretation of the letters or the symbol ">." We use *semantics* to mean the interpretation of the language to the world outside itself. Thus, a syntactically correct sentence can be true or false, or even relate to imaginary entities (such as hobgoblins), while being syntactically correct. The semantics deals with the external meaning of the sentences whereas the syntax deals with the internal structure of the language. Thus, the sign ">" is used, for example, to mean "is numerically greater than" and also, in the context of choice theory, to mean "is preferred to" as in the sentence "A is preferred to B." The statement is syntactically correct in both interpretations.

Natural languages are very good at semantics. We can say all sorts of interesting and subtle things about the world with the uses of natural language. Indeed, the whole richness of the world is captured in language.[1] However, natural languages are inflexible as far as syntax is concerned. We can rearrange things a little, but we cannot carry out more than basic logical deductions within them. Anything much beyond the traditional syllogism leads to cumbersome structures that are hard to understand and follow when expressed in natural languages. Mathematical languages have the opposite virtues and vices. Their descriptive capacity is limited. "My love is like a red, red rose" would only translate as an unwieldy collection of symbols with little aesthetic appeal and whose meaning would be obscure. The semantic relationship of a mathematical language to the real structure it is describing needs to be precise but often rather stripped down. However, as we commented earlier, they are excellent for carrying out logical deductions. The implications of a set of mathematical statements can be worked out and often result in amazing and counterintuitive conclusions. They can also assert with precision whether propositions are true or false within the given calculus, proving various propositions. We do not need to simply say that something "looks true," but we can show that it is true. "True," of course, relates to syntactic truth within the mathematical system. However, we can assert that if the premises are semantically true then the conclusions, however far they lie from the original premises, are likewise semantically true. The truth has been carried through various steps on which we can rely with total confidence. It is this versatility with complex logical operations that gives mathematical languages their great power. With mathematical systems we can deal with high orders of syntactical complexity that can, of course, reflect complex semantic systems.

Some Applications of Formal Methods in International Relations

Many of the applications of formal methods in international relations theory have been in the area of decisions and choice.[2] Rational choice theory and the closely related game-theoretic approaches are dominant here. It is hard to see how these could have developed without the use of mathematical methods. It is also hard to deny that they have been of great significance in the development of international relations theory. This of course emphasizes the common link between international relations and the rest of the social sciences. Rational choice theory and game theory developed from microeconomics although they have been applied to virtually every form of human behavior both as an explanatory and normative theory. Many of the most significant developments, such as Axelrod's work on cooperation,[3] have not been cultivated within a narrow disciplinary framework but apply to cooperation as a general human phenomenon. Such developments have important implications for international behavior and can become incorporated within international relations theory. However, this theory is all part of a more general social theory.

The initial applications of the theory of games to international relations came in the early 1960s with the work of Boulding, Rapoport, and Schelling.[4] This marked a big step, and the nature of deterrence and other conflict phenomena were greatly illuminated by this sort of analysis. Though now taken for granted, the insights developed by the formulation of such basic and simple games as chicken and prisoners' dilemma were profound. Nevertheless, after the big burst in the early 1960s, the development of the application of the theory of games to international relations seemed slow, though perhaps more so at the time than it seems in retrospect. Nigel Howard's development of metagames provided some development, but the applications to international relations were relatively few.[5] His later work on hypergames and drama theory has been more influential though arguably more neglected than it deserves.[6] The developments of game theory in international relations were nevertheless moving on with Brams's work, culminating, at least so far, in the theory of moves (TOM) reinforcing the tendency to look at games in the extensive form rather than the normal form as had earlier been more conventional. Kilgour, Zagare, and others have worked very much in the same sort of tradition. It is a tradition that comes directly out of the theory of games, though moving a long way from the original formulation (as one would hope and expect given the original work was first published in 1944). This work has been angled toward international relations, where such aspects of human behavior as deterrence have been prominent. However, it has more general application as all the authors are very aware, particularly in the case of TOM.[7]

Given that conflict and cooperation are central issues in international relations, it is not surprising that game theory and its offshoots have been prominent. However, they do not wholly define the field, and various general decision theory models such as the expected utility model have been powerfully employed, notably in the work of Bueno de Mesquita.[8] Expected utility models bring in the issues of risk and uncertainty in an explicit way. Given that the world is inherently very uncertain this seems like a necessary thing to do. Issues of uncertainty are quite prominent in recent discussions such as those of Claudio Cioffi-Revilla.[9]

Rational choice and game theory have been the dominant forms of analysis based on decisions, but it is a mistake to regard them as making up all of decision theory. Other decision theories such as prospect theory also have application in international relations, though more in potentiality than actuality so far. They too are stated in mathematical terms and would be hard to analyze otherwise.

One of the issues that the whole rational choice tradition has illuminated is the ambiguity of the concept of rationality itself when placed in a competitive context. The game of prisoners' dilemma itself exposes this ambiguity. Even when we have clearheaded actors, with coherent and transitive preferences, we cannot always say just what a rational action consists of. This issue, though a negative one, is very important as far as discussions of rational behavior are concerned. This has provoked a lot of discussion on the edge of formal theory itself about the whole nature of rationality in human conduct. Ainslie, Elster, Sen, and many others have participated in this debate.[10]

The centrality of decision theory in formal approaches to international relations (or any other approaches for that matter) is not surprising. We believe many phenomena in international relations can be explained as the consequences of decisions. However, not everything can, and there are some approaches that do not center on decisions, or, inasmuch as they imply decisions somewhere, they are taken as input where the output is the central issue. Classic amongst these are the Richardson models of arms races and hostility. There have been extensions of this at various times including the various hostility models of Dina Zinnes and her collaborators.[11] Schrodt has also developed Richardson-style models to discuss arms balances and other similar problems.[12] This class of model explores the consequences of simple input-output rules where the ensuing patterns are often counterintuitive. Despite the historical importance of Richardson's work in the development of our discipline, these sorts of model have tended to be secondary to the models based on various forms of decision theory.

The Nature of Formal Modeling

Broadly, formal modeling involves the use of mathematical, diagrammatic, and symbolic methods in the study of problems in international relations. The term is often used synonymously with "mathematical modeling," though perhaps here we should be cautious. Clearly the use of mathematical methods is an aspect of formal modeling. However, we might broaden the definition. Formal theory can be regarded as any theory that is expressed in any terms other than natural language. This would then include a statement of the one-shot prisoners' dilemma[13] as part of formal methods. This is a clear case of where something was obscure in natural language, but when stated more formally the concept became clear. It is a very simple problem. Once stated, the deductive steps are minimal and obvious. Nevertheless this simple statement of the problem has been enormously insightful in all branches of the social sciences. We might also include in formal methods any diagrammatic representation such as a flow diagram where we seek to illuminate a problem by representing it in a nonverbal manner. Often such diagrams are just a restatement of a verbal argument in different terms to make the argument clearer. No new information is added, and there need be no deductive steps involved in the argument that reveal unsuspected implications of the argument. If we use diagrams to illustrate a verbal argument, this is a wholly pragmatic issue and is judged solely by whether some or all the readers of the argument find it helpful.

However, deduction starts quite early. Once deductive arguments get complicated, they quickly need formal, mathematical methods to carry them through. This is no longer a matter of taste or convenience but of necessity. Richardson models are a clear case in point, though this is not an isolated instance.

Clearly we have to be careful with our vocabulary, so some elaboration on the basic terms will be useful. The words are not always used consistently, though the underlying concepts are. I follow the usage of R. B. Braithwaite in what follows.[14]

A *theory* is a set of generalizations about the world. The generalizations can be true or false, something that is determined by observation. A theory starts off with a set of postulates that are regarded as true for the purpose of the exercise. Other propositions are deduced from these postulates, and the whole set of propositions is the theory. The deduced propositions are called lower-level propositions within the theory. It is the theory as a whole that is testable against observation. Not all individual propositions need be testable (or refutable in Popperian terms).[15] The theory stands or falls as a whole as a description of the world.[16]

A *model*[17] is a simplified picture of reality. In structure it is the same as a theory. It starts from postulates from which other deductions are made. However, because of its simplified nature, it does not always follow that it is testable as the reality it describes is an artificial one. It is also in part the prototype of a theory. A model is progressively complicated to bring it closer to reality until it is sufficiently close to stand in as a picture of the reality. The boundaries between theory and model are sometimes rather vague (which also makes the issue of refutability more ambiguous in practice than it is in theory).

However, models are often used to explore the underlying structure of some process even when it is quite a way from a description of any international or other social process. The initial statement of the one-shot prisoners' dilemma is usually told in terms of an absurdly implausible story. Even iterated models of the prisoners' dilemma are a long way from any direct application to the real world except, from time to time, that of the psychological laboratory. However, they do appear to have some structural correspondence with "real" processes, and for that reason we think we can get some greater understanding of these processes such as the significance of time and the discount factor. It might lead us to theory, but it is a long way before we get there. As Jon Elster remarked, "Rational choice theory tells us what to look for, not what we will find." However, the real world even then intrudes on our models, and we can fit various findings into them. Usually we assume simple exponential discount functions. However, there is increasing evidence that people use hyperbolic discount functions despite the fact that this is in some sense "irrational" and can produce switching preferences over time. However, if we are hoping to get theories of how the world behaves rather than as we think it "ought" to behave then these must be incorporated into our models as precursors of what will go into our theories.

Mathematics are used, and need to be used, when there are significant deductive steps in the argument. A mathematical structure, sometimes called a *calculus*, starts from *axioms*, which are assumed to be true, from which theorems are deduced. Thus, they parallel the structures of models and theories. The abstract terms of the calculus are paralleled and interpreted in terms of the theory. Thus, if there is a correspondence between the axioms of the calculus and the postulates of the theory, the theorems of the calculus correspond to the lower-level propositions within the theory. A calculus can often be interpreted in many different contexts. Thus, differential equations can be used to describe arms races,[18] the growth of plants,[19] and the movements of bodies in motion (as in classical mechanics). We can have nonmathematical models and nonmathematical theories, but in general theories of any complexity are mathematically expressed.

The final purpose of any theory is to test it against the real world. There is obviously a close relationship between the use of formal methods and the use of statistical methods. Statistics deals with classes of events and generalizations. So, for the most part, do formal methods. Thus, many of the statistical tests used are tests of relationships such as linear relationships. This immediately relates statistics to formal theory, and the two are intertwined. To test relationships statistically one must also manipulate them into easily testable form, either in the sense of restating the relationships (testing for log-linearity instead of direct linearity for example) or in working out implications of a proposition to find those that are readily testable that will imply the truth also of the basic proposition under review. Any theory that is to be tested by statistical means is going to be at least minimally formal. Statistical theory itself is, of course, mathematically based, though this is a separate issue.

It should not be concluded from this that all formal methods necessarily require strong forms of measurement. Mathematics deals in qualitative shapes as well as measurement though such qualitative methods are not widespread in international relations. On the other hand a lot of work does depend only on ordinal measures where greater than and less than and equal to are the only categories. Quite a lot of decision theory, including basic games like prisoners' dilemma, can be posed in ordinal terms.

What Is Added by the Use of Formal Methods?

Formal languages, beyond the simplest, are technical languages. This raises the problem of communication and understanding across different academic cultures. We have to learn mathematics. Often the problem with understanding mathematical arguments is not a lack of knowledge of the mathematics involved so much as the lack of the habit of following mathematical arguments. One "reads" mathematics in a rather different way from the way one reads natural languages. This can be an impediment to the novice though it need not be an impediment to anyone interested in the results and the initial premises from which they have been derived.

Given that it takes time and effort to learn mathematical techniques, which is something of an ordeal for many people, why should we bother applying formal methods to the study of international relations? An argument one often hears—literally, for though I have heard it often in conversation it is rarely committed to paper—is that all formal theories do is restate the obvious in complicated language or move off into mathematical fantasies that have nothing to do with the real world. The discipline of international relations can move ahead quite satisfactorily without the intervention of mathematics.

In its extreme form, this argument is hard to justify, though in a more muted form something may be said for it. It is probably the case that some efforts at formal theory have been justified more by mathematical enthusiasm than by a substantive problem. Intrigued by the mathematics, scholars have pursued problems further and further away from any plausible application. Even this might be justified in that, prior to any investigation, it is often hard to know where it will lead. Most formal theorists are, I presume, like the author in confining the bulk of their output to the wastepaper bin. In this paper I argue that formal theory both has and will contribute much more than that. However, it is important for formal theorists to make some effort to communicate their results in nonmathematical language to those who are involved in other fields. This is often possible providing that the actual workings of the processes are taken on trust. Thus, using game-theoretic techniques, Wagner[20] has shown that a balance-of-power system does not require the five actors that some conventional theorists have asserted.[21] The working out of this result is complex and requires some knowledge of game theory. However, the outsider needs to know the initial postulates of the theory—that is, what Wagner has assumed—and the final result. It does not require much, if any, formal knowledge to understand these; indeed, these are the general concepts that go into a balance-of-power theory anyway. If these postulates are accepted, the rest follows. If these postulates are regarded as incomplete, the nonformal theories can suggest a new approach. This is not a question of not doing formal theory so much as making sure that there is a maximum of accessibility.

One major reason for at least attempting to apply mathematical methods to international relations is their extraordinary success in other disciplines. Physics, of course, is the paradigm case. From its earliest days, physics could develop only with the extensive use of mathematics. Only the most extreme of postmodernists would want to deny its great success. The use of mathematics in the natural sciences is generally uncontroversial. Likewise mathematics has been widely used with great success in the social sciences. Economics, in particular, has made big advances by the use of mathematical techniques. Even those who regard economics as going overboard in the overdevelopment of technique as opposed to substance nevertheless acknowledge the necessity of mathematical methods in developing even basic theory.[22] While economics stands as the physics of the social sciences, the application of mathematics has been widespread to other areas. While the extent of the application of mathematics to psychology, sociology, and so on is controversial, the application of some mathematics is widely if not universally accepted amongst practitioners of the various disciplines. Thus, it would seem foolish to neglect the possibility that similar methods in international relations and cognate subjects would also be fruitful. They may yield magnificent returns as some of the earlier practitioners such as Richardson hoped and even expected. That at least they would yield some profitable insights would almost be expected. To neglect the use of methods that have been so outstandingly successful in other areas would seem simply irresponsible. Further, there seems no special reason why the subject matter of international relations should mean that it is exempt from analysis by mathematical means. Scholars of international relations study a form of social behavior. If any form of social behavior is susceptible to mathematical analysis, then the presumption is that international relations would be also.

The Covering Law

The use of deductive methods became central with the covering law of explanation. An explanation of an event is an interpretation of an event in the context of a theory; in slightly different words, the event is seen as an instance of the theory. This form of explanation has been most clearly expounded by Hempel in his *covering law model of explanation*.[23] Hempel argues that all true explanations can be stated in this form, and an analysis of theories in international relations would seem to confirm that we, too, follow this pattern. One of the more explicit recent uses of this in international relations is in Geller and Singer.[24]

In the covering law model, we have a theory consisting of the statements $L(1)$, $L(2)$ . . . . $L(n)$. These statements are generalizations about sets of events (which can be in natural language or a formal language) that are deductively linked so that those that are not postulates are logically implied by groups of others. We also have a set of *initial conditions*: $C(1)$, $C(2)$ . . . . $C(m)$. These are statements about singular events. We have another set of singular events, $E(1)$, $E(2)$ . . . . $E(k)$, that are the events we want to explain. Thus the search for an explanation involves an inquiry into why, if the C's occur, we should expect the E's to occur. In a strict form of explanation (such as is commonplace in physics), the E statements and the L statements together *logically* imply the E statements. This is illustrated in the following diagram.[25]

$$C(1), C(2) \ldots \ldots \ldots C(m)$$
$$L(1), L(2) \ldots \ldots \ldots L(n)$$
$$\overline{}$$
$$E(1), E(2) \ldots \ldots \ldots E(k)$$

The point is that a logical deductive argument is carried out. While this does not necessarily imply the use of formal methods, once the argument gets at all complex they become necessary. Clearly this form of explanation in its strict form, though a commonplace in physics, tends to get blurred in the social sciences. Our facts in our theories are not as precisely defined as in physics, and our explanations are more commonly "explanation sketches" (in Hempel's terms) rather than strict explanations. However, this does not alter the need for the deductive argument and the mathematics that follows from that.

The covering law model is a standard approach to explanation in the empiricist or positivist approaches to the social sciences. Mathematics is not excluded if we adopt approaches that do not center on generalization, though their scope and range is more restricted. I have argued elsewhere that even approaches that on the surface deny the centrality of generalization in fact need some concept of generalization if they are to be any use at least in any policy context. This opens the door to a mathematical approach.

Some Counterarguments

It could still be argued that while the above arguments are satisfactory as far as other social sciences are concerned, international relations is different in some way. There is no scope for significant deductive arguments in this context. This argument is hard to accept. Apart from the successful cases where formal deductive methods have been used, it is hard to see what is distinctive about this form of human behavior that makes it exempt from the principles that apply to others. If significant deductive arguments are useful in other parts of the social sciences, it would seem odd if international relations were somehow different. It is an argument that has been used generally about social scientific methods in international relations but with as little basis.

It might appear that an analysis in terms of natural language is to be preferred to a formal analysis in that it is more widely understood. Formal theorists can understand natural language in a way in which the reverse does not happen. For this reason, only in situations where a formal analysis is manifestly superior should it be used.

This argument has two weaknesses. First, it is often not clear at the beginning what the payoffs of writing out a problem formally will be. It may turn out to be an exercise in futility. However, it may turn out to reveal a richness that was obscure at the beginning. In some ways, formal theorists resemble gold prospectors who get inured to the disappointments of mining dross by the promises of the occasional successful insight. In many ways problems are always worth trying out. Second, formal theorists are not obliged to make every step of every argument clear to everyone irrespective of their mathematical knowledge. Indeed, there can be debates amongst formal theorists, sometimes on purely technical matters, that would be unclear to outsiders. There is nothing particularly wrong in this. What is important is that when significant conclusions are reached that might be expected to be of general interest to the profession as a whole, efforts are made to communicate to the broader professional public in generally comprehensible language. The more technical our arguments, the more crucial should be our expository efforts. This is no more than we would expect of other technical areas. International relations specialists are interested in what comes out of the Soviet archives about, say, the Cuban missile crisis. However, we leave the technical arguments about the reliability or authenticity of some documents to the specialists whose debates might be incomprehensible to outsiders. At best, the outsiders would lack means of evaluating the evidence. Thus, we wait for the end results of the argument and expect them to be explained to us. This is similarly the case with work done in the formal theory tradition.[26]

This does not mean that all problems can be usefully analyzed by mathematical means. If description is dominant, then natural language is the most appropriate and will do the job better. Indeed, mathematical languages will add nothing except, perhaps, a little confusion. An account of the actions of the United Nations over the last five years will almost certainly be better done in natural language. However, an analysis of the power within UN committees might well have a useful formal aspect to it, drawing on the many powerful propositions from the formal theory of committees.

The Origins and Development of Formal Modeling in International Relations

Formal modeling became noticeable in international relations in the early 1960s. The works that took it from being a rather specialist niche, which excited a handful of scholars—usually not professionally involved in international relations—were those of Boulding, Rapoport, and Schelling. The approach became visible and hard to ignore except, possibly, by those who believed they had found the truth in traditional methods. Schelling concentrated on extending game theory to make it more readily interpretable in terms of international relations and practical conflict issues, though not always in a way that appealed to the standard game theorists. Both Boulding and Rapoport, though in rather different ways, used game theory and Richardson's interaction models to analyze general conflict problems, especially relating to international relations. Boulding further ransacked the economists' collection of models, particularly duopoly and oligopoly models, to interpret them in more general contexts. Rapoport, a mathematician but also a general polymath, concluded his book with a dialogue between a supporter of the capitalist system and a supporter of a communist system to illustrate the concept of what he called "debates." The dialogue, and the whole spirit behind it, has strong hints of what later became called constructivism.[27] Though this is not directly related to the concept of formal modeling, it is illustrative of the spirit of intellectual innovation that was characteristic of this whole style of thought.

Though this period saw a vastly increased interest in formal methods, the origins were much earlier. Richardson was the grandparent of formal methods as well as of statistical methods in international relations. His work goes back to the early 1920s when he published a monograph written while an ambulance driver in World War I. He developed this during World War II and the immediate postwar period (he died in 1953). His central mathematical work was his celebrated arms race model, now regarded as a central piece but initially ignored. Rapoport published an extended article in the first issue of the *Journal of Conflict Resolution* on "Lewis Fry Richardson's mathematical theory of war."[28] This is still the best exposition of Richardson's work and its breadth. The recognition of Richardson as an extraordinary thinker and pioneer in the development of international relations and peace research was confirmed with the importance given to him in the works by Boulding and Rapoport mentioned earlier.

The development of formal methods did not come in isolation, either intellectual or political. There were two factors that made the developments unsurprising in the late 1950s and early 1960s. First, the intellectual context of the time was one where the powers of mathematical analysis were being recognized more generally in the social sciences. Second, the political context was the cold war, which included fears of nuclear annihilation. A common feeling amongst those who were deeply concerned about the nuclear problem was that traditional international relations scholarship needed at best augmenting. It seemed to offer little prospect of peace. The dark pessimism of the realists such as Morgenthau who appeared to hold that what we had for an international system was the best we could hope for seemed unduly dreary. If the traditional methods could only help us bemoan our sad lot at a higher level of sophistication then perhaps other methods should be used that might offer some better prospect.

At least one should try. This, of course, applied to the whole of the social scientific approach to the peace research tradition and was not confined to formal methods as such. However, it was a significant stimulus to the formal approaches.

However, the whole development came in an intellectual as well as a political context. Economics had taken a powerful mathematical and statistical turn and appeared to promise results. Attempts to use mathematical analysis in all forms of social science from sociology to psychology were developing apace. Political science, often regarded as the nearest disciplinary neighbor to international relations, was using formal methods enthusiastically and could claim to have done so in limited forms since the eighteenth century when Condorcet formulated his famous paradox of voting. Votes rather naturally lend themselves easily to both theoretical and practical work, but the mathematization of political science has gone well beyond the analysis of voting. The move toward mathematization was associated with the view that the divisions into separate disciplines of the social sciences were arbitrary. The divisions into economics, psychology, and so on were convenient, possibly, but indicated no fundamental ontological differences (to use a word that was rarely used at the time and would not have been used in contemporary justifications of this argument). The basic issue was the study of human behavior where there was the presumption that this would be done in similar ways whatever the manifestation. Appropriate techniques were a matter of convenience, not of principle. Even these techniques, such as many mathematical techniques, had broad application over both natural and social sciences. In this context, the extension of formal methods into international relations and conflict studies was not only natural but almost inevitable.

The role of the political background of some of the early workers in the formal tradition was significant. Richardson was a Quaker pacifist, of the generation who were deeply influenced by World War I, which he had seen firsthand. He passionately believed in rebuilding a world in which peace was the norm. His work was a model of objectivity. Nevertheless, his underlying position was that we must alter the world but first we need to understand it as it is. Indeed, it would be impossible from reading his work to know what his political position was. Boulding and Rapoport were both within this same tradition, though it was World War II and the subsequent nuclear world that was the center of their political experience and concerns. They were studying the world with a long-term view of bringing about fundamental change. They certainly believed in change. Schelling occupies a more ambiguous position. He certainly provided a more fundamental analysis of conflict than the traditional theorists could, and nor was he a crude cold warrior. However, his view was less radical. He was more warmly welcomed than the others by the liberal end of the conventional establishment. There was a lot more work done using formal methods in what can be more clearly seen as a problem-solving tradition. All sorts of work in operations research went on at organizations such as the RAND Corporation into such issues as missile siting, convoy size and deployment, and all the other more down-to-earth aspects of military procedures that rest on the edge of practical strategy and international relations. Moving toward the more political and abstract realm of international relations theory and such issues as how to have agreements in contexts where there is cheating come close to a sort of Fabian approach to fundamental change.

Conclusion: What of the Future?

Formal approaches to international relations theory have added a lot to our understanding of the operation of the international system and bode well for doing rather more in the future. We know things, for example, about alliance behavior and the structures of conflict, quite apart from the structuring of problems to make them susceptible to statistical testing, that would not have been possible otherwise. This is all sufficient justification in itself.

What of the future of formal methods? We face the problem that Popper raised about the prediction of ideas. If one can predict an idea one has already had to have it so one is caught in a trap. All we can do is suggest some plausible lines of progress that may be shown in the future to have been good or bad guesses.

However, it is hard to suppose that deductive modeling is going to be less needed. As theory advances, it is more likely to become more deductively complex rather than less. Guetzkow's famous metaphor of "islands of theory" will expand and link up needing more not less formality to construct them adequately. Likewise polymetric techniques are likely to advance requiring more ingenious rearrangements of theoretical relationships to maximize the effective confrontation of theory with fact. Even simplification requires more formality: the derivation of simple patterns from complex ones requires insightful deduction.

The big successes of formal theory have mainly been with one form or another of decision theory, mainly rational choice theory. Indeed, sometimes formal theory is mistakenly referred to as if it were a near synonym of rational choice theory. In the classic debate, formal methods have tended toward agency rather than structure. This itself has been elaborated in the formal tradition by Starr and various coauthors. I would speculate that structural theories will become more and more developed from a mathematical point of view.

Other speculations are that simulation methods will be used more frequently and that these will generate a whole set of quasi-experimental worlds. These simulations can be of the structure of the system or of an artificial intelligence form that might (or might not) integrate more closely with choice theory.

We might also move to consider further still the presuppositions behind not just formal theory but in particular those of rational choice. Often, as some of the critics of rational choice have maintained, the apparent obviousness of the maximizing hypotheses makes one blind to the possibility that, as hypotheses about actual behavior, they may be wrong. Theories about choice are empirical theories and depend on their being accounts of how people actually choose. We can have doubts about some of the central principles of rational choice. For example, people do not calculate their degrees of belief as the theory of probability suggests they do; they do not necessarily have exponential discount functions even if such functions do lead to well-behaved patterns; they do not always use backward induction as they should as many experiments of iterated prisoners' dilemma with a known ending point show. Choice theories will have to embody these issues. People do not always behave as they "ought" to do from the point of view of the modeler. The conceptual problems also need to be dealt with with care. There is already a well-trodden field that elaborates the presuppositions of such concepts as "rationality," but there is further to go. The efforts to bring emotions into the analysis of choice represent welcome moves away from the aridity of earlier rational choice theory. Indeed, it would be better to get rid of the word *rational* altogether as it has prescriptive overtones that are inappropriate for a supposedly empirical analysis.

As the applications of formal methods in international relations are likely to increase rather than decrease, we should also pay more attention to making our results comprehensible to people who have neither the training nor the interest to engage in the technicalities of the problems. This does not mean that we have to make every technical exercise clear to everyone—far from it—or that everyone should be constantly explaining things to the nonmathematically inclined. It simply means that some of us should tackle the problem of exposition seriously. Formal approaches are an important and necessary means of tackling problems, but they are not the only way, nor are all problems suitable for formal analysis. Thus, we do not have to suppose we shall colonize the whole of international relations knowledge. We must, at all cost, avoid becoming a mathematical priesthood purporting to dispense knowledge from behind a secure barrier of incomprehensibility.

Notes

1. There is also the view, stemming from the later Wittgenstein, that language does not just reflect the world but actually constitutes the world. I would not deny that language is, at times, constitutive but assert that it also has a reflective role as in the correspondence view of language.
2. This paper is not intended as a comprehensive, or even a partial, survey of the applications of formal methods in international relations. I give various examples along the way to illustrate my argument. All these illustrations I use are, in my view, significant developments, but the omission of some work (and I omit most work) does not imply that I regard it as any less important.
3. Robert Axelrod, *The Evolution of Cooperation* (New York: Basic Books, 1984).
4. Kenneth Boulding, *Conflict and Defense* (New York: Harper and Row, 1962); Anatol Rapoport, *Fights, Games, and Debates* (Ann Arbor: University of Michigan Press, 1965); Thomas Schelling, *Strategy of Conflict* (Cambridge: Harvard University Press, 1960).
5. Nigel Howard, *Paradoxes of Rationality* (Cambridge: MIT Press, 1971).
6. Nigel Howard, "Drama Theory and Its Relationship to the Theory of Games," *Group Decision and Negotiation* 3, no. 2 (1994): 187–206.
7. Steven J. Brams, *Theory of Moves* (Cambridge: Cambridge University Press, 1994).
8. See Bruce Bueno de Mesquita, "The Contribution of Expected-Utility Theory to the Study of International Conflict," in *Handbook of War Studies,* ed. Manus I. Midlarsky (Boston: Unwin Hyman, 1989): 143–69.
9. Claudio Cioffi-Revilla, *Politics and Uncertainty: Theory, Models, and Applications* (Cambridge: Cambridge University Press, 1998).
10. George Ainslie, *Picoeconomics: The Strategic Interaction of Successive Motivational States within the Person* (Cambridge: Cambridge University Press, 1992); Jon Elster, *Ulysses and the Sirens* (Cambridge: Cambridge University Press, 1979); A. K. Sen, "Rational Fools: A Cri-

tique of the Behavioral Foundations of Economic Theory," *Philosophy and Public Affairs* 16, no. 4 (1977): 317–44.

11. Dina Zinnes, *Conflict Processes and the Breakdown of International Systems,* Merriam Seminar Series on Research Frontiers (Denver: University of Denver Press, 1983); Dina Zinnes and Robert Mulcaster, "Hostile Activity and the Prediction of War," *Journal of Conflict Resolution* 28, no. 2 (1984).

12. Philip Schrodt, "Richardson's N-Nation Model and the Balance of Power," *American Journal of Political Science* 22, no. 2 (1978).

13. The position of the apostrophe in "prisoners'" is deliberate. There are two of them, and the word is plural. The dilemma only arises because there are more than one. It is, so to speak, jointly owned.

14. R. B. Braithwaite, *Scientific Explanation* (Cambridge: Cambridge University Press, 1955).

15. Karl Popper, *The Logic of Scientific Discovery* (New York: Basic Books, 1959).

16. This point is widely misunderstood, particularly by critics of an empiricist or positivist approach. Not all propositions within a theory need be directly observable. If this were required it would impoverish the natural as well as the social sciences. See Braithwaite, *Scientific Explanation,* and Michael Nicholson, *Causes and Consequences in International Relations: A Conceptual Study* (New York: Pinter, 1996).

17. This use of *theory,* at least in the sense of a scientific theory, is fairly generally accepted, as is the use of *axiom.* The words *model* and *postulate* are not always used consistently. Axiom is used as I (following Braithwaite) have used it though sometimes it is used also to include what I am calling a postulate.

18. Lewis F. Richardson, *Statistics of Deadly Quarrels* (Pittsburgh: Boxwood Press, 1960).

19. D'Arcy Thompson, *Growth and Form* (Cambridge: Cambridge University Press, 1917).

20. Harrison Wagner, "The Theory of Games and the Balance of Power," *World Politics* 38, no. 4 (1986): 546–76.

21. Joseph Frankel, *International Relations in a Changing World* (Oxford: Oxford University Press, 1988).

22. The eminent economist Joan Robinson once remarked, "I knew no mathematics and therefore had to think instead." This was meant as a jibe at the mathematical economists. Her work, by the standards of economics at the time and still more modern economics, is undoubtedly not mathematical. However, her skillful use of diagrammatic methods would put her firmly in the ranks of the formal theorists if they were applied to international relations even today.

23. Carl G. Hempel, *Aspects of Scientific Explanation: And Other Essays in the Philosophy of Science* (New York: Free Press, 1965).

24. Daniel S. Geller and J. David Singer, *Nations at War: Scientific Study of International Conflict* (Cambridge: Cambridge University Press, 1998).

25. This diagram is very minimally formal. There is no deduction involved nor does it contain anything that is not explained in natural language

in the preceding paragraph. However, I think it makes the argument clearer, which it probably does for some readers and not for others. Its justification is purely heuristic.

26. I think this issue is important. I argue a similar point in "What's the Use of International Relations," *Review of International Studies* 26, no. 2 (2000).

27. Constructivism emphasizes the interpretation and understanding of things and events and argues that these interpretations can alter, though not necessarily easily. Alexander Wendt argues this in *The Social Theory of International Relations* (Cambridge: Cambridge University Press, 1999). Of particular interest in light of Rapoport's approach is K. M. Fierke's *Changing Games, Changing Strategies* (Manchester, England: Manchester University Press, 1998).

28. Anatol Rapoport, "Lewis Fry Richardson's Mathematical Theory of War," *Journal of Conflict Resolution* 1, no. 1 (1957): 249–99.

CUMULATION, SYNTHESIS, AND RESEARCH DESIGN FOR THE POST–FOURTH WAVE

Harvey Starr

Theory, Logic, and Method in the Post–Fourth Wave

It is both fitting and useful for the International Studies Association to ask its members to reflect on where we are in the study of international/transnational/global politics and relations, and where the study might be going. It is similarly useful to think about areas of advance as well as the puzzles and problems that remain, and how we can do better. It is also appropriate to do so at the start not only of a new century but a new millennium. Thus, in a memo to the participants in the millennial reflection panels held at the 2000 International Studies Association annual meeting, Michael Brecher and Frank Harvey noted:

> The goal of the ten millennium Reflection panels, then, is to challenge proponents of specific paradigms, theories, approaches and substantive issue areas to confront their own limitations, stimulate debate about their most significant accomplishments and shortcomings, and discuss research paths for the years ahead. On the eve of a new millennium, scholars of International Studies have an opportunity and an obligation to engage in genuine self-criticism as a guide to identifying important theoretical, methodological and epistemological credentials and prospects of International Studies.

While this point in time is a propitious one for reflection, the members of the quantitative methods panel have not had to wait for the millennium to engage in a variety of self-reflective and stock-taking activities. Their career-long search for cumulation, better theory, and the best ways to test and evaluate that theory is quite evident. For example, more than a quarter of a century ago, I addressed stock taking and cumulation in the discussion of the application of quantitative methods to the study of international phenomena.[1] More than a decade ago, Ben Most and I addressed a set of impediments to cumulation, which included a self-critical appraisal of the failure of quantitative scholars to match theory and logic to research design and method. We identified these three elements—theory, logic, and method—as the components of the "research triad." The research triad served as the core of our presentation, as we argued that "scholars need to recognize the existence of a research triad . . . and that each leg of this triad is critical for advancing our knowledge of international phenomena."[2] Scholars were likened to "jugglers" as "each element of the triad needs to be held in the air at the same time in a complex set of interrelationships, indicating that for the juggler to be successful, all of the balls (elements of the triad) must be kept going simultaneously."[3] Part of the charge to members of the millennial reflection panels was to identify and promote "intra-subfield consensus." As such, I think that I can do no better than to continue the call for attention to the research triad and the promotion of creative and rigorous research design—no matter what subfield is under investigation, what specific theoretical framework is used to guide the research, or what specific methodologies are used to evaluate and compare theoretical frameworks.

While Most and Starr pointed to a set of ongoing feedback loops among the elements of the triad, as well as the more specific elements of research design,[4] the driving element always was *theory*. Thus, theory must be at the forefront of our endeavors, whatever the subfield or whatever the methodology employed. Clearly, I do not think this is unique to me or members of the quantitative methods panel; see, for example, the 1985 symposium in *International Studies Quarterly*, where international relations scholars from very different methodological and substantive camps all agreed on the centrality of rigorous theorizing.[5]

The think pieces we were enjoined to prepare for the millennial reflection panel in order to facilitate discussion and debate were asked to address one or more of six tasks. A careful reading of these tasks indicates that they are specifically related to questions of cumulation and synthesis. Specifically, task number two was "to assess where we stand on key debates and why we have failed to resolve them," while task five was "to address the broader question of progress in international studies." Task four was "to explore ways to achieve fruitful synthesis of approaches." In addition to drawing our attention once again to the research triad, these tasks lead me to maintain my position that researchers should use some form of an agent-structure theoretical framework, as I continue to see that approach as the most useful way to synthesize across levels of analysis, disciplines, and different forms of causal relationships.

After directing some comments toward tasks two and five, I will argue for some form of agent-structure framework (partially addressing task six regarding an "agenda of topics") and note that this approach presents us with three major methodological challenges.

A final element of introduction is in order. As the latter decades of the twentieth century have been filled with various "post"-ists and "post"-isms, perhaps I can describe this essay as thinking about the study of international phenomena in terms of a "post–fourth wave." In the 1960s Karl Deutsch characterized the study of international relations as going through four "waves," starting first with international law, then to a second focusing on diplomatic history and international organization. Deutsch noted "a third wave of advance . . . underway since the 1950s. It has consisted in the reception of many relevant results and methods from the younger of the social and behavioral sciences such as psychology, anthropology, and sociology."[6] While the third wave continued, a fourth began in the 1960s: "the rise of analytic and quantitative research concepts, models and methods, a movement toward the comparative study of quantitative data and the better use of some of the potentialities of electronic computation."[7] The third wave led to questions with massive data requirements—data that previously had not been considered necessary or relevant. Obviously, if such data had not even been thought of, it had not been collected. Therefore, much of the activity in the third and fourth waves found itself concerned with data collection and analysis; much of the work of the fourth wave continued to be inductive and descriptive. It had also begun to be aware of, and take advantage of, the astounding capabilities of computers.

I think we are in a post–fourth wave period that has been fueled by significant advances in computational and data-handling technology (both hardware and software) and by a massive influx of mathematical and formal models. I'm not sure that the stage we are now in clearly qualifies as a "fifth wave"—after all Lewis F. Richardson was building mathematical models in the decades before World War II (covering such phenomena as arms races or diffusion), and computers were being used in data analysis with regularity by the late 1950s and early 1960s. However, it seems clear to me that the range of the "analytic" techniques now being used, the frequency of their use, and their sophistication involve a qualitative (pardon the expression!) movement beyond the fourth wave that Deutsch described. The number and caliber of mathematical and formal models being employed and their technical complexity, investigating every level of analysis and choice situation (most based on microfoundations of economic choice), constitute a significant difference from Deutsch's fourth wave. A reading of the papers presented by Zinnes, Bueno de Mesquita, and Brams on the quantitative methods panel (in this volume) strongly confirms this view. The formal nature of the post–fourth wave is important, because it can be inclusive of, and synthesize, both the research triad and agent-structure approaches.

In large part, the fourth wave continues with the tasks of empirically testing and evaluating these formal models. This is an important component of the fourth wave, and I think the extent of this empirical testing of formal models in international politics is more extensive than the picture presented by Zinnes in her paper. I do agree with Zinnes that "a mathematical model may be beautiful and provide wonderful insights, but it is not a theory about international politics until it has been subjected to an evaluation. Story and data must meet." This is the heart of the research triad—the linkage between theory and research.

Both the fourth wave and the post–fourth wave involve the testing of formal models, both for evaluation of existing models and the generation of better models (theory). Again, I agree with Zinnes that this is not easy. In many cases the task of testing formal constructs constitutes a formidable challenge to our ability to generate appropriate research design. However, in terms of the research triad, formal models both require and reflect a high degree of theoretical grounding. Formal models translate theory into mathematical and logical constructs. As such, they ensure the internal logical consistency of the formalized translation of theory.[8] As noted, the challenge then confronting the researcher is somehow to capture these formalized relationships in empirical representations and evaluations. The relationships among theory, formalized models, research design, and research results epitomize the research process described by Most and Starr,[9] as well as the scholar who must "juggle" all three components of the research triad.

Cumulation/Progress and Theory

Tasks two and five essentially address the issue of cumulation. The cumulation of knowledge in a specific discipline or area also served to focus the discussion in Most and Starr.[10] Most and Starr argue that theory *must* be central to research and propel the research process.[11] The centrality of theory in the research enterprise is also key to Zinnes's notion of "integrative cumulation"[12] or Bueno de Mesquita's focus on "progress"[13] in a Lakatosian sense. The obvious position any student of research design must support is that the methods selected by any researcher must be appropriate to the questions being investigated. Those questions, in turn, must be theory driven. Thus, as noted earlier, any researcher must begin with well-grounded and well-specified theory. The importance of theory is obvious. Russett and Starr write, "Theory organizes and simplifies reality; thus helping to separate the important from the trivial by pointing out what we really wish to look at and what is unimportant enough to ignore. This is why theory is so important—it affects not only which answers we come up with, but also what questions we ask in the first place!"[14] Most and Starr stress the dynamic feedback loops that exist among theory, research design, and findings, as each informs and modifies the other.[15] Theory thus not only affects the design and the research product but is itself continually modified and updated by the research process and the results of that process, in a dynamic combination of induction and deduction. As the research process unfolds and theory is modified, the researcher may be led to investigate additional phenomena originally omitted from the study.

This view means that theory is central to the actual enterprise of empirical research. Given the current state of international relations "theory" at some U.S. institutions as well as abroad, it is important that basic issues concerning methodology (and epistemology) that link theory, research design, and the actual enterprise of research are discussed and returned to the forefront of the scholarly enterprise. This *must* be argued explicitly because, for some academics, the idea of "theory" has been, and too often continues to be, used to mean only broader philosophical worldviews or ideologies. As such, theory has been divorced from research by those who use the term in this way. Social scientists need to be reminded that theory's central contribution rests in the way in which it informs, shapes, and is in turn shaped by empirical research, that theory is a tool in the study of the world of politics. The theory-research loop is crucial here. This loop is irrelevant when theory is conceived of as ideology—where the answers are known, and, thus, research is irrelevant. Only when theory is seen as central to research, and not used as ideology, can it be the basis for integrative cumulation.

This theory-research feedback loop was a prominent component of Most and Starr's *Inquiry, Logic, and International Politics.*[16] The work in that book, and with other colleagues since then, was concerned with a set of key issues in the logic of inquiry that directly addressed this relationship. These issues also helped to comprise a truly critical logic that challenged researchers to examine the theoretical bases of their research. This involved clarifying the logical consistency of the relationship between theory and research design. It also involved the researcher considering the logical structure of the components of his or her research designs. In sum, the set of issues presented by Most and Starr that comprised the critical logic included the form of the relationship under study; matching the logic of theory/models to the logic of research design; development of process models; broader versions of the agent-structure problem; identifying the appropriate units of analysis; case selection; and such vital concepts as "substitutability" and "nice laws."

Perhaps most important for both cumulation and synthesis, the critical logic—along with its subcomponents and its attendant issues—was *not* limited to any specific area of international politics or political science.[17] Nor is it limited to any specific methodological tradition. This critical logic *is* indeed able to deal with most critiques that are directed at systematic empirical work from outside the scientific method–based tradition of inquiry.[18] That is, most of the critiques raised by those critical of "positivism" (always an ambiguously used concept) can be subsumed under issues raised in the critical logic of Most and Starr. Using the critical logic of Most and Starr, the scholar need not "stand outside" the scientific method tradition to raise and deal with such issues as "choice posing as truth" or "reality as a social construction" or the broad issue of relativism.[19] To repeat, the key point here is that the critical logic and its components apply across methodologies and to all aspects of research design—as long as one's true enterprise is to investigate some aspect of the empirical world.

The Synthetic Use of Agent-Structure Approaches: Three Challenges

The opportunity-and-willingness construct[20] is based on the work of Harold and Margaret Sprout. This construct is simply one version of a more general agent-structure approach and is captured in the "ecological triad" of the Sprouts. The ecological triad consists of the entity, the environment, and the entity-environment relationship. The *first challenge* I want to raise reflects a major methodological problem scholars currently face—and will constitute a major future challenge; it is *how to get at* the entity- environment relationship. This is, again, simply one version of the more general "agent-structure problem."[21]

The original article by Starr ("'Opportunity' and 'Willingness' as Ordering Concepts in the Study of War") was only vaguely suggestive of the ways in which opportunity could relate to willingness and how willingness might relate to opportunity. Yet the nature of these (inter)relationships is essential to theory building and testing. As Elster notes in discussing "opportunities" and "preferences": "Scholars disagree on the relative importance of preferences and opportunities in explaining behavior."[22] This was a key question throughout Most and Starr's *Inquiry, Logic, and International Politics*, one that was approached in a number of ways. While a set of logical analyses demonstrated the joint necessity of opportunity and willingness in explanation, other parts of the book, such as the simulation analyses of system structure and willingness in chapter 6, began to lead toward a focus on willingness that is most strongly articulated in Friedman and Starr's ultimate development of an empirical framework based on methodological individualism.[23] The relationship between opportunity and willingness is further developed in Cioffi-Revilla and Starr.[24] Here, through the use of Boolean logic, the authors demonstrate how opportunity and willingness as elements in first-order causality are related to substitutability, which is central to second-order causality.

Looking at opportunity and willingness and then adding the important auxiliary concept of substitutability presented by Most and Starr, Cioffi-Revilla and Starr distinguish between a first-order causality of world politics (willingness and opportunity) at the analytical level and a deeper second-order causality of substitutability at the operational level. The first-order (necessary) elements of opportunity and willingness are linked by the Boolean *and*, while the range of possible modes of (sufficient) second-order substitutability are connected by the Boolean *or*. Cioffi-Revilla and Starr then formalize and analyze the political uncertainty of international behavior, along with willingness, opportunity, and their substitutability, at both the analytical and operational levels. In so doing, they mathematically derive a number of interesting insights into the agent-structure problem, especially in regard to the relationship between agency and structure. This article clearly demonstrates the many possible ways in which the opportunity-and-willingness framework can be developed and the important nonintuitive implications that can be derived through formal analyses.

Friedman and Starr investigate the opportunity-and-willingness framework as it relates to the broader debate in the literature concerning the agent-structure relationship.[25] The agent-structure problem refers to questions concerning the interrelationship of agency and structure and to the integration of this dialectical relationship into the explanation of social phenomena. The agent-structure problem raises a variety of issues in the philosophy of science and the logic of inquiry. Friedman and Starr argue that the current treatment of the agent-structure problem in the international relations literature is problematic. Using the opportunity-and-willingness framework and related concepts such as substitutability, they critique the confusion among ontological, epistemological, and methodological issues and analyses. For example, they argue that the postulation of causal interrelationships among agency and structure requires that these concepts be defined autonomously and encompass explicitly delimited parameters of variability. The structurationist view that each must be endogenized is incomplete, ignoring the basic nonrecursive nature of agency and structure (opportunity and willingness). The use of opportunity and willingness also promotes recognition that structuration-theoretic approaches to international politics inadequately attend to the variability of agency identity and interest, and to the social structural foundations of this variability. From these and other metatheoretic considerations, Friedman and Starr derive a methodological individualist model of the dialectical interrelationship between multidimensional and dynamic sociopolitical contexts and individual international political elite choice processes.

This methodological individualist perspective is clearly picked up by models of expected utility, prospect theory, and other formal models of choice, where factors of structure/opportunity are built into the payoff structure, resource constraints, the form of the game, and so on. This is one reason why I have found these approaches so useful and why developments in methodology must continue in the areas of choice (agency) under a variety of conditions of constraint (structure). A key problem in getting at the opportunity-and-willingness relationship is often due to the *lack of variance* within the opportunity structure. That is, it is very difficult to find enough cases where the different structural or environmental conditions necessary to evaluate a model exist. Recall also that Most and Starr in their discussion of necessity, sufficiency, and research design note that it is not enough to study the presence of some independent variable *y* or some dependent variable *y*, but *not-x* and *not-y* as well.[26] It is for this reason that in both Most and Starr and in the ongoing Two-Level Security Management Project,[27] I have argued that the use of *simulations* can be most helpful, and have moved in that direction.

Given the lack of cases and variance,[28] simulations permit the control and experimentation necessary to look for causal relationships. Using simulation we are able to analyze a model for its internal consistency and to examine the plausibility of its assumptions by generating implications for hypothetical systems of states (or any other set of "environed entities"). Simulations, such as that created for the Two-Level Security Management Project, can demonstrate that the model's predictions conform to the implications of other accepted theories and to the empirical findings of previous studies. And, as with other formal models, they can reveal nonintuitive relationships.[29]

A *second challenge*, briefly noted earlier, concerns the *form* of the relationships investigated with an agent-structure model. That is, given opportunity and willingness, substitutability, and nice laws, how do we construct research designs to deal with the logical differences between models of necessity and sufficiency? In particular, how do we conduct the empirical analysis of *necessity*? For example, analysts such as Frank Harvey[30] have usefully and appropriately raised the issue that theories or models of deterrence are models of *necessity* not sufficiency but that critics of those models test them with designs only appropriate for sufficiency. It is interesting to highlight the parallels between critics of rational models of deterrence and the critics of Bueno de Mesquita's expected utility theory, as discussed by Most and Starr in *Inquiry, Logic, and International Politics.* In both cases analysts are proposing models of *how people are supposed to behave* if certain processes are at work. Neither process is itself observable; indeed, deterrence is about actions *that do not occur!* Both "theories" set out conditions that must be present in order for certain outcomes—the results of these processes—to occur: that is, necessary conditions. Neither theory is presented in an "if-then" structure that represents sufficiency. *However,* while the conditions may obtain, the proposed results may not appear. This startles the critics of such approaches!

Yet this is exactly what is to be expected with models of necessity. And it is what makes them difficult to test. One of our ongoing challenges, then, is to design methods to study nonobservable phenomena or outcomes that do not occur. As Most and Starr point out in regard to expected utility, the number of cases that occur in a cell where the conditions of expected utility obtain but no conflict initiation occurs is irrelevant.[31] And, again, we're trying to analyze behavior that does not occur. Note carefully that this corresponds directly to arguments by Lebow and Stein,[32] and similar critics, that deterrence theory fails *because* while all the conditions for deterrence are present, there is "no deterrence." In Bueno de Mesquita's expected utility analysis, no conflict initiation reflects the nonoccurrence of behavior. With deterrence, critics do not realize they are in the same boat, because a lack of deterrence is reflected in some party actually behaving—initiating an attack or making a challenge of some kind. Using the research triad of logic, theory, and research design, it is clear what is happening. The critics of such models of necessity *think* that the sort of behavior they can see permits them to treat the relationship as a sufficient relationship. It does not. Note that by using deterrence we can illustrate the methodological challenges posed by the study of necessity:

a. if deterrence is successful there is no behavior to see;
b. if deterrence fails behavior does occur and can be observed;
c. thus, critics study deterrence failure because it is observable;
d. in so doing they *think* they are solving the *not-y* problem, which must be solved to establish sufficiency;
e. they conclude that the factors of rational deterrence theory do not predict to successful deterrence, that either there is no relationship or there is no sufficient relationship.

The former is not true; the latter is essentially irrelevant. Logic has helped us understand these deterrence debates. Some promising research designs, following Harvey and others, include the use of Boolean analyses and comparative studies in order to study necessity.

The *third challenge* concerns how we are to investigate the phenomenon of *substitutability* (and the related idea of nice laws). As noted in Cioffi-Revilla and Starr, substitutability is closely related to opportunity and willingness, providing multiple paths to either opportunity or willingness—"alternative modes of redundancy."[33] More generally, substitutability indicates that any single cause may have multiple effects and that any single effect may have multiple causes. Different problems may lead to similar responses or that a given problem may be dealt with in multiple ways. Thus, for any given set of conditions, the same policy choice is *not* equally likely across time or space for elites.[34]

Substitutability (as well as nice laws) thus lies at the heart of the use of agent-structure frameworks, where the choices of agents are analyzed in regard to the contextual structures within which they exist. It is not simply that substitutable modes (or redundancy) are related to greater "complexity" in the world; these modes actually make political behavior in a complex world more possible.

The combination of opportunity and willingness with substitutability as a way to deal with the agent-structure problem reveals the complexity and uncertainty in international phenomena (a complexity that has not been adequately addressed by either realism or neorealism or most variants of transnational liberalism). Yet as Cioffi-Revilla and Starr demonstrate, "the fundamental uncertainty of politics is scientifically tractable."[35] With concepts such as nice laws, substitutability, context, and adaptation, the opportunity-and-willingness framework can deal with both the analytical and operational levels of theory and give us a better grasp as to what behaviors are more or less likely to occur under what conditions.

The challenge of *how* to study substitutability is discussed at length in Starr as part of a special issue of the *Journal of Conflict Resolution* on the use of substitutability in the study of international politics.[36] The recognition of substitutability complicates research design as it forces the analyst out of single-variable or single-indicator ways of thinking about political phenomena. Only by understanding the broader concept or phenomenon under study could one fully grasp exactly what one should be investigating in terms of the full range of operational observations. If some range of behaviors

were all substitutable means for achieving some foreign policy outcome, then the whole range would need to be included in any particular study. Focusing on only one would mean a failure to provide
full coverage of the possible outcomes and lead to incomplete results
that failed to cumulate (or even make sense when compared). The
results would fail to capture the theory or model being tested (as
only one part was being tested). And, returning to the logic component of the research triad, focusing on only one possible outcome
(the "successful" outcome that is observed) leads to the logical problems that exclude the study of sufficient relationships.

The authors of the special issue of the *Journal of Conflict Resolution* provide important clues as to how we can study substitutability. Some note that the status quo, or "no action," must be part
of the model. They also argue that the substitutability problem
"translates" to a time-series situation, concerned with sequences of
responses that require data dealing with temporal variance.[37] With
such time-series needs in mind, the best techniques to deal with
empirical estimation are sought. Both Regan and Bennett and Nordstrom argue that the use of multinomial logit analysis is the most
appropriate way to deal with the data in substitutability situations:
analyses where the dependent variable is presented in multiple,
unordered categories. The possibility of multiple outcomes that capture the same overriding concept—such as security or viability—
clearly presents the analyst with substantial problems of research
design. Choices that have not been taken need also to be considered
in our analyses, as difficult as that may be. The fact that there are
multiple possible outcomes—directed at different internal and external audiences playing two-level games—may also complicate
analyses that are based on a straightforward trade-off between two
possible policies or actions.

Conclusion

I have briefly—too briefly—tried to indicate some of the methodological challenges that face students of world/global/international
politics/relations as we enter the twenty-first century. Cumulation
and "progress" in the study of global phenomena will depend on the
quality and rigor of our theories and our methods. Synthesis will
follow broad agent-structure approaches that cut across more standard levels of analysis and disciplinary boundaries. The challenges

facing researchers arise from finding the appropriate methods by which to study the agent-structure problem. These include

- how to cut into the continuous feedback loops between agent and structure—between endogenous and exogenous factors;
- how to design studies of necessity;
- how to find the correct methodological tools for studying phenomena that do not occur, for studying *not-x* and *not-y* and not just selecting on either the independent or dependent variables; and
- how to craft the proper designs and methods to study substitutability.

I also think we must encourage the use of computer simulations to overcome problems of variance in opportunity/structure. All of the aforementioned will be needed to test fully the empirical implications of the formal models that are being developed to investigate literally every aspect of world/global/international politics/relations. Formal models, whether developed from economics, game theory, expected utility theory, or other sources will most certainly constitute the main analytical approach of the post–fourth wave, as a natural means to synthesize agency and structure, and choice (willingness) given constraints (opportunity). The prospects for continued cumulation and progress in the expansion of our knowledge are both daunting and exciting.

Notes

1. Harvey Starr, "The Quantitative International Relations Scholar as Surfer: Riding the Fourth Wave," *Journal of Conflict Resolution* 18, no. 2 (1974): 336–68.
2. Benjamin A. Most and Harvey Starr, *Inquiry, Logic, and International Politics* (Columbia: University of South Carolina Press, 1989), 2.
3. Ibid., 10.
4. Gil Friedman and Harvey Starr, *Agency, Structure, and International Politics* (London: Routledge, 1997).
5. Bueno de Mesquita began his reply to the other articles by saying, "I am greatly encouraged by the extent of agreement regarding the advantages of axiomatic, deductive theorizing over *ad hoc* hypothesis testing reflected in the exchange between myself, Robert Jervis and Stephen Krasner. Convergence on this critical epistemological issue is far more important than the remaining differences over quantification, case study

analysis, and the like." Bruce Bueno de Mesquita, "Reply to Stephen Krasner and Robert Jervis," *International Studies Quarterly* 29, no. 2 (1985): 151.

6. Karl Deutsch quoted in Starr, "The Quantitative International Relations Scholar as Surfer," 345.

7. Deutsch quoted in ibid., 345.

8. In discussing the strengths and contributions of game theory in his quantitative methods panel paper (in this volume), Bueno de Mesquita includes game theory's reliance on explicit logic, along with its transparency in assumptions, reasoning, and propositions. These features ensure that the scholar must be involved in rigorous theorizing.

9. Most and Starr, *Inquiry, Logic, and International Politics*, ch. 1.

10. Ibid.

11. See also Harvey Starr, "Visions of Global Politics as an Intellectual Enterprise: Three Questions without Answers," in *Visions of International Relations*, ed. Donald J. Puchala (Columbia: University of South Carolina Press, 2000).

12. Dina A. Zinnes, "The Problem of Cumulation," in *In Search of Global Patterns*, ed. James N. Rosenau (New York: Free Press, 1976).

13. Bueno de Mesquita, "Reply to Stephen Krasner and Robert Jervis"; or Bruce Bueno de Mesquita, "The Contribution of Expected-Utility Theory to the Study of International Conflict," in *Handbook of War Studies*, ed. Manus I. Midlarsky (Boston: Unwin Hyman, 1989). See also "Symposium: Methodological Foundation of the Study of International Conflict," in *International Studies Quarterly* 29, no. 2 (1985): 121–54.

14. Bruce Russett and Harvey Starr, *World Politics: The Menu for Choice*, 5th ed. (New York: Freeman, 1996), 30.

15. Most and Starr, *Inquiry, Logic, and International Politics.*

16. Ibid.

17. See, for example, the title of Claudio Cioffi-Revilla and Harvey Starr, "Opportunity, Willingness, and Political Uncertainty: Theoretical Foundations of Politics," *Journal of Theoretical Politics* 7, no. 4 (1995): 447–76.

18. See especially Friedman and Starr, *Agency, Structure, and International Politics.*

19. These are among the "five major insights which constitute the promise of postmodernism," which are presented in John Vasquez, "The Post-Positivist Debate: Reconstructing Scientific Enquiry and International Relations Theory after Enlightenment's Fall," in *International Relations Theory Today*, ed. Ken Booth and Steve Smith (University Park: Pennsylvania State University Press, 1995), 218. While it would take another paper to demonstrate fully, I hold that the critical logic (and/or positions it can represent or lead to) is capable of dealing with each of these insights. It is not that postmodernism does not have useful things to say, only that such comments *can* be generated by critical investigation from within the scientific tradition. For a much fuller development of this argument, see Friedman and Starr, *Agency, Structure, and International Politics.* I have not been persuaded by the postpositivist or postmodernist position that the world eludes our ability to study it

in any intersubjective way. Individuals do so every day; scholars across the social sciences and natural sciences have done so successfully for decades (if not centuries). See Pauline Rosenau, *Post-Modernism and the Social Sciences* (Princeton: Princeton University Press, 1991); Vasquez, "The Post-Positivist Debate"; Oyvind Osterud, "Antinomies of Postmodernism in International Studies," *Journal of Peace Research* 33, no. 4 (1996): 385–90; and Oyvind Osterud, "Focus on Postmodernism: A Rejoinder," *Journal of Peace Research* 34, no. 3 (1997): 337–8, for examples of the counterarguments that I find compelling.

20. See Harvey Starr, "'Opportunity' and 'Willingness' as Ordering Concepts in the Study of War," *International Interactions* 4, no. 4 (1978): 363–87; and Most and Starr, *Inquiry, Logic, and International Politics*, ch. 2.

21. Friedman and Starr (*Agency, Structure, and International Politics*, 3) elaborate:

> Agency and structure are the defining components for the understanding of human interaction within a society and of the explanation of social phenomena. The agent-structure problem refers to the general set of questions concerning the interrelationship of these two components, and to the ways in which explanations of social phenomena integrate them.
>
> International political systems, like all social systems, are comprised of agents and structures. What is more, agency and structure are interrelated. This basic tenet of social theory is shared by the three most widely acclaimed modern social theorists—Durkheim, Weber, and Marx.

See also Alexander Wendt, "The Agent-Structure Problem in International Relations Theory," *International Organization* 41, no. 3 (1987): 335–70.

22. Jon Elster, *Nuts and Bolts for the Social Sciences* (Cambridge: Cambridge University Press, 1989), 15.

23. Friedman and Starr, *Agency, Structure, and International Politics*.

24. Cioffi-Revilla and Starr, "Opportunity, Willingness, and Political Uncertainty."

25. Friedman and Starr, *Agency, Structure, and International Politics*.

26. Most and Starr, *Inquiry, Logic, and International Politics*.

27. For example, Marc V. Simon and Harvey Starr, "Extraction, Allocation, and the Rise and Decline of States," *Journal of Conflict Resolution* 40, no. 2 (1996): 272–97; and Marc V. Simon and Harvey Starr, "A Two-Level Analysis of War and Revolution: A Dynamic Simulation of Response to Threat," in *Decision-Making on War and Peace: The Cognitive-Rational Debate*, ed. Nehemia Geva and Alex Mintz (Boulder, Colo.: Lynne Rienner, 1997).

28. For example, in looking for systems with different polarity, as in Most and Starr, *Inquiry, Logic, and International Politics*, ch. 6; or the different conditions regarding internal and external conflict and the rise and decline of states, as in Simon and Starr, "Extraction, Allocation, and the Rise and Decline of States"; or the number of democracies in the system,

the number of endangered democracies, and countries with different configurations of neighbors, as in Marc V. Simon and Harvey Starr, "Two-Level Security Management and the Prospects for New Democracies: A Simulation Analysis," *International Studies Quarterly* 44, no. 3 (2000): 391–422.

29. Additionally, as Simon and Starr note: "In a sense, we use simulations as what Eckstein (1975) called a 'plausibility probe' to determine what kind of empirical work is warranted—to lead to further empirical analysis." Simon and Starr, "Extraction, Allocation, and the Rise and Decline of States," 275.

30. Frank Harvey, "Rigor Mortis or Rigor, More Tests: Necessity, Sufficiency, and Deterrence Logic," *International Studies Quarterly* 42, no. 4 (1998): 675–707; Frank Harvey, "Practicing Coercion: Revisiting Successes and Failures Using Boolean Logic and Comparative Methods," *Journal of Conflict Resolution* 43, no. 4 (1999): 840–71.

31. Most and Starr, *Inquiry, Logic, and International Politics*, 56–7.

32. Richard N. Lebow and Janice Gross Stein, "Rational Deterrence Theory: I Think Therefore I Deter," *World Politics* 41, no. 1 (1989): 208–24.

33. Cioffi-Revilla and Starr, "Opportunity, Willingness, and Political Uncertainty," 456–57.

34. See, for example, Patrick M. Regan, "Substituting Policies During U.S. Interventions in Internal Conflicts," *Journal of Conflict Resolution* 44, no. 1 (2000): 90–106. Nice laws are similarly related to context and the complexity of choice within complex notions of context. This term refers to "'sometimes true,' domain specific laws" (Most and Starr, *Inquiry, Logic, and International Politics*, 98). Most and Starr remind us that while we should aim for generality, the "right type of law" is one that is clearly specified, that the relationships among variables that it proposes will work only under specified conditions. Most and Starr question whether social scientists will ever generate important "universal" laws. They note, however, that "it may be useful to recognize that there could very well be laws that are in some sense 'good,' 'domain specific,' or 'nice' even though the relationships they imply are not necessarily very general empirically. . . . it may be more productive to think of laws each of which is always true under certain conditions (or within certain domains) but which is only 'sometimes true' empirically because those conditions do not always hold in the empirical world." Most and Starr, *Inquiry, Logic, and International Politics*, 117.

35. Cioffi-Revilla and Starr, "Opportunity, Willingness, and Political Uncertainty," 468.

36. Harvey Starr, "Substitutability in Foreign Policy: Theoretically Central, Empirically Elusive," *Journal of Conflict Resolution* 44, no. 1 (2000): 128–38; See Glenn Palmer, ed., *Substitutability in Foreign Policy: Applications and Advances,* special issue of *Journal of Conflict Resolution* 44, no. 1 (2000).

37. See Regan, "Substituting Policies During U.S. Interventions in Internal Conflicts"; and D. Scott Bennett and Timothy Nordstrom, "Foreign Policy Substitutability and Internal Economic Problems in Enduring Rivalries," *Journal of Conflict Resolution* 44, no. 1 (2000): 33–61.

Accomplishments and Limitations of a Game-Theoretic Approach to International Relations

Bruce Bueno de Mesquita

Game-theoretic reasoning emerged as an important form of analysis in international relations, especially regarding security studies, with the publication in 1960 of Thomas Schelling's *The Strategy of Conflict.* The remainder of the 1960s saw a proliferation of carefully reasoned, policy-relevant studies grounded in the techniques of formal logic and rational choice modeling. A small sampling includes Daniel Ellsberg's application of expected utility reasoning to deterrence strategy, Martin McGuire's investigation of secrecy and arms races, Anatol Rapoport and Albert Chammah's examination of the prisoner's dilemma in the context of cooperation and conflict, Bruce Russett's study of the calculus of deterrence, and many others.[1] Over the course of the next thirty or forty years, game theory became analytically more sophisticated, contributed greatly to the acquisition of cumulative knowledge in international relations, and gradually emerged as a tool for generating hypotheses worthy of empirical study and as a contributor to policy debate. Game-theoretic analyses today increasingly are closely linked to empirical tests and to questions of great policy significance.

This essay summarizes one person's views of the strengths and contributions of game theory as a tool for studying international relations and assesses the limitations inherent in the current state of the science. I do not review individual studies here in any depth, focusing instead on broad patterns and generalizations. The interested reader should see several excellent reviews and evaluations of this literature, as well as my own lengthier discussions of it.[2]

Contributions of Game Theory to Studies of Social Phenomena

Game theory, and rational choice models more broadly conceived, make at least five contributions to the study of human interaction, including the study of international relations. These include (1) the provision of a motivational foundation for action; (2) an explanation of strategic behavior; (3) an ability to integrate other theories and approaches; (4) cumulative knowledge; and (5) insights into methodological issues influencing analyses of decision making. With the possible exception of its attentiveness to strategic decisions, game theory cannot claim a unique position in advancing any of these components of the study of international relations. No theory or methodology can make such a claim. But formal models, particularly game-theoretic models and spatial models, offer specific and important advantages in contributing to progress on all five of the fronts I have mentioned. What is more they have succeeded in doing so despite the fact that only a tiny fraction of international relations scholars employ these models, perhaps at present not more than two dozen out of, for instance, the more than three thousand members of the International Studies Association. In the pages that follow, I explore this claim, highlight important achievements, and then turn to a discussion of some of game theory's limitations.

Motivation for Action

Rational choice approaches provide a motivational foundation for action so that the link between correlation and causation is readily discerned. Rational choice models of international relations stipulate that decision makers are interested in maximizing their welfare. Theorists differ in their perspective regarding the content behind this motivation, with some looking at the maximization of the national interest,[3] while others investigate individual decision-maker interests,[4] thereby distinguishing the welfare of leaders from the well-being of their states. By emphasizing motivations, such models ensure that political strategy enters into the explanation of international affairs, with emphasis on how domestic and foreign institutions, and international structures, constrain, but do not determine, behavior.

The assumption that decision makers are rational is not a subject of inquiry in models that accept this perspective but rather an initial condition that, in conjunction with other assumptions, leads to implications about choices and actions. The rationality assumption says no more than that decision makers do what they *believe* is in their best interest given the information they possess at the time a choice is made. The "other assumptions" can relate to whether the "decision maker" is a state treated as a unitary actor, a group with shared interests, or individuals with perhaps competing or conflicting interests. Additionally, a rational choice theory might stipulate that all actors maximize the same thing, whether it be national power, security, or welfare, or the individual's term in office, policy goals, religious fervor, and so on. Alternatively, different actors might be assumed to maximize different interests or different goals, such as relative gains or absolute gains, personal political gain or national security, and so on. The assumption of rationality does not restrict the range or complexity of objectives decision makers want to achieve in theory or in reality.

Despite its flexibility, the rationality assumption helps formulate the microfoundations for causal arguments by tying action to objectives. Other approaches, such as psychological theories of cognitive dissonance, groupthink, and so on, can also help provide microfoundations so that they form part of a relatively small set of approaches that facilitate a focus on what motivates action. Ultimately, the explanations offered by alternative theories can only be judged on the basis of their logical integrity and their empirical bite. Although some might argue that internal consistency is not critical,[5] without it we can make no sense of what a theory does or does not claim. Likewise, without empirical testing we can make no headway in choosing among internally consistent theories that make different predictions about behavior and outcomes.

Strategic Interaction

Game theory is a body of reasoning designed explicitly to attend to the logic of strategic interaction. Strategic interaction, in which decision makers select a course of action taking into account expectations about how others will respond, is central to all of international affairs. One consequence of the emphasis on strategic interaction is that propositions derived from game theory models are contingent hypotheses. This is true because any decision maker's actions are contingent on what he or she believes will prompt the most favorable response. Therefore, what one chooses to do depends on how others are expected to respond.

Non–game-theoretic points of view often assume away or greatly simplify the most interesting features of strategic interaction in international affairs. In the course of doing so, they frequently make noncontingent, linear predictions. For example, it is commonplace to find realists arguing that greater military advantage over an adversary is always better than less advantage.[6] Yet there are numerous instances of weaker states emerging victorious in military confrontations with stronger states. The observable military balance is contingent on a willingness to use available resources. Asymmetries in motivation, for example, can offset the apparent military superiority of one or the other combatant.[7] Of course, it is not necessary to use game theory to form contingent hypotheses, but because all game theory models rely on the logic of strategic interaction, the use of game theory is sufficient to make contingent predictions.

The very idea of equilibrium in game theory depends on contingent expectations. Decision makers consider alternative courses of action. They weigh the expected consequences of choosing one path or another, perhaps across many choices. In each case, they consider what they believe other decision makers will do, and then they, like all decision makers, choose the action that they think most advances their goals. Their actions are restricted to the set that enhances their welfare over all other actions, not at every step of the way, but in terms of the expected payoff at the end of the game.

Psychological theories, like game theory models, provide motivations for action, thereby fulfilling the first of the five conditions I discuss. They do not, however, provide clear and explicit rules for decision making in situations involving strategic interaction. That is, psychological theories lack an equivalent to game theory's notion of equilibrium. Even as highly developed and formalized a psychological theory as prospect theory contains no foundation from which to discuss how anticipated responses by others shape decision making. For example, consider the well-known experimental observation that individuals told by a physician that they have a 10 percent chance of recovery (and, implicitly, a 90 percent chance of dying) given a proposed medical procedure are unlikely to choose the procedure, whereas those told they have a 90 percent chance of recovery (and, implicitly, a 10 percent chance of dying) tend to elect the procedure. Prospect theorists, lacking a theory of strategic interaction, point to this result as evidence that standard expected utility axioms are violated. Yet a simple signaling game readily predicts the observed behavior.

Imagine a physician bound by professional ethics to report accurately to her patients the average recovery rate from a medical procedure. The physician may believe that her patient has a better or worse than average chance of recovery but is restricted to report the average recovery rate. By choosing to frame the rate as a recovery rate or a failure rate, the physician conveys additional information that she believes will help the patient make a more informed choice. The patient, comprehending the signal, takes the additional information into account and chooses accordingly. Because prospect theory and other psychological theories lack a well-formed approach to strategic interaction, they are unable at this time to achieve the subtlety of game-theoretic accounts when choices involve strategy or the transmission of private information. Instead, they interpret their experimental results as a challenge to all models grounded in expected utility's axioms, whereas many—though perhaps not all—of the experimental findings make perfectly good sense in a setting that includes strategic interaction. For problems involving strategic choice—and this surely includes most interesting problems in international relations—game theory is significantly advantaged over other approaches.

Integrating Approaches

Models based on game theory facilitate incorporation of the concerns and assumptions of structural, behavioral, constructivist, and psychological theories and so can help to integrate the important knowledge derived from these other approaches. Game theory readily synthesizes knowledge from diverse perspectives while retaining the logical rigor imposed by its axiomatic foundations. It does so because these other approaches do not contradict game theory assumptions.

Structure is a central element in games of sequential decision making in which choices are constrained by the situation decision makers find themselves in. Indeed, a significant body of research exists revolving around the theme of structure-induced equilibria. This literature examines how structures (such as bipolarity or multipolarity, balance of power or preponderance of power, etc.) and political institutions (such as democracy, autocracy, or monarchy, federalism or unitary governance, etc.) shape choices, influencing the strategies decision makers reject or accept.

Through a strategic analysis of preferences and beliefs game theory provides a means to examine attitudes, perceptions, uncertainties, and learning on the part of decision makers. At the same time, game theory provides a systematic means of analyzing and predicting behavior across large classes of events whether they involve sincere behavior, credible commitments, bluffing, or other forms of strategic decision making. These all seem to be crucial elements in the study of international affairs. Other approaches may take these features into account, but game theory is the only method with which I am familiar that explicitly requires attentiveness to all of these concerns.

Having said that, we should keep in mind that there is not a single game theory of international relations. Rather, game theory is a mathematical foundation from which to construct different, often competing theories. As such, game theory is an axiomatically based tool for studying decision making. In international relations, game theory provides a method for explaining and analyzing strategic behavior. The quality of any given theory, of course, depends on the insights of the researcher. Game theory as a method is beneficial because it ensures that crucial factors, including the ones I have enumerated, as well as explicit, transparent arguments, are taken into account. With normal language it is easy for clever rhetoric to mask logical inconsistencies. With the greater precision of mathematics, formal models reduce the risk that *seemingly* consistent arguments substitute for *actually* consistent arguments. Since inconsistent arguments are incoherent, either "predicting" everything or nothing, the explicit logic of game-theoretic analysis is a boon to weeding out ill-conceived theories while still leaving room for the proverbial thousand flowers to bloom.

A few examples help illustrate how rational choice models, especially game-theoretic ones, clarify logical relationships between seemingly competing theories or help separate internally consistent implications from less rigorously surmised associations within extant theories. Power transition theory purportedly predicts that the likelihood of major, system-transforming wars increases when rivals are approximately equal in power, one is growing faster than the other, and the rivals disagree over the rules and norms governing international intercourse.[8] Kim and Morrow, Powell, and Bueno de Mesquita and Lalman offer formal representations of power transition theory.[9] Each finds support for some of that theory's core hypotheses, but each also raises doubts about other, central portions of the power transition argument. None of the formal models, for instance, finds that equal power between rivals is either necessary or sufficient for war. The formal models suggest new propositions as well as challenging some original ones, and point to more nuanced tests (on, for example, differences in risk-taking propensities between challengers and targets that are associated with war). Power transition predictions about allies are shown to be a special case of a more general argument about allies and war, an argument that subsumes the seemingly contradictory predictions stated by power transition theorists and balance-of-power theorists.[10]

Though not unique in its ability to integrate ideas or compare arguments, game theory's formalism conveys an advantage. To assess the logical implications of alternative assumptions or alternative statements of a theory, it is necessary first to stipulate *precisely* what the theory says or what it includes and excludes. When assumptions and their logical connections are explicit, it is straightforward to alter one or another component of a theory to ascertain how the theory's predictions are modified by the change. In doing so, we learn whether the theory's predictions follow from its assumptions; follow but are not robust against minor changes in the assumptions; follow and are robust to changes in assumptions; or do not follow. This kind of systematic, detailed evaluation of a theory is hard to do and, therefore, is rarely done outside the formal literature in international relations. Within that literature, however, it is common.[11]

Cumulative Knowledge

No approach or methodology corners the market on generating cumulative knowledge about international relations. Game-theoretic models, because of their formalism, however, offer some important advantages in the efficient discovery of cumulative knowledge. They do so because explicit assumptions make it easy to determine what the logical consequences are of relaxing one or another condition, substituting alternative assumptions, or restricting the theory further by adding new assumptions as discussed earlier. In this way, anomalous cases can be carefully explored and modified theories constructed that may account for known facts and the seeming anomalies, while also uncovering new facts. Fearon's audience costs argument has just this quality, as does Powell's research into guns versus butter or Morrow's assessment of endogenous regime formation.[12]

The past few years have witnessed the development of a body of research dedicated to testing competing rational actor models, thereby helping to distinguish the empirical content of alternative formulations.[13] Reiter and Stam, for instance, contrast competing explanations of the democratic peace.[14] Some argue that democracies win wars more often than do their adversaries because democratic norms lead to greater support for war efforts among the citizenry. Others argue that democracies win more often because leaders risk losing their jobs if their state is defeated in war and so select the wars to enter carefully, negotiating and offering concessions in those instances where they do not believe they will prevail militarily. Because at least some of these arguments have been formulated in explicit, game-theoretic terms, the contingencies under which democracies are expected to fight and win are spelled out with sufficient detail to construct tests of the alternative explanations.

Gelpi and Grieco[15] also contributed significantly to this debate by identifying conditions under which audience effects, as predicted by Fearon, are expected to increase the willingness of democracies to fight and when institutional constraints, as predicted by Bueno de Mesquita and Lalman, diminish the willingness of democracies to fight. These at least partially competing hypotheses (depending on the contingent conditions) both derive from formal, game theory models of international interaction. Smith has similarly expanded the general understanding of international interaction, specifically regarding the reliability of alliances, by using game theory to focus attention on the interdependency between alliance formation, alliance reliability, and conflict initiation.[16] Schultz and Morrow have expanded our understanding of the nexus between domestic affairs and international conflict in their models in which decision makers maximize personal welfare rather than national welfare.[17] These studies raise significant questions about the common notion that partisanship should end at the water's edge, suggesting political and national benefits to be derived from partisan competition in foreign policy. The tie between the formal literature and empirical tests has led to more sophisticated testing and to progress in understanding the contingencies under which war is more or less likely,[18] under which alliances are more or less reliable,[19] under which threats of sanctions are likely to succeed or fail,[20] under which deterrence is effective or ineffective,[21] and so forth. The empirical track record associated with game-theoretic approaches to international relations is growing in breadth, depth, and the significance of findings.

Methodological Insights

Game theory contributes broadly to international relations research, even among non–game theorists, by drawing greater attention to endogenous choices and their implications for path dependence; selection effects in theory and in data and how they can distort inferences from historical analysis; the importance of independence between arguments and the evidence used to evaluate their merits if we are to distinguish between description, explanation, and prediction; and prediction as a means of evaluating the potential of scientific inquiry to help improve future international affairs. These four items—endogeneity, selection effects, independence between argument and evidence, and prediction—represent areas where rational choice models are especially helpful in clarifying empirical problems that frequently arise in other modes of analysis.

By endogeneity I mean choices or conditions determined by the logic of the situation rather than given or assumed from outside. For instance, in neorealism the structure of the international system is taken as given, as exogenous, but neorealists state that their objective is to explain changes (as well as constancy) in system structure. Their stated objective indicates that they believe the system's structure is endogenous, yet they do not lay out a theory of choice that helps explain the relationship between individual actor choices and consequences for system structure. Quite the contrary, they deny the existence of such a link. Yet when individual leaders choose to form alliances, build domestic military capabilities, or conquer others' territory, they make choices that can alter the polarity and balance of power in the international system. They also contemplate choices that can precipitate countermoves by their rivals, leading to still further changes in the system's structure. Thus, their choices are constrained by their expectations about the consequences of their actions, one set of which has to do with the international structure. In this more game-theoretic view, the structure is endogenized rather than taken as given.

Selection effects are closely tied to endogeneity and are central to understanding the nature of contingent hypotheses. For example, as mentioned earlier, Smith shows that one nation is more likely to attack another if the would-be attacker believes the target's allies are unreliable.[22] If the target's allies are believed to be reliable then the likelihood of attack is diminished, and when attacks take place, allies are more likely to prove unreliable. Thus, tests of the reliability of allies cannot look only at cases following an attack as the attacker is likely to have selected targets based on the reliability of its target's allies. Failure to attend to this selection effect can lead to grossly misleading empirical inferences.

Independence between the statement of hypotheses and the evidence for or against the hypotheses is essential if we are to develop a better understanding of how the world of international politics works. There is no inherent advantage to induction or deduction in arriving at "correct" answers to the puzzle of how the world works. There are, perhaps, efficiencies to be gained in beginning deductively and then progressing to induction. Hypotheses derived from first principles provide ideas to test that are not derived from observed patterns in known data. Because the deduced propositions from an axiomatic model follow logically from the assumed initial conditions, the propositions have the advantage of being closely based on causal logic. In this way the researcher gains the efficiency of evaluating the hypotheses by looking at data chosen to approximate the initial conditions of the theory, rather than being chosen based on known values for the dependent variable. If the propositions or hypotheses are borne out, then confidence is built in the theory. Inductive research, in contrast, typically derives hypotheses from the observed patterns in the data. Then, until a second, independent data set is generated, the first data set has not provided a test of any hypotheses, but rather a description of the hypotheses. Unfortunately, it is the rare social science study that collects a second, independent data set and then tests to see if the *precise* explanation extracted from the first data set (or case study) holds in the second. If the structure of the hypotheses changes from data set to data set, then the evidence refutes the original hypotheses, new hypotheses describe current data (which may be refuted by the original data set), and yet another independent data set may be required to evaluate the new claims. One great advantage of out-of-sample testing is that it provides a useful way to evaluate whether a hypothesis derived from one body of data is robust in the face of new bodies of data.

Out-of-sample testing moves knowledge forward by providing predictive tests. As formal models do not derive their hypotheses from the data, they facilitate prediction because they offer specific, contingent descriptions of how variables relate to each other rather than merely describing some known data. Then predictive tests are as readily conducted as ex post tests. Of course, with genuinely predictive tests there is no danger that the ex ante, stated hypothesis is designed to fit the known outcome because there is not yet a known outcome. Induction does not preclude real prediction as evinced by empirical models of economic performance and presidential election outcomes. But few empirical theories are applied to prediction, whereas formal models are as readily tested on future events as on past events. Elsewhere I have summarized some of the literature concerning formal models and prediction in international relations.[23]

Summary of Benefits

The emphasis on strategic interaction inherent in game theory coupled with its explicit logic, transparency in assumptions, and reasoning and propositions have led to substantial progress in knowledge. Game-theoretic models and empirical tests of them have advanced our understanding of alliance formation, reliability, and termination. They contributed significantly to the debate on the democratic peace, providing theoretical bases on which to account for the known empirical regularities, as well as suggesting novel empirical insights. Rational choice models are at the core of deterrence theory and played a central role in the development of nuclear and conventional strategy throughout the cold war. Recent research on economic sanctions as a tool of diplomacy shows the limitations of sanctioning as a strategy. Much of that research is grounded in game theory.[24] A burgeoning literature on the paths to cooperation in international affairs grows directly out of investigations of repeated games.[25] Knowledge of the factors leading to conflict initiation, escalation, and termination have been significantly improved by game-theoretic analyses. I could go on but will stop here to turn attention to the limitations of this approach. Clearly, much remains to be done, with the promise of benefits from this approach—an approach still in its infancy and lacking a critical mass of scholars—being greater than the substantial accomplishments to date.

Limitations

Since its initial formal statement in the 1940s,[26] game theory has made tremendous technical progress. The earliest formulations assumed that players were bound to honor promises they made. Cooperative games of this sort precluded the possibility of investigating such inherently interesting problems as the prisoner's dilemma. After all, a key feature of that game is that players can promise to cooperate and fail to do so because nothing other than their self-interest governs their behavior. By the 1950s, noncooperative game theory emerged as a means to consider situations in which players could renege on promises. The 1950s also saw the emergence of the critical solution concept for noncooperative games, the Nash equilibrium. A Nash equilibrium is a complete plan of action for each player (i.e., a strategy) such that no player believes he can be better off by switching to a different strategy.

By the 1960s, Harsanyi showed how to model games in which players were, in colloquial parlance, uncertain of what game they were playing.[27] That is, he showed how to examine situations in which, for example, players were uncertain about prior moves in the game (that is, the history of play) or, loosely, about the payoffs their fellow players attach to particular outcomes. With his insights it became possible to address much higher levels of uncertainty than had previously been possible in game theory. With the introduction of subgame perfection as a refinement of Nash's equilibria, sequential games and their game trees came into their own, largely supplanting "normal form" games. Now analysts could evaluate how the sequence of action influences behavior and, in the process, could eliminate on logical grounds many Nash equilibria. Only a subset of Nash equilibria survive the subgame perfection requirement that players are restricted to making best replies, thereby eliminating incredible threats. Progress continued apace throughout the 1980s and up to the present. With the development of sequential equilibria, Bayesian perfect equilibria, and other refinements, it became possible to deal increasingly effectively with still more complex forms of uncertainty, larger numbers of players, learning, and one-stage, multistage, and infinitely repeated games.

By any yardstick, game theory has matured markedly over the past six decades, but much remains to be done. Game theory endures significant limitations, some of which are being overcome as the state of knowledge improves, others of which are inherent to the approach and are unlikely to be removed, though they can be improved upon by borrowing from other perspectives. I divide my discussion along these lines. First I discuss limitations that may be resolved in time. Then I turn to limitations that reflect the complementarity between rational actor models and other perspectives.

Information

Game theory models are demanding in terms of information assumptions. I hasten to add, however, that the demands regarding information are not what many critics seem to think they are. For instance, any game must contain some element of common knowledge. Critics often mistakenly believe that this means that every bit of information in a game-theoretic setting must be known by everyone. This is odd since game theory has always dealt with problems of uncertainty in the guise of incomplete and/or imperfect information. Many of the structurally simplest games, such as the prisoner's dilemma or chicken, involve decision making under uncertainty. Huge strides, as already noted, have been made in adding sophistication and rigor to the treatment of uncertainty and of learning in game theory models. However, some element of any game must be common knowledge. That is, each player must know the element, each player must know that everyone else knows it, and each player must know that everyone else knows that each player knows it, and so on. This requirement means that games that involve learning must start with the premise that everyone knows everyone else's prior (initial) beliefs (though not their prior knowledge, which can be private). Players can disagree about prior expectations, thereby holding different beliefs, but games assume that everyone knows what the prior beliefs held by others are, whether they agree with them or not. Several prominent game theorists are working on alternative approaches to remove this constraint, so this is an area where we can expect significant progress in the future.

Multiple Equilibria

Many games have multiple Nash equilibria. For games with multiple equilibria (and even many simple games like chicken or battle of the sexes contain multiple equilibria), game theory can predict a probability distribution over actions but cannot say definitively when one action or another will be taken provided each such action is part of an equilibrium strategy. However, there have been and continue to be important steps toward reducing the problem of multiple equilibria. Solution concepts like subgame perfection, universal divinity, Bayesian perfect equilibria, and so forth "refine away" many Nash equilibria, thereby making predictions more precise. Each refinement is itself a Nash equilibrium so that all of the foundational rigor established through the application of Nash equilibria is preserved. Consider the following simple example.

Table 1 depicts a normal-form payoff matrix for battle of the sexes. Player A prefers to go to the opera with B (A's utility if both choose opera is 3) over going to the movies with B (in which case A's utility is 1), but A prefers going to the movies with B over going to the opera or the movies alone (in each case A's utility for going alone is 0). B's utility for going to the movies with A is 3 and for going to the movies alone is 0, while B's utility for going to the opera with A is 1 and for going to the opera alone is 0. That is, A and B prefer to coordinate, doing something together rather than doing something alone, but they disagree over what they would most like to do together. This simple game as stated has three equilibria: both go to the opera; both go to the movies; or A goes to the opera with probability .75 and A goes to the movies with probability .25, while B goes to the opera with probability .25 and to the opera with probability .75.

The game matrix in table 1 is consistent with three games written out as trees, also called the extensive form (see figure 1). In the top-left game, player A moves first. Of the three Nash equilibria for the game in table 1, only one survives as a subgame perfect Nash equilibrium. The equilibrium strategies are depicted with dotted lines. B's plan of action is to choose the movies if A chooses the movies and to choose the opera if A chooses the opera. A's plan of action is to choose the opera, so that the outcome is that A and B go to the opera together. The top-right game shows B moving first, again with dotted lines depicting the equilibrium actions. B's threat to go to the movies is not credible in the top-left game, just as A's threat to go to the opera is not credible in the top-right game. The lighter dotted line in the bottom game indicates that when B chooses, B does not know what choice A made. I have not depicted the equilibria for this game as they are the same as in table 1. Yet the top two games each contain only one equilibrium although each, if written in matrix or

Table 1. Battle of the Sexes

		Player B	
		Opera	*Movies*
Player A	Opera	3,1	0,0
	Movies	0,0	1,3

normal form, would look exactly like table 1. This illustrates several principles.

Refinements of the Nash equilibrium improve the precision of game-theoretic predictions by eliminating some strategies from the equilibrium set. Whether these refinements improve predictive accuracy, however, remains unknown. To my knowledge there are no systematic empirical tests of the match between outcomes and predictions under alternative refinements. When games contain mixed strategy equilibria, such as the probabilistic choices of movies and opera just discussed, game theory predicts the probability distribution of actions. In such situations, the prediction can be evaluated only against a large number of cases as the theory makes no prediction about a specific case, but rather a prediction about the distribution of choices across cases. Then a single case can neither be said to support nor to contradict the theory's prediction. Of course, as the

Figure 1.

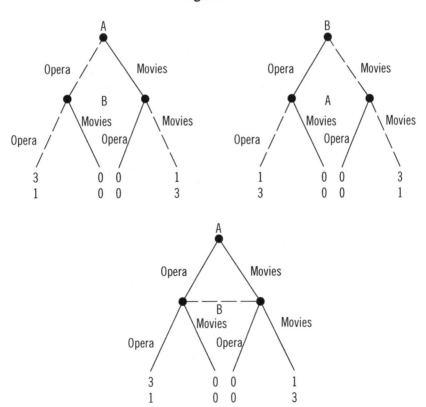

previous example also illustrates, not all games contain multiple equilibria.

Game theorists have not stopped with refinements of the Nash equilibrium in efforts to refine and improve prediction. Other efforts, such as quantal response equilibria, introduce non-Nash refinements that nevertheless are grounded in a rigorous, axiomatic foundation.[28] These refinements are designed partially to address the reality that people make errors in their choices and partially to address estimation problems in models with perfect information. There is considerable additional research on improving the criteria for selecting among equilibria, but this is not the place for an extended discussion of these technical matters.

Despite the improvements in equilibrium selection concepts, much remains to be done. Here is an area with clear complementarity between approaches. Constructivism focuses on socially created views of reality. As such, it may develop into a theory of how people choose among alternative strategies. It is a possible way to resolve the issue of common conjectures. Nash assumed that people share common conjectures about how others would play a given game and that this would lead to equilibrium selection. Focal points likewise were seen as ways that people would choose one equilibrium strategy over another. But no game theorist has a theory about the formation of common conjectures or about the formation of preferences. Constructivism and the empirical literature on socialization are two possible sources for identifying behavioral bases for selecting among equilibria and for predicting and explaining the formation of preferences over outcomes. Constructivism lacks a theory of action, like equilibrium theory in games, but game theory lacks a view on how preferences, focal points, and common conjectures are formed or communicated. Together, constructivism, or theories of socialization, and game theory might provide a powerful body of insights with which to resolve equilibrium selection.[29] It is a pity, then, that more constructivists have not been attracted to the idea of using their insights to test empirically whether their approach can help discriminate preferences over equilibria. Perhaps this will prove to be a promising and fruitful area of future research.

Skill and Bounded Rationality

Another well-known limitation of game theory is that all players are assumed to play with equal skill. That does not, however, mean that everyone plays the same way. The concept of player types is prominent in game-theoretic investigations of situations with limited information, especially when one does not have a clear idea of what outcome others prefer or by how much. Signaling games, for instance, have become prominent as a means to address the problems that arise regarding player types and the credibility of their actions. Players can learn more about the true preferences and intentions of other players through close observation of their actions. By distinguishing between cheap talk signals and costly signals, game theory has refined the analyst's ability to distinguish conditions under which a bluff is credible from those in which it is not.

One prominent approach to addressing the reality that skills are not equally distributed is the vast literature on bounded rationality. Little of the bounded rationality literature confronts problems of strategic interaction, focusing instead on simpler decision-theoretic problems. Most prominent are the efforts, mentioned earlier, by Kahneman and Tversky to develop prospect theory.[30] Unfortunately, there is little real-world, nonlaboratory empirical evidence beyond anecdotes to substantiate the claims for prospect theory, and few of its adherents in international relations are carefully attentive to its demanding mathematical structure. Nevertheless, prospect theory holds out the possibility of evolving into an axiomatic foundation for explaining rational, but non–utility-maximizing, behavior.

One recent effort to compare prospect theory with an expected utility model highlights some important, generally overlooked limitations of prospect theory and raises questions about its practicality or power as a predictive tool.[31] In this study, a prospect theorist chose the elements of the Northern Ireland Good Friday Agreements as a vehicle for comparing the two approaches. Data were collected on the Good Friday Agreements in May 1999, and explicit predictions were made about the implementation, delay, watering down, or outright breakdown of talks surrounding each element and the whole package. In August 2000, the researchers identified what actually had happened and compared the results to the predictions. Several important lessons were learned from the exercise. First, the expected utility approach made detailed predictions about the actions of each decision maker over time, as well as predicting the consequences of those actions for decisions taken on each element and the whole of the Good Friday Agreements. Prospect theory could only be precise about predicting who among the decision makers was expected to be risk averse and who was expected to be risk acceptant. It allowed less precise predictions about outcomes. Still, explicit conditions were stipulated that would falsify the less precise prospect theory predictions. The expected utility model made eleven predictions, each of which turned out to be correct. The prospect theory predictions were correct between four-elevenths and seven-elevenths of the time, depending on how some are interpreted. The conditions that were stipulated in advance as falsifying the specific prospect theory claims in fact occurred in this case so that the theory was not upheld. Of course this is only one test, so too much should not be made of it. Nevertheless, it is the first systematic, ex ante test of the effectiveness of the prospect theory viewpoint in comparison with a standard, expected utility–grounded game theory model.

Theories of bounded rationality address an important limitation of game theory models, but they do not yet address those limitations effectively. In particular, bounded rationality models proliferate the range of actions predicted to be possible. That is, in models of bounded or limited rationality, the sequence in which options present themselves determines actions while no theory of what governs the sequence of choices is provided. A fundamental factor—the order in which options are presented to players—is taken as exogenous rather than as strategically shaped by rivals. Theories of bounded rationality, then, are capable only of weak, vague (sometimes nonfalsifiable) predictions rather than the more precise (and falsifiable) predictions possible with game theory. Even when game-theoretic predictions are somewhat vague, as in cases of multiple equilibria, bounded rationality models are vaguer, with even more equilibria.[32] Theories of bounded rationality, rather than simplifying or clarifying expectations, lead to a proliferation of equilibria beyond those supported in rational choice models.

A promising approach for solving many of the information restrictions of game theory is to blend game theory with evolutionary models. Evolutionary games are beginning to enjoy considerable attention.[33] Evolutionary models allow players to have different levels of skill or insight in strategic situations and then select players on the basis of their success. In the short term, many inefficient strategies survive, but this literature generally shows that over the longer run, strategies and players fail to survive on the basis of their inefficiency so that eventually evolutionary processes seem to favor players who choose Nash equilibrium strategies. This is encouraging both for rational choice theorists and for non–rational choice theorists who utilize the power of evolutionary models. Indeed, I suspect that in the long run, game theory as we now know it will give way to just such dynamic, evolutionary models. For now, however, game theory provides a simpler mathematical structure than do evolutionary models within which to investigate strategic interaction in international affairs. As the tools for dealing with computational complexity improve, we may perhaps look forward to evolutionary models or dynamic games replacing the comparative static analysis prevalent in current game theory.

Conclusions

As a tool for studying international affairs game theory is, relatively speaking, in its infancy. Despite the recency of the approach and the paucity of researchers trained in its use, game theory and other rational choice approaches already have had a significant impact on how we think about and test theories of international affairs. Rational actor models yield subtle, contingent propositions, many of which have already been tested and found to be consistent with the historical record. But game theory also poses challenges to the analyst. These challenges concern ways to improve or reduce dependence on demanding conditions. Still, even when the demands of assumptions are stringent, rational actor models offer a tool that facilitates testing the effects of relaxing or substituting alternative assumptions while maintaining analytic rigor and transparency. Other approaches lack this degree of clarity and logical precision. In the end, we are unlikely to uncover whatever laws govern human interaction until we impose rigorous standards on the logical consistency and empirical assessment of our theories. Rational choice models are one important step in that direction.

Notes

1. Daniel Ellsberg, "The Crude Analysis of Strategic Choice," *American Economic Review* 51 (1961): 472–89; Martin McGuire, *Secrecy and the Arms Race* (Cambridge: Harvard University Press, 1965); Anatol Rapoport and Albert M. Chammah, *Prisoner's Dilemma: A Study in Conflict and Cooperation* (Ann Arbor: University of Michigan Press, 1965); Bruce M. Russett, "The Calculus of Deterrence," *Journal of Conflict Resolution* 7 (June 1963): 97–109.
2. David Lalman, Joe Oppenheimer, and Piotr Swistak, "Formal Rational Choice Theory: A Cumulative Science of Politics," in *Political Science: The State of the Discipline*, 2d ed., ed. Ada Finifter (Washington, D.C.: American Political Science Association, 1993); Bruce Bueno de Mes-

quita, *Principles of International Politics* (Washington, D.C.: Congressional Quarterly Press, 2000); Jacek Kugler and Yi Feng, eds., special issue of *International Interactions* 23, no. 3 (1997); Michael Brown, Owen Cote Jr., Sean Lynn-Jones, and Steven Miller, eds., *Rational Choice and Security Studies* (Cambridge: MIT Press, 2000).

3. Steven J. Brams, *Superpower Games* (New Haven, Conn.: Yale University Press, 1985); Emerson Niou, Peter Ordeshook, and Gregory Rose, *The Balance of Power* (New York: Cambridge University Press, 1989); Robert Powell, *Nuclear Deterrence Theory: The Search for Credibility* (New York: Cambridge University Press, 1990); Robert Powell, *In the Shadow of Power: States and Strategy in International Politics* (Princeton, N.J.: Princeton University Press, 1999); Woosang Kim and James D. Morrow, "When Do Power Shifts Lead to War?"*American Journal of Political Science* 36 (1992): 896–922; Bruce Bueno de Mesquita and David Lalman, *War and Reason* (New Haven, Conn.: Yale University Press, 1992); Alastair Smith, "Alliance Formation and War," *International Studies Quarterly* 39 (1995): 405–25.

4. James D. Fearon, "Domestic Political Audiences and the Escalation of International Disputes," *American Political Science Review* 88 (1994): 577–92; James D. Fearon, "Signaling Foreign Policy Interests: Tying Hands versus Sinking Costs," *Journal of Conflict Resolution* 41 (February 1997): 68–90; Bruce Bueno de Mesquita and Randolph Siverson, "War and the Survival of Political Leaders: A Comparative Study of Regime Types and Political Accountability," *American Political Science Review* 89 (1995): 841–55; Kenneth A. Schultz, "Domestic Opposition and Signaling in International Crises," *American Political Science Review* 92 (1998): 829–44; Bruce Bueno de Mesquita, James D. Morrow, Randolph Siverson, and Alastair Smith, "An Institutional Explanation of the Democratic Peace," *American Political Science Review* 93 (1999): 791–807.

5. Stephen Walt, "Rigor or Rigor Mortis? Rational Choice and Security Studies" *International Security* 23, no. 4 (1999): 5–48.

6. Henry Kissinger, *White House Years* (Boston: Little, Brown, 1979); Paul K. Huth, *Standing Your Ground: Territorial Disputes and International Conflict* (Ann Arbor: University of Michigan Press, 1996).

7. Alexander L. George, David K. Hall, and William E. Simons, *The Limits of Coercive Diplomacy* (Boston: Little, Brown, 1971); Bueno de Mesquita, *Principles of International Politics.*

8. A. F. K. Organski, *World Politics* (New York: Knopf, 1958); A. F. K. Organski and Jacek Kugler, *The War Ledger* (Chicago: University of Chicago Press, 1980); Jacek Kugler and Douglas Lemke, eds., *Parity and War* (Ann Arbor: University of Michigan Press, 1996); Ronald L. Tammen, Jacek Kugler, Douglas Lemke, Allan C. Stam III, et al., *Power Transitions: Strategies for the 21st Century* (New York: Chatham House/Seven Bridges Press, 2000).

9. Kim and Morrow, "When Do Power Shifts Lead to War?"; Robert Powell, "Uncertainty, Shifting Power, and Appeasement," *American Political Science Review* 90 (1996): 749–64; Bueno de Mesquita and Lalman, *War and Reason.*

10. Bueno de Mesquita, *Principles of International Politics*, 413–14.

11. Christopher K. Butler, *Superpower Dispute Initiation: Status-Quo Evaluations and Strategic Timing* (Ph.D. dissertation, Michigan State University, 2000); Byeonggil Ahn, "When Hawks are Doves and Doves are Hawks: Domestic Conditions and Foreign Conflicts," *Journal of International and Area Studies* 6, no. 1 (1998): 21–44; Powell, "Uncertainty, Shifting Power, and Appeasement"; Kim and Morrow, "When Do Power Shifts Lead to War?"

12. Fearon, "Domestic Political Audiences and the Escalation of International Disputes"; Powell, *In the Shadow of Power*; James D. Morrow, "Modeling the Forms of Cooperation: Distribution versus Information," *International Organization* 48 (1994): 387–423.

13. For a small sample of such investigations, see for instance Christopher Gelpi and Joseph Grieco, "Democracy, Crisis Bargaining, and Audience Costs: Analyzing the Survival of Political Elites" (paper presented at the annual meetings of the American Political Science Association, Boston, 1998); D. Scott Bennett and Allan C. Stam III, "Comparative Theory Testing: Expected Utility versus All Comers" (paper presented at the annual meeting of the International Studies Association, Minneapolis, 1998); D. Scott Bennett and Allan C. Stam III, "A Universal Test of an Expected Utility Theory of War," *International Studies Quarterly* 44 (2000): 451–80; Dani Reiter and Allan C. Stam III, "Democracy, War Initiation, and Victory," *American Political Science Review* 92 (1996): 377–89; Erik Gartzke, "War Is in the Error Term," *International Organization* 53 (1999): 567–88.

14. Reiter and Stam, "Democracy, War Initiation, and Victory."

15. Gelpi and Grieco, "Democracy, Crisis Bargaining, and Audience Costs."

16. Smith, "Alliance Formation and War."

17. Schultz, "Domestic Opposition and Signaling in International Crises"; James D. Morrow, "Electoral and Congressional Incentives and Arms Control," *Journal of Conflict Resolution* 35 (June 1991): 243–63.

18. Bennett and Stam, "A Universal Test of an Expected Utility Theory of War."

19. Smith, "Alliance Formation and War."

20. Lisa L. Martin, *Coercive Cooperation: Explaining Multilateral Economic Sanctions* (Princeton, N.J.: Princeton University Press, 1992); Alastair Smith, "The Success and Use of Sanctions," *International Interactions* 21, no. 3 (1996): 229–45.

21. Jacek Kugler and Frank C. Zagare, "The Long-Term Stability of Deterrence," *International Interactions* 15, no. 3 (1990): 255–78; Frank C. Zagare, *The Dynamics of Deterrence* (Chicago: University of Chicago Press, 1987); Frank C. Zagare and D. Marc Kilgour, "Asymmetric Deterrence," *International Studies Quarterly* 37 (1993): 1–27; Samuel Wu, "To Attack or Not to Attack: A Theory and Empirical Assessment of Extended Immediate Deterrence," *Journal of Conflict Resolution* 34 (September 1990): 531–52.

22. Smith, "Alliance Formation and War."

23. Bueno de Mesquita, *Principles of International Politics*, ch. 17.

24. Martin, *Coercive Cooperation*; Smith, "The Success and Use of Sanctions."
25. Rapoport and Chammah, *Prisoner's Dilemma*; Michael Taylor, *Anarchy and Cooperation* (New York: Wiley, 1976); Robert Axelrod, *The Evolution of Cooperation* (New York: Basic Books, 1984).
26. John von Neumann and Oskar Morgenstern, *Theory of Games and Economic Behavior* (Princeton, N.J.: Princeton University Press, 1944).
27. John C. Harsanyi, "Games with Incomplete Information Played by 'Bayesian' Players," *Management Science*, ser. a, 14 (1967–68): 159–82, 320–34, 486–502.
28. Richard D. McKelvey and Thomas R. Palfrey, "Quantal Response Equilibria for Extensive Form Games," *Experimental Economics* 1, no. 1 (1998): 9–41.
29. I benefited from discussions with James D. Morrow in developing ideas about the linkage between common conjectures and constructivism.
30. See for instance Daniel Kahneman and Amos Tversky, "PT: An Analysis of Decision under Risk," *Econometrica* 47 (1979): 263–291; Daniel Kahneman and Amos Tversky, "Choices, Values, and Frames," *American Psychologist* 39 (1984): 341–50; Rose McDermott, *Risk-Taking in International Politics: Prospect Theory in American Foreign Policy* (Ann Arbor: University of Michigan Press, 1998).
31. Bueno de Mesquita, *Principles of International Politics*; Bruce Bueno de Mesquita, Rose McDermott, and Emily Cope, "The Expected Prospects for Peace in Northern Ireland," *International Interactions* 27, no. 2 (2001): 129–67.
32. Kenneth Binmore, *Essays on the Foundations of Game Theory* (Oxford, England: Blackwell, 1990); Thomas J. Sargent, *Bounded Rationality in Macroeconomics* (Oxford, England: Clarendon, 1993).
33. Axelrod, *The Evolution of Cooperation*; David P. Barash, *Sociobiology and Behavior*, 2d ed. (New York: Elsevier, 1982); Andrew Farkas, *State Learning and International Change* (Ann Arbor: University of Michigan Press, 1999).

GAME THEORY IN PRACTICE

Problems and Prospects in Applying It
to International Relations

Steven J. Brams

Introduction

In the last twenty or so years, there has been a surge of interest in modeling both national security and international political economy issues using the tools of game theory.[1] I will not try to cite this now extensive literature here but instead will (1) outline four major theoretical problems that have bedeviled various attempts at game-theoretic modeling of international relations (IR) and (2) propose an alternative approach, called the "theory of moves," that is grounded in game theory and that I and others have found attractive in modeling dynamic play. I argue that it captures the thinking of decision makers and realistically delineates their strategic choices in a parsimonious but historically informed way. Thereby I will indicate how some of the failures of game theory over the past half century, especially in modeling the dynamics of strategic choice in IR, can be ameliorated by an alternative, though controversial, theory.[2]

I illustrate how the theory can be applied to the well-known game of prisoners' dilemma. I then use the theory to analyze Anwar Sadat's peace initiative to Israel in 1977, which startled the world but eventually led to a peace treaty between Egypt and Israel in 1979. Sadat's bold attempt to break the impasse between the two countries and end a thirty-year conflict seems, in retrospect, to be the product of an eminently rational statesman, though it probably cost Sadat his life when he was assassinated in 1981.

Modeling Problems

I start by outlining four major pitfalls that plague game-theoretic modeling of IR phenomena and processes.

1. Misspecifying the Rules

A game is "the totality of rules that describe it."[3] To be sure, what constitute rules is not a simple matter. Generally speaking, rules both prescribe and proscribe behavior. Any game-theoretic models, therefore, should propose rules of play that reflect how players think and act in the strategic situation being modeled.

Based on this reality check, standard game theory often misses the mark. Players do not usually

- choose strategies simultaneously, or independently of each other, as assumed in the normal or strategic form of a game that can be represented by a payoff matrix; or
- adhere to a specified sequence of choices, as assumed in the extensive form of a game that can be represented by a game tree.

Rather, play usually starts at some initial state, or status quo point. Players look ahead to ascertain whether they can do better by moving or staying in this state. Their choices will vary, depending on the initial state and the rules that indicate what kinds of moves are possible and the means that best satisfy their goals.

Generally accepted rationality postulates, applied to the normal or extensive game forms, are frequently violated. For example, sometimes players choose dominated strategies in prisoners' dilemma, or they do not use backward induction, starting from the endpoints of a game tree, when prisoners' dilemma is repeated and the number of rounds is known. These violations, I suggest, are remediable, but they require different rules of play to render them rational and intelligible.

2. Confusing Goals with Rational Choice

Most people have goals, whether implicit or explicit, and they choose the best means to satisfy them, subject to environmental constraints like incomplete information. Emphatically, these constraints do not impair their rationality. Thus, if a person's goals are short term, then he or she will be rational with respect to them; if long term, this person's behavior may be quite different.

Some theorists have suggested that short-term goals mirror a thin kind of rationality and long-term goals a thicker or deeper kind. But, in fact, the observable differences in the behavior of the thin and thick types usually arises from their different goals, not their rationality or lack thereof. Put another way, thin types are not being irrational but instead choosing (rationally) *not* to look deeply or far ahead, presumably because this is too costly.

Rationality is a concept appropriately applied to the efficiency or efficacy of the means, or instruments used, to attain desired ends. What are the costs and benefits of different means, and are people making efficacious choices to achieve their ends? Rationality does *not* concern the ends themselves, which are neither rational nor irrational. To be sure, it is an important developmental question how people come to harbor the goals that they do, but that question is not pertinent to any instrumental notion of rationality that game theory postulates.

3. Arbitrarily Reducing the Multiplicity of Equilibria

Many games have multiple Nash equilibria; the 2×2 game of chicken, for example, has two equilibria in pure strategies and one in mixed strategies. Worse, in repeated play, almost any outcome of any game can be supported as a Nash equilibrium under certain conditions. With this embarrassment of riches, a game-theoretic model may not be helpful in narrowing down a plethora of stable outcomes to a few precise predictions.

Some theorists argue that norms like reciprocity, when they take hold in a population, can induce cooperative outcomes in collective-action situations, thereby helping actors avoid inefficient equilibria. Indeed, there is a good deal of empirical evidence to support not only the reciprocity norm but also the buildup of trust, and the nurturing of reputations of honesty and probity, to stabilize cooperation in games.

Unfortunately, these explanations for cooperation are often ad hoc: they do not follow from tenets of rationality in the games being studied. Rather, reciprocity, reputation, and trust are imported as behavioral assumptions, in part because these characteristics of game play are actually observed. Institutions may also play a role in fostering cooperation, but they are not as robust in IR as in domestic politics.

An important theoretical direction of game theory has been to endogenize some of its more restrictive assumptions by coarsening information structures, relaxing common knowledge of rationality, offering refinements of Nash equilibria, and the like. In effect, the definition of a game is altered by changing what players know, how they apprehend others' calculations, and the nature of the outcomes they seek.

For example, there are now several models that demonstrate how cooperation can emerge from repeated play of prisoners' dilemma when information is incomplete. But repeated play is very much an artifact when modeling player choices over time. Do players really play a single so-called stage game again and again, with no variation in its strategies, outcomes, or payoffs, accumulating payoffs at each stage?

In fact, strategies are often in flux, and possible outcomes are constantly changing, undermining the assumption of repeated play of a single stage game. Also problematic in the modeling of IR games, such as protracted wars, is that payoffs may not be realized in stages but only after considerable time has elapsed.

While evolutionary game theory and ecological models offer more sophisticated dynamics, they are complex, even if they narrow down the equilibria to relatively few. In addition, few IR processes seem plausibly modeled by a dynamic involving the random matching of players—with possible mutations—as assumed in biological-evolutionary models.

4. Forsaking Backward Induction

On the one hand, backward induction is "the oldest idea in game theory" that has "maintained its centrality to this day."[4] On the other hand, real players do not painstakingly work backward from the endpoints of a game tree, with many levels and a multitude of branches, to try to determine what they should do at the start of play. Rather, players develop heuristics and use rules of thumb that simplify this process, not because they are short-term thinkers and have abandoned their intelligence but because they have found good approximations to backward induction. But whence these rules, if not from robust and time-tested simplifications that approximate the calculations of backward induction?[5]

Thus, we should not dismiss backward induction too quickly. We use simple contingent strategies, like tit for tat, because they work well most of the time, even if they are not optimal in every situation. As I shall argue next, players make more exacting calculations in specific games, looking two, three, or four moves ahead, especially when the outcome is important to them.

TOM: An Alternative Approach

What I call the *theory of moves* (TOM) embeds extensive-form games within the normal form, deriving advantages of both forms: the nonmyopic thinking of the extensive form disciplined by the economy of the normal form.[6] In my view, the rules of TOM, which allow players to move and countermove within a payoff matrix, capture the changing strategic nature of situations that evolve over time. TOM's ability, as well, to incorporate differences in power—moving, order, or threat—reflects an asymmetry of player capabilities in many IR games.

Because prisoners' dilemma is a central focus of IR, let me illustrate the nonmyopic perspective that TOM provides by showing what constitutes rational play in the simple 2 × 2 version of prisoners' dilemma:

- If the play starts at the *noncooperative outcome,* players are stuck, no matter how far ahead they look, because as soon as one player departs, the other player, enjoying its best outcome, will not move on. *Outcome:* the players stay at the noncooperative outcome, which makes it a "nonmyopic equilibrium."
- If play starts at the *cooperative outcome,* then neither player will defect, because if it does, the other player will also defect, and they both will end up worse off. Thinking ahead, therefore, neither player will defect. *Outcome:* the players stay at the cooperative outcome, which makes it a nonmyopic equilibrium.
- If play starts at one of the *win-lose outcomes* (best for one player, worst for the other), the player doing best will know that if it is not magnanimous, and consequently does not move to the cooperative outcome, its opponent will move to the noncooperative outcome, inflicting on the best-off player its next-worst outcome. Therefore, it is in the best-off player's interest, as well as its opponent's, that the former act magnanimously, anticipating that if it does not, the noncooperative outcome (next to worst for both), rather than the cooperative outcome (next to best for both), will be chosen. *Outcome:* the best-off

player will move to the cooperative outcome, where play will stop.

These rational moves, grounded in backward induction, are not beyond the pale of most players. They are frequently made by those who look beyond the immediate consequences of their own choices.[7] Such farsighted players *can* escape the dilemma in prisoners' dilemma—as well as poor outcomes in other games—provided play begins at a state other than the noncooperative one in prisoners' dilemma.[8] Hence, TOM does not predict unconditional cooperation in this game but, instead, makes it a function of the starting point of play.[9]

TOM's history-dependent approach has been applied to the fifty-six other 2 × 2 strict ordinal *conflict games*—in which players can rank outcomes, but there is no outcome that is mutually best—and its predictions empirically tested in several IR studies.[10] Not only have its predictions been generally supported, but it has also explained well the dynamics of these conflicts.

I turn next to a real-life application of TOM that makes a prediction different from classical game theory. It illustrates how a deliberate move by one player (surpriser) to a Pareto-inferior state (i.e., one worse for both players) may induce the other player (surprisee) to implement an outcome better for both. This case suggests how surprise can engender cooperation rather than conflict in foreign policy, though it may entail risk.

Sadat's Peace Initiative

The disengagement of forces after the October 1973 Yom Kippur War, engineered by U.S. secretary of state Henry Kissinger, left Israel in control of the Golan Heights of Syria and the Sinai Peninsula of Egypt, the same territory it had captured in the Six Day War in June 1967. With no settlement in sight four years after the Yom Kippur War, there seemed every prospect of still another Arab-Israeli war when Anwar Sadat, president of Egypt, reported "thinking along the following lines":

Why shouldn't I go to the Israelis directly? Why shouldn't I stand before the Knesset and address the Israelis themselves as well as the whole world, putting forward the Arab cause and stating its dimensions? I conjured up what the reaction might be to such a move, which no one would expect. It would be said that it would be an uncalculated gamble.[11]

Although Sadat offers, as justification, such philosophical musings as "This is my fate" and "The hour is coming, have no doubt,"[12] it seems that there was considerable calculation behind his gamble, despite his impulsive nature.[13] For one thing, he wanted "to show the Israelis they were dealing with a new style of Arab leadership," not "monsters who wanted only to drive Israel into the sea."[14] For another, he was dismayed by the prospect of a reconvening of the Geneva Peace Conference between Israel and its Arab neighbors, which was supported by the superpowers but which Sadat believed was fraught with procedural obstacles and would end in stalemate.[15]

After his historic visit to Jerusalem on November 19–21, 1977, Sadat could accurately claim that "the Israeli people themselves became a pressure group in favor of peace."[16] As for other Arab leaders, Sadat bitterly remarked that after the Yom Kippur War, "when the entire Arab world made a lot of money out of oil and added to their wealth, Egypt by contrast was drained of its resources";[17] indeed, she faced a severe economic crisis in 1976–77.[18]

Sadat acknowledged that "we knew we could not fight the United States,"[19] which would likely side again with Israel if there were another war. More than any other factor, Telhami claims that it was the economic and military power of the United States that moved Egypt from the Soviet toward the American camp and a willingness, under U.S. auspices, to negotiate with Israel.[20]

Israeli leaders also felt that the United States must be a principal participant in the peace process.[21] In addition, Israel's

> military thinking had changed considerably as a result of the 1973 war. Secure borders were still considered vital, but it was recognized that dynamic and mobile warfare could to a large extent compensate for natural borders. . . . As a result of less steadfast American backing, Israel's bargaining position also changed . . . weakened by the Carter administration's more sympathetic policy toward the Arab states and Egypt in particular.[22]

Thus, when Sadat made his peace initiative to the Egyptian parliament on November 9, 1977, Prime Minister Menachem Begin, though caught unprepared, took only four days to extend an official invitation for Sadat to come to Jerusalem "to conduct talks for a permanent peace between Israel and Egypt."[23]

While the "psychological barrier" was broken,[24] it was more than psychology that produced what I call the Sadat initiative game (table 1). Egypt's (Sadat's) choices were to initiate (I) or not initiate (Ī) a lasting peace by visiting Jerusalem, and Israel's (Begin's) choices were to cooperate (C) or not cooperate (C̄) with this initiative. A brief description of the resulting four possible outcomes and the preferences of the players for each follows (I proceed clockwise from the upper-left outcome in table 1).[25]

1. ĪC—(4,1). Israel undermines her bargaining position by being cooperative—presumably, by offering concessions—before Egypt takes the first step and commits herself to a permanent solution to their conflict. (This would be especially damaging to the reputation of Begin, who was the newly elected prime minister from the hawkish Likud party.) What is worst (1) for Israel is, in this case, best for Egypt (4), because any resulting agreement between the two countries would favor Egypt insofar as it requires fewer concessions from her.

2. ĪC̄—(2,3). Without a peace initiative from Egypt or cooperation from Israel, the status quo stays in place. Continuing occupation of the Sinai is next worst (2) for Egypt, whereas it is next best (3) for Israel since her security is ensured, though at a high price.

3. IC̄—(1,2). Israel's frustration of Egypt's peace initiative is Egypt's worst (1) outcome because Sadat's big gamble is to no avail. But this outcome is quite unsatisfactory (2) for Israel as well, because she will lose American support and almost surely have to fight another war with Egypt, which will have little recourse to try to regain its lost territory.

4. IC—(3,4). Israel's favorable response to Egypt's peace initiative not only breaks the psychological barrier but also offers a good prospect of permanent peace. With appropriate security guarantees, this is the best (4) outcome for Israel and the next best (3) for Egypt, which will face the wrath of its Arab neighbors and the loss of monetary support from other Arab countries for negotiating a separate peace.

In the 2 × 2 game in table 1,[26] Egypt has a dominant strategy of not initiating peace: it is better whatever strategy Israel chooses. Anticipating this choice, Israel's best response is not to cooperate, resulting in payoffs of (2,3) at the status quo of ĪC̄. This is the unique Nash equilibrium, from which neither player would have an incen-

Table 1. Sadat Initiative Game

		Israel	
		Cooperate (C)	*Don't cooperate (C̄)*
Egypt	Don't initiate (Ī)	(4,1) Premature concessions by Israel; victory for Egypt	(2,3) Status quo; Sinai remains occupied
	Initiate (I)	**(3,4)** Negotiated settlement but conflict for Egypt with other Arab countries	(1,2) Initiative frustrated, presaging new war

Note. (i,j) = (payoff to Egypt, payoff to Israel).
4 = best; 3 = next best; 2 = next worst; 1 = worst.
Nash equilibrium underscored.
Nonmyopic equilibrium in boldface.

tive to depart unilaterally, making status quo the outcome that classical game theory would predict when both players are assumed to choose their strategies independently.

To be sure, Sadat, by taking the initiative and choosing I, changed the 2 × 2 game into a 2 × 4 game—in which he moves first and Begin responds—which makes IC, associated with (3,4), a dominant-strategy Nash equilibrium in the resulting 2 × 4 game. Although Sadat moved first, it still leaves open the question that both Arabs and Israelis have struggled to answer: Why did Sadat take the initiative that he did?[27]

The answer, I submit, is that it is rational, according to TOM, for Egypt to move to (1,2) and Israel to countermove to (3,4), resulting in a better outcome for both players than they receive at the status quo of (2,3). This is because if Egypt moves from the status quo of ĪC to IC̄, changing the state from (2,3) to (1,2), Israel will suffer too unless it responds by moving from IC̄ to IC, which gives Israel its best state of (3,4).

Notice that the latter state, which is a negotiated settlement, is better for both players than the status quo of (2,3). It is, therefore, in *both* players' interest that Egypt seize the initiative and move, temporarily, to (1,2), thereby affording Israel the opportunity to countermove to (3,4). On the other hand, if Israel had taken the initiative and moved first to $\overline{\text{IC}}$ from $\overline{\text{IC}}$, Egypt—going from (2,3) to (4,1)—would have had no incentive subsequently to move on to a negotiated settlement at (3,4). Thus, TOM also explains why it was Egypt, not Israel, that had to seize the initiative that would break the deadlock at (2,3).

After the peace accords negotiated at Camp David in September 1978 were translated into a peace treaty that was signed in April 1979, both sides clearly benefited from Sadat's dramatic visit to Jerusalem. In retrospect, there seems to be nothing irrational about Sadat's first move, because it did precisely what Sadat intended it to do in breaking the "psychological barrier."

Discussion

I do not pretend that all surprise can be captured in the switch by a player from a dominant to a dominated strategy, as illustrated in game 27. However, both the Sadat case of diplomatic surprise and the case of military surprise modeled in Brams's "The Rationality of Surprise"—namely, the Japanese attack on Pearl Harbor in December 1941—suggest that such switches may well catch a target completely off guard, generating great shock.

It turns out that a move by one player (say, Row) from its dominant-strategy Nash equilibrium, which in turn induces a countermove by Column to a different state, is rational in exactly six 2 × 2 games. In three of these games, this is to Column's benefit as well as Row's (both Egypt and Israel benefited from Sadat's visit to Jerusalem), but in the other three games it is only to Row's benefit (see "The Rationality of Surprise," which defines a generic surprise game).

In classical game theory, the incentive to move from a unique dominant-strategy Nash equilibrium in a 2 × 2 game also has a rational-choice justification, but it is awkward. It requires comparing the Nash equilibrium in the 2 × 2 game with the Nash equilibrium that Row can induce, if it moves first, in a 2 × 4 game. If the equilibrium in the 2 × 4 game is better for Row, then Row would have an incentive to move first.

TOM, by contrast, does not presume different games. Rather, play starts at states, with the order of moves endogenous. Players move and countermove according to rules of play and rationality rules that enable them to look ahead and anticipate ending up at a nonmyopic equilibrium from each state. Thus, (3,3) is a nonmyopic equilibrium from any state except (2,2) in prisoners' dilemma, whereas (3,4) is a nonmyopic equilibrium from all states in game 27.

The surprise of the Sadat peace initiative stems from thinking that the player with the dominant strategy (Egypt) would never have an incentive to depart from its strategy. The reason is that the outcome induced by the other player's best response, which is (3,4) in game 27, has no equilibrium status, not to mention state (1,2) that the players must pass through to get to (3,4) from (2,3).

According to TOM, however, IC is the unique nonmyopic equilibrium in game 27, wherever play starts. Hence, the players will be motivated to move there and realize payoffs of (3,4). The migration of Sadat and Begin from the status quo to a negotiated settlement is, therefore, not so surprising.

The fact that there was so much surprise leads me to postulate that, even if the game played was one of complete information (i.e., each player knows the other player's strategy choices and preferences for states, as given in table 1), there was incomplete information about either the rules of play or the rationality rules. Indeed, there was probably incomplete information about both player preferences and the rules, but it is the latter kind of incomplete information that has been much less studied, either empirically or theoretically. Because different rules may generate radically different equilibrium results, it is important to try to ascertain those that are most plausible in a situation.

The rules of TOM, in my opinion, are highly plausible in many situations. Players often do think more than one step ahead and are able to determine the series of moves and countermoves that they and an opponent are likely to make.

Without diminishing the standard explanations for surprise, especially in war, including lack of warning and noise,[28] it seems to me that a neglected alternative explanation is *anticipation failure.* This occurs when the surprised (myopic) player fails to anticipate the nonmyopic thinking of the other player.[29]

In the case of Sadat's peace initiative, the initially myopic player (Israel) acted very much according to TOM *after* it got over its initial shock. Had Sadat's dramatic gesture been anticipated, Begin might have tried to steal some of his thunder. But, as I showed earlier, Israel could not have induced (3,4) in game 27. Moreover, because Israel stood to benefit from the train of events that Sadat's move set off, it would have been foolish of Begin to try to undermine Sadat's efforts.

Conclusions

TOM incorporates into the framework of game theory an initial state in a payoff matrix; the moves and countermoves required to reach a nonmyopic equilibrium; and threat, moving, and order power that reflect asymmetries in the capabilities of the players (which I have not discussed here). It also allows for incomplete information, which in some games may lead to misperceptions and even flawed play.[30]

Because TOM postulates that players rank outcomes but not attach cardinal utilities to them, it seems eminently applicable to strategic situations in which it is hard to estimate players' precise valuations of the outcomes. In addition, it overcomes some problems of classical game theory by providing realistic rules for dynamic play, restricting nonmyopic equilibria to those that can be reached from where play commences, and using backward induction that enables players to make farsighted calculations.

What TOM offers that classical game theory does not is a simple and dynamic rationale for the players' making their moves and countermoves, which was observed in the empirical case analyzed herein. In specific games, it provides detailed prescriptions for optimal play, depending on where play starts and the powers of the players, that could aid foreign policy decision makers, especially in crises.[31]

But TOM is no panacea. It has been mostly developed for two-person games, whereas strategic situations in IR, including alliances and collective-action situations more generally, are often best modeled as n-person games.[32] While TOM can be extended to more complex games, more general theoretical structures need to be built, based on plausible rules of play. In my view, these need to take into account (1) players' strategic choices of coalition partners and (2) the courses of actions that flow from these choices.[33] Power differences among those coalitions that form, and the history of play that delimits equilibria—by ruling out later choices that are precluded by earlier ones—should provide foundations for a more general dynamic theory.

Notes

1. This paper is adapted from my paper "Game Theory: Pitfalls and Opportunities in Applying It to International Relations" (*International Studies Perspectives* 1, no. 3 [2000]: 221–32), in which the Iran hostage crisis of 1979–81 is used as the illustrative case study instead of, as here, Sadat's peace initiative in 1977; the latter is drawn from Steven J. Brams, "The Rationality of Surprise: Unstable Nash Equilibria and the Theory of Moves," in *Decisionmaking on War and Peace: The Cognitive-*

Rational Debate, ed. Nehemia Geva and Alex Mintz (Boulder, Colo.: Lynne Rienner, 1997), 103–29 (updated version, with a response and rebuttal, in *Mathematica Japonica,* 49, no. 2 [1999]: 293–316). In both this article and "Game Theory," technical details are omitted that can be found in Steven J. Brams, *Theory of Moves* (Cambridge: Cambridge University Press, 1994); Brams, "The Rationality of Surprise"; and other works on the theory of moves that are cited later. I gratefully acknowledge the support of the C. V. Starr Center for Applied Economics at New York University.

2. See the following recent exchange on the theory: Randall W. Stone, "The Use and Abuse of Game Theory in International Relations: The Theory of Moves," *Journal of Conflict Resolution* 45, no. 2 (2001): 216–44; Steven J. Brams, "Response to Randall Stone: Heresy or Scientific Progress?" *Journal of Conflict Resolution* 45, no. 2 (2001): 245–54.

3. John von Neumann and Oskar Morgenstern, *Theory of Games and Economic Behavior,* 3d ed. (Princeton, N.J.: Princeton University Press, 1953), 49.

4. Robert J. Aumann, "Backward Induction and Common Knowledge of Rationality," *Games and Economic Behavior* 8, no. 1 (1995): 6.

5. Backward induction itself is not always robust; it may be sensitive to the parity of the number of rounds of play and the boundedness of the game (i.e., whether it will end after some finite number of rounds). Steven J. Brams and D. Marc Kilgour, "Backward Induction Is Not Robust: The Parity Problem and the Uncertainty Problem," *Theory and Decision* 45, no. 3 (1998): 263–89.

6. Steven J. Brams, "Theory of Moves," *American Scientist* 81, no. 6 (1993), 562–70; Brams, *Theory of Moves.*

7. As a case in point, consider the following statement by Theodore C. Sorensen about the deliberations of the Executive Committee (Excom) during the October 1962 Cuban missile crisis: "We discussed what the Soviet reaction would be to any possible move by the United States, what our reaction with them would have to be to that Soviet reaction, and so on, trying to follow each of those roads to their ultimate conclusion." Quoted in Ole R. Holsti, Richard A. Brody, and Robert C. North, "Measuring Affect and Action in International Reaction Models: Empirical Materials from the 1962 Cuban Missile Crisis," *Journal of Peace Research* 1, no. 1 (1964): 188.

8. However, Willson's nonmyopic rules, which allow for backtracking, provide an avenue of escape by rendering even a sequence of moves that carries the players from the noncooperative to the cooperative state in prisoners' dilemma rational. Alternatively, I show how credible threats can induce cooperation in prisoners' dilemma and related games. See Stephen J. Willson, "Long-Term Behavior in the Theory of Moves," *Theory and Decision* 45, no. 3 (1998): 201–40; Stephen J. Willson, "Axioms for the Outcomes of Negotiation in Matrix Games," *Mathematical Social Sciences* 39, no. 3 (2000): 323–48; Brams, *Theory of Moves,* ch. 5.

9. Under the TOM rules of play that allow players to move and counter-

move within the payoff matrix, prisoners' dilemma is, of course, no longer the classical version of this game. Because there is almost always some status quo in most IR games, however, I believe it more realistic to start play at states rather than have players commence by making simultaneous or independent strategy choices. Contrast the cooperation that emerges from this framework, based on backward induction, with that that emerges from a framework that postulates ad hoc behavioral assumptions, like reciprocity.

10. Brams's *Theory of Moves* includes analyses of the Cuban missile crisis in 1962 and the U.S. bombing of Vietnam in 1972. Other applications of TOM to IR can be found in Brams, "The Rationality of Surprise"; Steven J. Brams, "To Mobilize or Not to Mobilize: Catch-22s in International Relations," *International Studies Quarterly* 43, no. 4 (1999): 621–40; Zeev Maoz and Ben D. Mor, "Enduring Rivalries: The Early Years," *International Political Science Review* 17, no. 2 (1996): 141–60; Tansa George Massoud, "Theory of Moves and the Persian Gulf War," in *The Political Economy of War and Peace*, ed. Murray Wolfson (Amsterdam: Kluwer Academic, 1998), 247–66; Ben D. Mor, *Decision and Interaction in Crisis: A Model of International Crisis Behavior* (Westport, Conn.: Praeger, 1993); Ben D. Mor, "The Middle East Peace Process and Regional Security," *Journal of Strategic Studies* 20, no. 1 (1997): 172–202; Ben D. Mor and Zeev Maoz, "Learning and the Evolution of Enduring International Rivalries: A Strategic Approach," *Conflict Management and Peace Science* 17, no. 1 (1999): 1–48; Marc V. Simon, "When Sanctions Can Work: Economic Sanctions and the Theory of Moves," *International Interactions* 21, no. 3 (1996): 203–28; Lester A. Zeager, "Negotiations for Refugee Repatriation or Local Settlement: A Game-Theoretic Analysis," *International Studies Quarterly* 42, no. 2 (1998): 367–84; Lester A. Zeager, "The Role of Threat Power in Refugee Resettlement: The Indochinese Crisis of 1979" (preprint, Department of Economics, East Carolina University); Lester A. Zeager and Jonathan B. Bascom, "Strategic Behavior in Refugee Repatriation: A Game-Theoretic Analysis," *Journal of Conflict Resolution* 40, no. 3 (1996): 460–85.

11. Anwar Sadat, *Those I Have Known* (New York: Continuum, 1984), 104–5.

12. Ibid., 105.

13. Michael I. Handel, *The Diplomacy of Surprise: Hitler, Nixon, Sadat* (Cambridge: Center for International Affairs, Harvard University, 1981), 324–25; Eric Silver, *Begin: The Haunted Prophet* (New York: Random House, 1984), 177.

14. Sadat, *Those I Have Known*, 105.

15. Frank Gervasi, *The Life and Times of Menachem Begin: Rebel to Statesman* (New York: Putnam, 1979), 48–54; Handel, *The Diplomacy of Surprise*, 318–20.

16. Sadat, *Those I Have Known*, 106.

17. Ibid., 106.

18. Handel, *The Diplomacy of Surprise*, 322–23.

19. Sadat, *Those I Have Known*, 107.

20. Shibley Telhami, *Power and Leadership in International Bargaining: The Path to the Camp David Accords* (New York: Columbia University Press, 1990), 13.
21. Janice Gross Stein, "Prenegotiation in the Arab-Israeli Conflict: The Paradoxes of Success and Failure," in *Getting to the Table: The Processes of International Prenegotiation,* ed. Janice Gross Stein (Baltimore: Johns Hopkins University Press, 1989), 179.
22. Handel, *The Diplomacy of Surprise,* 265–66.
23. Moshe Dayan, *Breakthrough: A Personal Account of the Egypt-Israel Peace Negotiations* (New York: Knopf, 1981), 75.
24. Anwar Sadat, *In Search of Identity: An Autobiography* (New York: Harper and Row, 1978), 300–302.
25. After developing this game, I reread Maoz and Felsenthal and discovered, to my amazement, that they had used exactly the same game to model Sadat's peace initiative. However, their strategies focus on the concrete terms of the eventual peace treaty: for Egypt, to recognize or not recognize Israel; for Israel, to withdraw or not withdraw from the Sinai. They interpret Sadat's visit to Jerusalem as being a self-binding commitment to peace that was made especially credible by its public nature. TOM shows *why* Sadat moved first—and why Begin responded as he did—but it says nothing about why Sadat felt it necessary to create such a public spectacle: not being trusted by the Israelis, he wanted to convince them with a well-nigh irrevocable commitment to peace. Zeev Maoz and Dan S. Felsenthal, "Self-Binding Commitments, the Inducement of Trust, Social Choice, and the Theory of International Cooperation," *International Studies Quarterly* 31, no. 2 (1987): 177–200.
26. Game 27 in Brams, *Theory of Moves.*
27. This question is asked in, for example, Ishmail Fahmy, *Negotiating for Peace in the Middle East* (Baltimore: Johns Hopkins University Press, 1983); Dayan, *Breakthrough.*
28. See Brams, "The Rationality of Surprise," for citations.
29. It is worth noting that a game-theoretic model incorporates the choices of *both* players, whereas the surprise literature distinguishes two schools of thought: the "victim's school," whose "central goal is to uncover the factors that constrain a victim's attempt to avert surprise"; and the "surpriser's school," which "seeks to explain the means an actor is likely to use to deceive an adversary." Alex Roberto Hybel, *The Logic of Surprise in International Conflict* (Lexington, Mass.: Lexington Books, 1986), 3. A game may be seen as a way of combining these different perspectives in a payoff matrix, which links the strategies and preferences of both the victim and the surpriser and is a powerful device that Schelling highlighted a generation ago (Thomas C. Schelling, "What Is Game Theory?" in *Contemporary Political Analysis,* ed. James C. Charlesworth [New York: Free Press, 1967], 224–32). Even earlier, Schelling suggested a dynamic approach to the study of surprise attack that has much in common with the dynamics incorporated in TOM. See Thomas C. Schelling, *The Strategy of Conflict* (Cambridge: Harvard University Press, 1960).

30. Examples are given in Brams, *Theory of Moves.*
31. For its recent application to the Northern Ireland conflict, see Steven J. Brams and Jeffrey M. Togman, "Agreement through Threats: The Northern Ireland Case," in *Being Useful: Policy Relevance and International Relations Theory,* ed. Miroslav Nincic and Joseph Lepgold (Ann Arbor: University of Michigan Press, 2000), 325–42.
32. Steven J. Brams and D. Marc Kilgour, "Fallback Bargaining," *Group Decision and Negotiation* (forthcoming 2000), and Willson, "Long-Term Behavior in the Theory of Moves," among others, have offered extensions to n-person games.
33. Steven J. Brams, Michael A. Jones, and D. Marc Kilgour, "Single-Peakedness and Disconnected Coalitions," *Journal of Theoretical Politics* (2002).

REFLECTIONS ON QUANTITATIVE
INTERNATIONAL POLITICS

Dina A. Zinnes

Like other members of the millennial reflections panels, I received a set of questions to guide my comments. To a large extent, however, I found the questions hard to answer within the context of a panel on quantitative methods. I am not, for example, sure that there are "unresolved debates" in regard to quantitative methods; I don't know what "theoretical insights" we have had regarding methodology; nor am I clear as to the meaning of "a fruitful synthesis of approaches" within this context. So while I will reflect on the uses and abuses of methodology in the general field of international studies/relations, it will be more of a personal statement about where we have been, where we seem to be going, and what we need to consider in the decades ahead.

First, where have we been? To answer this question I had a graduate student look through the past decade of the main journals in political science to determine the number of international relations (IR) articles in each journal and the percentage of those that used either statistics or mathematical modeling or both. I was curious as to whether there had been an increase (or decrease) in the use of quantitative methods and particularly whether there were differences in trends between the use of statistics or the use of mathematical modeling. I was also interested in two subquestions: (1) was there a strict dichotomy between the use of statistics and modeling or were there some attempts to use both? and (2) was mathematical modeling primarily game theoretic?

The survey covered *American Political Science Review* (*APSR*), *American Journal of Political Science* (*AJPS*), *Journal of Conflict Resolution* (*JCR*), *Conflict Management and Peace Science* (*CMPS*), *Journal of Peace Research* (*JPR*), and of course *International Studies Quarterly* (*ISQ*) for the years from 1990 through 1999. Table 1 provides the results of this investigation, reported in two five-year intervals. With the exception of *JPR*, especially from 1990 to 1994, we discover that, based on these journals, most of the published work in the field is quantitative—that is, it uses either statistics, mathematical modeling, or both. We also see that quantitative research in IR has not decreased but increased or held steady (*ISQ*). However, quantitative research in our field is heavily dominated by statistical analyses as seen by comparing the numbers in columns 3 and 4. Indeed, with the exception of *APSR*, the use of statistical analyses has increased from the 1990–94 period to the 1995–99 period, while the use of mathematical models, with the exception of *JPR*, has held constant or decreased slightly. Moreover, a comparison of columns 4 and 5 with column 6 quickly demonstrates that the overwhelming form of mathematical modeling is game theory. Finally, column 5 shows that very few quantitative articles contain both mathematical models and statistical analyses.

So this is where we have been. Where are we going? If the "trends" over the two subperiods are any indication, it appears that while we are moving in the quantitative direction, we are doing so largely through the use of statistical analyses. Moreover, given that most mathematical models are game theoretic, the questions of international politics subjected to mathematical modeling are seen principally through the eyes of rational actors. Finally, the separation of the two forms of quantitative analysis—very little research contains both mathematical models and statistical analyses—suggests that most mathematical models go untested, and this does not seem to be changing.

I find these results disturbing on several counts. The typical statistical study begins with an argument, formulated verbally, from which one or more hypotheses are generated. Data are collected and statistics are used to assess the likelihood that the hypothesis is false, or conversely that the data are adequate to conclude that the hypothesis is supported by the data. But what is the relationship between the verbal argument and the hypothesis? Without the use

Table 1. Quantitative Methods in International Relations Research

Journal	Year	Articles per Issue	IR Articles	Statistics Articles	Modeling Articles	Both	Games	Other
APSR—Total	90–94	185	26	11	8	2	8	2
APSR—Total	95–99	211	22	11	7	4	8	1
APSR—Totals	90–99	396	48	22	15	6	16	3
AJPS—Total	90–94	187	17	8	7	2	7	2
AJPS—Total	95–99	224	17	16	0	1	1	0
AJPS—Totals	90–99	411	34	24	7	3	8	2
JCR—Total	90–94	139	81	44	22	6	18	10
JCR—Total	95–99	161	100	63	21	7	18	10
JCR—Totals	90–99	300	181	107	43	13	36	20
CMPS—Total	90–94	23	20	7	8	1	1	7
CMPS—Total	95–99	28	26	11	8	3	3	8
CMPS—Totals	90–99	51	46	18	16	4	4	15
JPR—Total	90–94	124	85	23	7	2	5	4
JPR—Total	95–99	127	98	39	12	0	2	10
JPR—Totals	90–99	251	183	62	19	2	7	14
ISQ—Total	90–94	73	64	22	14	2	9	7
ISQ—Total	95–99	95	83	33	12	4	7	9
ISQ—Totals	90–99	168	147	55	26	6	16	16

of a formal language—that is, a mathematical model—it is next to impossible to demonstrate that the hypothesis actually flows from the argument. The statistical analysis of the hypothesis thus becomes, by default, the "theory" that is being evaluated. The argument that supposedly produced the hypothesis is essentially irrelevant. But the argument that was meant to produce the hypothesis is usually where the interesting ideas are found, the place where the researcher is explaining why certain things happen. We have reduced what may have been a rich interpretation of the international world to an often uninteresting if-then statement. Consequently if IR research is becoming increasingly quantitative through the ever greater use of statistics, we are replacing possible explanation with far less interesting statements about what is associated with what.

This is not to decry the use of statistics. Statistics are extremely important in helping us make decisions about the noisy world of data. What is unfortunate then is not the increasing use of statistics but that we have not correspondingly increased our use of formal languages to help us tie the hypotheses being tested with the arguments that supposedly produce them. The disturbing fact is that the use of mathematical models has not increased over the last decade. The increasing use of statistical analyses has fooled us into thinking that we have become more "theoretical," whereas in actual fact it might reasonably be argued that we have become less theoretical.

Thus what is needed in the years to come is a far greater emphasis on the use of mathematical models to carefully represent our arguments, theories, about the international world so that we can demonstrate beyond a reasonable doubt what conclusions do indeed flow from an argument. Only then can we say that the test of a hypothesis gives us confidence in our argument; only then will we become more theoretical as a field.

How do we do this? The first step is to move statistics courses out of the limelight of graduate programs. These should not be among the first courses that graduate students meet in their training as they produce a mind-set that makes potential researchers see everything through "if . . . then . . ." glasses. The first courses of a graduate program should force the student to think in terms of puzzles, things that don't make sense, don't fit with the way we think about the world, and teach the student how to "tell stories" that fit these anomalies into what we know about the way the world works.

This is the beginning of theorizing. The next step is to teach the student how to translate these stories into a mathematical language so that it is possible to empirically evaluate various aspects of our stories. Only after we have developed the theory (= story) and made it precise using a formal language should we turn to statistics to help us determine whether conclusions from our theory are indeed supported by data. Statistics should come toward the end of a graduate program; these courses should be the caboose rather than the engine of a research program.

But how do we teach the translation of stories into formal languages? The fact that most research involving mathematical models is game theoretic in nature indicates that we need to broaden our horizons. Game theory is an important and exciting way to translate stories into a formal language. But it is not the only formal language available, and indeed it may not be the best formal language for the story that is being told. Mathematical languages, like natural languages, come in different shapes and sizes—some are better than others for expressing certain ideas. I understand that the language of the Eskimo is rich in its ability to talk about snow but less adequate to express other ideas. Similarly, game theory is an excellent modeling language for capturing conflictual decision-theoretic situations, but not all stories involve rational actors. Our graduate programs must therefore include introductions to more than a single modeling language and provide the student with some feeling for how to make appropriate choices between languages.

But having learned that the nature of theorizing lies in telling stories about puzzles and even having learned how to choose among modeling languages and translate a story into an appropriate mathematical structure is not sufficient. We now need to go the last mile. A mathematical model may be beautiful and provide wonderful insights, but it is not a theory about international politics until it has been subjected to an evaluation. Story and data must meet. And this raises some very interesting and curious issues. How does one "test" a game-theoretic model? Does the estimation of the parameters of a dynamic model constitute a test of that model? Because statistics and mathematical modeling have gone their separate ways, questions like these have seldom been addressed. But if we are unable to assess our models, if indeed we do not know how to falsify our theories, then they are nothing more than fun fairy tales.

So in conclusion, we have made considerable progress in making the field of international politics answer to the real world by becoming more aware of the need to empirically test our ideas. But we have a long way to go in making our ideas, our theories, explicit and an even longer way before we understand how to test our models.

REFLECTIONS ON MILLENNIA, OLD AND NEW

The Evolution and Role of Quantitative Approaches to the Study of International Politics

James Lee Ray

Introduction

As we enter the new millennium, the time seems right for a broad retrospective, introspective, and prospective analytical review of all categories of human endeavor, even including the academic study of international politics. This paper focuses on the evolution of the subfield of international politics over the last forty years, with a particular emphasis on the development of quantitative approaches. It focuses on its shortcomings but also points out what to this author at least seem worthy of being considered some accomplishments. It concludes with a few brief prescriptions for the future. It is presumptuous of me (and, to be fair to myself, of any one person) to take on such a task. I have two excuses. One is that the task was assigned to me. The other is that for good or ill I currently occupy something of a "gatekeeper" role in the field, that is, editor of a journal. That being the case, my views on these matters may be of some interest to practitioners in the field (assuming they are desirous of getting their works published, no matter how idiosyncratic and otherwise lacking in intrinsic merit they may be).

Where Have We Been?

The International Studies Association was created more than forty years ago. At that time, the academic field of international politics was, according to a general conception, much wrapped up in the debate fostered mostly by the appearance of Hans Morgenthau's *Politics among Nations* regarding the utility of "realism" versus "idealism."[1] This preoccupation of the 1950s was about to be replaced, in the 1960s, by the "behavioralist" revolution.

These may seem relatively simple, straightforward statements. But one of the points of this essay is that it is quite difficult to characterize, organize, and categorize in any comprehensive way all of the research efforts even in a relatively small field such as the academic study of international politics. If we analyze two editions of *International Politics and Foreign Policy*, edited by James Rosenau,[2] we can find evidence supporting the view of the 1950s as dominated by the debate between realists and idealists, while in the 1960s attention focused instead on the behavioral revolution. For example, the 1961 version of this volume contained not a single selection authored by J. David Singer. In the later 1969 edition, there are five selections authored or coauthored by Singer, including one focusing on "The Behavioral Science Approach to International Relations."[3]

But a closer look at the 1961 version of *International Politics and Foreign Policy* reveals that in fact the behavioral revolution has roots and origins that predate significantly the onset of the 1960s. That volume (based on works originally published in the 1950s, for the most part) has a substantial number of works based on and/or advocating quantitative, statistical, mathematical, and "scientific" approaches to the study of international politics. Richard C. Snyder advocates game theory as a tool of analysis.[4] There is an early exemplar from the Project on International Conflict and Integration at Stanford under Robert North, relying on content analysis to provide a reproducible, statistical analysis of the onset of World War I.[5] One also finds a contribution by Karl Deutsch advocating quantitative studies of international politics,[6] and other articles urging practitioners in the field to investigate the utility of computer simulations[7] and experiments,[8] as well as mathematics.[9] And of course, Rapoport devoted his contribution to a discussion of the work by Lewis Fry Richardson on arms races, and "Richardson published a mathematical treatment of the causes of war . . . as long ago as 1919."[10] In short, the idea that the behavioral revolution in international politics burst upon the academic scene in the 1960s is rather misleading; that movement can, in fact, be seen as well under way by the arrival of the 1960s.[11]

A review of academic work in the field in the 1950s and 1960s also provides a basis for what is probably a healthy sense of "the more things change, the more things etc., etc." "Realists" and "idealists" fought passionate battles in the 1950s. In the 1990s, Steve Smith observes that "what is termed idealist thinking is still powerful in contemporary theoretical debates, and realism still probably dominates the teaching of the discipline."[12] *International Security* just last year published a lively exchange regarding the utility of mathematical, deductive "rational choice" versus more intuitive and inductive approaches to the study of international politics.[13] Rapoport observes that "the contribution of . . . [those] inclined toward mathematical theorizing is in showing that it does not matter where the cycle of observation-hypothesis-theory-verification begins. It may be at times useful to begin with theory *in abstracto* and at other times with the compilation of data. The cycle must be traversed several times anyway before a coherent picture can arise."[14]

Though it is a healthy antidote against faddism, perhaps, to see such continuity in debates over the last four decades, such continuity can also lead to skepticism. Perhaps the field is just spinning its wheels, continually engaged in the same old debates over and over again?

I believe such skepticism should be resisted and that there are sound bases for doing so. One can, for example, get some sense of progress by reading the editor's introduction to Oliver Benson's contribution to the earlier *International Politics and Foreign Policy* on the use of computers: "Professor Benson explores the possibility of using high speed computers in research in the international field. Other disciplines have found that these newly developed machines facilitate the handling of problems which once seemed unresearchable. What at one time might have required thousands of man-hours can now be accomplished in but a few computer-minutes. It would seem that students of international politics and foreign policy cannot afford to ignore the potentialities of these aids to research."[15]

If one reviews the two Rosenau readers, one can see (with some benefit of hindsight) a striking lack of attention to economic factors or variables, either as explanatory factors or as issues to be addressed in a theoretical fashion. This began to change, perhaps, with neo-Marxist (or neo-Marxist-Leninist) analyses of the Vietnam War.[16] Attention to economic factors was reinforced in the 1970s by the onset of détente between the United States and the Soviet Union (and thus a decrease in the extent to which the traditional issues of security and war seemed to deserve priority) and serious international economic problems associated importantly with OPEC's oil price increases in 1973 and 1979. The result was the emergence of what has become a thriving subfield of international political economy,[17] as well as increased sensitivity to nonstate actors such as multinational corporations.[18] This subfield experienced some de-emphasis perhaps, with the rebirth of the cold war in the 1980s (and the resulting reemphasis on matters of national security and international conflict). However, what might be termed the second end of the cold war at the end of the 1980s has brought about a rekindling of interest in nongovernmental actors[19] and a solidification of the place in the study of international politics of international political economy.[20] Surely this entry and integration of economic matters into the subfield of international politics represents real, tangible progress for it over the last forty years.

According to Vasquez, "an increasing portion of the field . . . has until recently moved further and further away from quantitative analysis. . . . [But] the tide has turned the other way with findings on the democratic peace increasing the interest in scientific research even among senior scholars who had long been hostile to such modes of analysis."[21] Tracing research on the relationship between regime type and international conflict does in fact offer important insights, perhaps, into the evolution of quantitative approaches to the study of international conflict over the last three or four decades. James Rosenau's article on "pre-theories" posited that one of the more important fundamental distinctions between states for attempts to understand foreign policies was type of political system.[22] Several empirical analyses from that era[23] provided evidence that democratic states are somewhat less conflict prone than autocratic states, but the evidence was not all that striking, and the finding had no apparent or lasting impact on the field. Dean Babst argued on the basis of a reasonably thorough review of data on interstate wars that no two democratic states had ever fought a war against each other.[24] Rummel devoted five whole volumes[25] to developing a theoretical structure supporting the idea that "the fundamental variable relating to the occurrence of international . . . war . . . is political rights, civil liberties, and economic freedom within nations. The less freedom within two nations, the more likely violence is between them; and between democracies, war should not occur at all."[26] These volumes had little apparent or immediate impact. Nor did Rummel's articles following up on this theme[27] draw much attention, except from critics who disputed his claims.[28] Not until the 1990s did research on the "democratic peace" draw all the attention that led Vasquez to conclude as the new millennium approaches that it constitutes an important indication as well as a source of inspiration for a "rebirth" of sorts of quantitative approaches to the study of international politics.[29]

It has been argued by this author and others that this sequence of developments regarding the unfolding of the democratic peace research program can be explained primarily by international political developments in the "real" world.[30] According to this argument, early work on peace between democratic states attracted little attention or support because of the cold war atmosphere surrounding it. Perhaps, however, there is a simpler, even more parsimonious explanation (which will, however, surely strike some as stunningly naive). It is possible that the recent fate of the democratic peace research program in terms of the amount of attention and support it has received can be explained primarily by reference to the quality of the evidence, and even the coherence of the theoretical structure on which it has been based.

Rummel provided a massive theoretical structure on which to base his observation that no two democratic states have fought wars against each other.[31] But the most specific systematic empirical evidence he provided in support of that assertion was basically limited to a review of data on interstate wars generated by the Correlates of War Project.[32] An attempt by Small and Singer to analyze the relationship between democracy and peace in a somewhat more thorough fashion provides an intriguing baseline against which to compare more recent research efforts.[33] Small and Singer had no annual data on regime type for the time period on which they focused. Therefore, they could not compare rates of warfare for democratic pairs of states with those of pairs of states not jointly democratic. (What they did instead was to compare wars in which democratic states participated with wars in which they did not.) They noted on the basis of the same kind of visual inspection of available data on wars relied on by Rummel (as well as Babst)[34] that democratic states had rarely if ever warred against each other. But they concluded that this was because wars are most often fought between neighbors, and "bourgeois democracies do not border upon one another very frequently over much of the period since 1816."[35] That conclusion, too, had to be based on a kind of summary review of information on the geographic location of states vis-à-vis each other, because computerized data on contiguity were not readily available then and were certainly not utilized by Small and Singer. Starting with Maoz and

Abdolali, and into the 1990s, such analyses as those by Maoz and Russett, Bremer, and Oneal and Russett have benefited from several types of progress achieved by quantitatively oriented analysts of international politics since the 1970s.[36] Annual observations of regime types have become available.[37] Computerized data on contiguity have allowed analysts such as Bremer and Maoz and Russett to establish beyond much doubt that the relationship between democracy and peace persists even when contiguity is controlled for.[38] These more recent analysts have also been able to control for a rather lengthy list of possibly confounding variables in a way that was simply not available to Small and Singer in the 1970s. They have done so using databases consisting of hundreds of thousands of cases that would have been difficult at best to deal with in the 1970s. And recent research has been based on analytical techniques[39] and refinements[40] unknown to international relations (IR) specialists in the 1970s.

I also believe that the democratic peace research program shows signs of having an impact in the area of theory that may ultimately be at least as important as that created by the empirical observation regarding the absence of wars between democratic states. These theoretical developments focus on substituting for basic realist and neorealist assumptions regarding states seeking power or security the alternative assumption that state leaders place the highest priority on staying in power.[41] This basic assumption provides theoretical purchase enabling the integration of the "two-level games"[42] faced by all state leaders and a means for integrating domestic and international factors within explanations of foreign policies and international politics in a manner increasingly attractive to an expanding sector of global politics specialists.[43] It may not be hopelessly naive, then, to conclude that the increased attention paid to and the impact of research on the relationship between regime type and interstate conflict in the 1990s is not simply a function of changing political tastes brought on by current events. Perhaps it is instead more importantly produced by the improvements in the quality of the evidence, as well as the theoretical bases on which this rapidly growing stream of research relies.

Where Are We (and Where Should We Be) Going?

As insensitive as this essay may appear up to this point, it is in fact not true that I am unaware that "the idealist/realist/behaviouralist progression is in fact a narrow, and particularly political, reading of international theory. Where, for example, is class, or ethnicity, or gender in this self-image? Where are the concerns of developing countries to be found in this canon? It is, in fact, a Western/white/male/conservative view of international theory."[44]

So far excluded from discussion in this review have been feminist contributions to IR theory or any mention in general of the "post-positivist" contributions making up the "third wave."[45] In principle, I am certainly favorably disposed to the idea that the increase in diversity among specialists in IR in the last ten or twenty years is a good thing. It would be even better if communication among these diverse specialists were more effective. While cognizant of the possibility that my perceptions on this point are a product of my own shortcomings, what I see occurring in recent years among much of this diverse population of IR specialists are miscommunication, misperceptions, and misunderstandings.

As partisan as I may be, however, I would not claim that all of these misperceptions are the fault of specialists making up part of the third wave who fail to comprehend what "scientific-," quantitative-, or rational choice–oriented specialists are up to. I can see how quantitatively oriented specialists in particular help create misperceptions and misunderstandings about what they aim to accomplish, for example.

In fact, I myself am confused about the ideal model or theory or product toward which large-N analysts are striving. The typical multivariate model consists of one relationship of special interest and then several obligatory control variables included in what most often appears to me to be a sort of haphazard, arbitrary fashion. Is the ideal-typical model or theory capable of being summarized in some sort of extra-large multivariate equation? A set of simultaneous equations? A computer simulation? What? (I have my own ideas, but unfortunately space limitations preclude their full discussion here.)

And somehow, second-wave specialists have convinced third-wave specialists, it seems to me, that we consider ourselves capable of being entirely objective, above prejudice, that what it means to be scientific, in our view, is to be sufficiently detached to allow the data to speak for themselves. Perhaps some second-wave specialists even believe that. Perhaps in the new millennium specialists making up the second wave can be more clear about the ultimate aims of their research endeavors and dispel this notion that to be scientific means somehow to be "above" emotions, commitment, or ideological convictions.

And perhaps third-wave specialists could communicate more clearly, too, in the new millennium. I for one am aware that many third-wave specialists (as well as many second-wave specialists, actually) are suspicious of the tendency for IR theory to focus on interaction among states. It is less clear to me what alternative type of political structure postpositivist or postmodernist (or even feminist) specialists would prefer to see take the place of states as the type of political unit preeminent in the current global political system.

UN secretary-general Kofi Annan has observed recently that "during the 1990s there has been a remarkable and little-noticed reduction in global warfare. More old wars have ended than new ones begun."[46] He refers almost entirely to internal, civil, ethnic conflicts. He notes also that between 1992 and 1998, the number of democratically elected governments in the world increased by about a third, and that "the evidence is in line with the well-established, if little publicized finding that democracies have far lower levels of internal violence than non-democracies. . . . In an era when more than 90% of wars take place within, not between states, the import of this finding for conflict prevention should be obvious."[47]

In short, Kofi Annan sees the emergence of stronger and more democratic states as a trend and a solution to the scourge of political violence. Granted, many new states have emerged in recent decades, and many of them are woefully weak and ineffective. Does this indicate that the time has come to move beyond the state? Toward what?

Ken Booth is one of those analysts who is obviously quite critical of the current state of "academic international relations theory" and of its emphasis on interactions among states.[48] He is quite clear about what else he is against. "We do," he declares with admirable candor, "have an enemy, and an enemy of global proportions at that." He concludes that "the enemy is us. Western consumerist democracy . . . is the problem. . . . In a capitalist-constituted world the consumer is sovereign."[49]

From this it is clear to me that Booth is opposed to democracy, at least in its current "Western" form, as well as capitalism. But what is he for? What would he prefer to substitute for "Western consumerist democracy"? Eastern aesthetic autocracy? To be fair, I should note that Booth does call for a "community of communities" within a much looser state framework, and for decision-making power to

devolve downward to regional and local groups, as well as upward
to continental and global functional organizations.[50] To me, this image raises more questions than it answers. Would these communities
be democratic? Would they be capitalist or market oriented? (Would
consumers, in other words, be somehow less "sovereign"?) Why
should we believe that they would be less consumerist or better able
to deal with pressing problems than national governments? (Have
local or state governments in the United States, for example, been
consistently more "progressive" or effective or admirable than the
national or federal government?) What will prevent the most powerful state governments from dominating "global organizations" in
the future the way they do now? What if some less-"enlightened"
states refuse to devolve power to local and regional groups, perhaps
expressly for the purpose of taking advantage of those states who do?
And finally, considering all the problems that seem to result in important part from weak state governments in many parts of the
world, is a decline in the influence, strength, and competence of
states (and their governments) something to be welcomed or encouraged?

One hope I have for the new millennium is that it will be easier
to discern what opponents of "statecentric" theories or models are
proposing and why they think these proposals should be adopted or
advocated by the field of global politics as a whole.

Notes

1. Hans J. Morgenthau, *Politics among Nations* (New York: Knopf, 1948).
   As Hoffmann said: "The theory which has occupied the center of the
   scene in this country during the last ten years is Professor Morgenthau's
   'realist' theory of power politics." See Stanley Hoffmann, "International
   Relations: The Long Road to Theory," *World Politics* 11, no. 3 (1959):
   346–77, reproduced in *International Politics and Foreign Policy*, ed.
   James N. Rosenau (New York: Free Press, 1961), 421–37. Morgenthau
   became something of a bête noire for advocates of the behavioral revolution in the 1960s, who tended to see him as the leading advocate of
   traditional, antiquantitative, and antiscientific work in international
   politics. Hoffmann's point in the article just cited is to advocate historical and philosophical approaches to international politics. One
   might assume, then, that he would be sympathetic to Morgenthau's realist approach. However, Hoffmann categorizes Morgenthau with advocates of "scientific approaches" such as Morton Kaplan and Karl
   Deutsch and is energetically critical of all of them.
2. James N. Rosenau, *International Politics and Foreign Policy* (New York:
   Free Press, 1961, 1969).

3. J. David Singer, "The Behavioral Science Approach to International Relations: Payoffs and Prospects," in James N. Rosenau, *International Politics and Foreign Policy,* 2d ed. (New York: Free Press, 1969), 380–91. It may also be interesting to note in light of the image of Singer that evolved in later years as an enthusiastic advocate of scientific methods, with an emphasis on inductive, statistical (as opposed to mathematical and deductive) approaches, that one of Singer's contributions to the second edition of the Rosenau volume was entitled "Inter-Nation Influence: A Formal Model." It is, perhaps, equally intriguing, and consonant with the theme here regarding the difficulties confronted by efforts to characterize theories, approaches, and perhaps most of all, theorists, to take note of the conciliatory theme with which Singer concludes his article advocating the "behavioral science approach": "It is . . . important that . . . [scientific research] not proceed at the expense of, and unrelated to, the excellent work that the traditional scholars have done for decades. . . . We can be expected to move steadily in the integrative direction, with the 'traditionalist' and the 'behavioralist' both reaching out in the other's direction, borrowing, adapting, and recombining in such a way as to gain the great benefits of the newer approach while retaining all that is valuable in the older." Singer, "Inter-Nation Influence," 69.
4. Richard C. Snyder, "Game Theory and the Analysis of Political Behavior," in Rosenau, *International Politics and Foreign Policy* (1961), 381–90.
5. Dina Zinnes, Robert C. North, and Howard E. Koch Jr., "Capability, Threat, and the Outbreak of War," in Rosenau, *International Politics and Foreign Policy* (1961), 469–82.
6. Karl W. Deutsch, "Toward an Inventory of Basic Trends and Patterns in Comparative and International Politics," in Rosenau, *International Politics and Foreign Policy* (1961), 450–60.
7. Oliver Benson, "A Simple Diplomatic Game," in Rosenau, *International Politics and Foreign Policy* (1961), 504–11.
8. Herbert Goldhamer and Hans Speier, "Some Observations on Political Gaming," in Rosenau, *International Politics and Foreign Policy* (1961), 498–503.
9. Anatol Rapoport, "The Mathematics of Arms Races," in Rosenau, *International Politics and Foreign Policy* (1961), 492–97.
10. Ibid., 492.
11. Nevertheless, the 1960s can accurately be viewed as a decade of great ferment and change in the field. The Rosenau 1969 edition retained only five out of the fifty-five contributions in the 1961 version.
12. Steve Smith, "The Self-Images of a Discipline: A Genealogy of International Relations Theory," in *International Relations Theory Today,* ed. Ken Booth and Steve Smith (University Park: Pennsylvania State University Press, 1995), 1–37.
13. Stephen M. Walt, "Rigor or Rigor Mortis? Rational Choice and Security Studies," *International Security* 23, no. 4 (1999): 5–48; Bruce Bueno de Mesquita and James D. Morrow, "Sorting through the Wealth of Notions," *International Security* 24, no. 2 (1999): 56–73; Lisa L. Martin,

"The Contributions of Rational Choice: A Defense of Pluralism," *International Security* 24, no. 2 (1999): 74–83; Emerson M. S. Niou and Peter C. Ordeshook, "Return of the Luddites," *International Security* 24, no. 2 (1999): 84–96; Robert Powell, "The Modelling Enterprise and Security Studies," *International Security* 24, no. 2 (1999): 97–106; Frank Zagare, "All Mortis, No Rigor," *International Security* 24, no. 2 (1999): 107–14. See also Jonathan Cohn, "When Did Political Science Forget about Politics? Irrational Exuberance," *New Republic*, October 25, 1999, <http://www.tnr.com/magazines/tnr/archive/1099/102599/coverstory 102599.html>.

14. Rapoport, "The Mathematics of Arms Races," 497. Rapoport concludes that "one suspects that questions of scientific strategy have no general answers." Ibid. Compare Rapoport's statement with that of Ordeshook of almost forty years later: "Regardless of the mathematical rigor of models, we need to drop the view of science as an enterprise directed by academics armed with theorems and lemmas or by experimentalists scurrying about in white smocks. Science proceeds less coherently, through induction and deduction. . . ." Cited by Walt, "Rigor or Rigor Mortis?" 48.

15. Benson in Rosenau, "A Simple Diplomatic Game," 504.

16. Harry Magdoff, *The Age of Imperialism* (New York: Monthly Review Press, 1969); Gabriel Kolko, *The Roots of American Foreign Policy* (Boston: Beacon Press, 1969).

17. Robert O. Keohane and Joseph S. Nye Jr.'s *Power and Interdependence* (Princeton, N.J.: Princeton University Press, 1977) is one important precursor.

18. Raymond Vernon, *Sovereignty at Bay* (New York: Basic Books, 1971). Charles F. Kindleberger's *The World in Depression, 1929–1939* (Berkeley: University of California Press, 1973) also deserves mention in this context.

19. For example, Jessica Mathews, "Power Shift," *Foreign Affairs* 76 (January–February 1997): 50–66.

20. As indicated quite neatly, perhaps, by the appearance of the second edition of Keohane and Nye's *Power and Interdependence* in 1989, as well as the fifth edition of Joan Edelman Spero and Jeffrey A. Hart's *The Politics of International Economic Relations* (New York: St. Martin's Press, 1997).

21. John A. Vasquez, *The Power of Power Politics: From Classical Realism to Neotraditionalism* (Cambridge: Cambridge University Press, 1998), 2.

22. James N. Rosenau, "Pre-Theories and Theories of Foreign Policy," in *Approaches to Comparative and International Politics*, ed. R. Barry Farrell (Evanston, Ill.: Northwestern University Press 1966), 27–92.

23. Maurice East and Philip M. Gregg, "Factors Influencing Cooperation and Conflict in the International System," *International Studies Quarterly* 11, no. 3 (1967): 244–69; Stephen A. Salmore and Charles F. Hermann, "The Effect of Size, Development, and Accountability on Foreign Policy," *Peace Science Society Papers* 14 (1969): 16–30; Maurice A. East and Charles F. Hermann, "Do Nation-Types Account for Foreign Policy

Behavior?" in *Comparing Foreign Policies*, ed. James N. Rosenau (New York: Wiley, 1974), 209–69; Dina A. Zinnes and Jonathan Wilkenfeld, "An Analysis of Foreign Conflict Behavior of Nations," in *Comparative Foreign Policy*, ed. Wolfram F. Hanrieder (New York: McKay, 1971), 167–213.

24. Dean Babst, "A Force for Peace," *Industrial Research* 14 (April 1972): 55–58. An earlier version of this paper was published as Dean Babst, "Elective Governments—A Force for Peace," *Wisconsin Sociologist* 3, no. 1 (1964): 9–14.

25. R. J. Rummel, *Understanding Conflict and War*, vols. 1–5 (New York: Sage, 1975–1981).

26. R. J. Rummel, "Roots of Faith II," in *Journeys through World Politics*, ed. Joseph Kruzel and James N. Rosenau (Lexington, Mass.: Lexington, 1989), 323.

27. R. J. Rummel, "Libertarianism and International Violence," *Journal of Conflict Resolution* 27, no.1 (1983): 27–71; R. J. Rummel, "A Test of Libertarian Propositions on Violence," *Journal of Conflict Resolution* 29, no. 3 (1985): 419–55.

28. For example, Steve Chan, "Mirror, Mirror on the Wall . . . Are the Freer Countries More Pacific?" *Journal of Conflict Resolution* 28, no. 4 (1984): 617–48; Erich Weede, "Democracy and War Involvement," *Journal of Conflict Resolution* 28, no. 4 (1984): 649–64.

29. Vasquez, *The Power of Power Politics*.

30. James Lee Ray, "Promise or Peril? Neorealism, Neoliberalism, and the Future of International Politics," in *Controversies in International Relations Theory*, ed. Charles W. Kegley Jr. (New York: St. Martin's Press, 1995), 335–55; and, for example, Nils Petter Gleditsch, ed., *Focus on Democracy and Peace*, special issue of *Journal of Peace Research* 29, no. 4 (1992): 369–434.

31. Rummel, *Understanding Conflict and War*.

32. J. David Singer and Melvin Small, *The Wages of War, 1816–1965: A Statistical Handbook* (New York: Wiley, 1972).

33. Melvin Small and J. David Singer, "The War-Proneness of Democratic Regimes, 1816–1965," *Jerusalem Journal of International Relations* 1 (summer 1976): 50–69.

34. Babst, "Elective Governments"; Babst, "A Force for Peace."

35. Small and Singer, "The War-Proneness of Democratic Regimes, 1816–1965," 67.

36. Zeev Maoz and Nasrin Abdolali, "Regime Types and International Conflict, 1816–1976," *Journal of Conflict Resolution* 33, no. 1 (1989): 3–35; Zeev Maoz and Bruce Russett, "Alliance, Contiguity, Wealth, and Political Stability: Is the Lack of Conflict among Democracies a Statistical Artifact?" *International Interactions* 17, no. 3 (1992): 245–67; Zeev Maoz and Bruce Russett, "Normative and Structural Causes of Democratic Peace, 1946–1986," *American Political Science Review* 87, no. 3 (1993): 624–38; Stuart Bremer, "Dangerous Dyads: Conditions Affecting the Likelihood of Interstate War, 1816–1965," *Journal of Conflict Resolution* 36, no. 2 (1992): 309–41; John R. Oneal and Bruce Russett, "The Classical

Liberals Were Right: Democracy, Interdependence, and Conflict, 1950–1985," *International Studies Quarterly* 41, no. 2 (1997): 267–94.

37. Ted Robert Gurr, *Polity Data Handbook* (Ann Arbor, Mich.: Inter-University Consortium for Political and Social Research, 1978); Ted Robert Gurr, Keith Jaggers, and Will H. Moore, *Polity II Handbook* (Boulder: Department of Political Science, University of Colorado, 1989); Keith Jaggers and Ted Robert Gurr, "Tracking Democracy's Third Wave with Polity III Data," *Journal of Peace Research* 32, no. 2 (1995): 469–82.

38. Bremer, "Dangerous Dyads"; Maoz and Russett, "Normative and Structural Causes of Democratic Peace, 1946–1986." In addition, Gleditsch provides evidence that democratic states have not in fact been separated geographically substantially more than nondemocratic pairs of states. Nils Petter Gleditsch, "Geography, Democracy, and Peace," *International Interactions* 20, no. 4 (1995): 297–323. For an early example of an interest in the impact of "distance" on relationships between them, see Quincy Wright, *A Study of War* (Chicago: University of Chicago Press, 1942, 1965): 1466–72.

39. Gary King, *Unifying Political Methodology* (New York: Cambridge University Press, 1989).

40. Nathaniel Beck, Jonathan N. Katz, and Richard Tucker, "Taking Time Seriously: Time-Series-Cross-Section Analysis with a Binary Dependent Variable," *American Journal of Political Science* 42, no. 4 (1998): 1260–88.

41. Bruce Bueno de Mesquita, James D. Morrow, Randolph M. Siverson, and Alastair Smith, "An Institutional Explanation of the Democratic Peace," *American Political Science Review* 93, no. 4 (1999): 791–807.

42. Robert D. Putnam, "Diplomacy and Domestic Politics: The Logic of Two-Level Games," *International Organization* 42, no. 3 (1988): 427–60.

43. James Lee Ray, "A Lakatosian View of the Democratic Peace Research Programme: Does It Falsify Realism (or Neorealism)" (paper delivered at the annual convention of the International Studies Association, Washington, D.C., February 16–20, 1999), and in "Progress in International Relations Theory," ed. Colin Elman and Miriam Fendius Elman (manuscript, 1999).

44. Smith, "The Self-Images of a Discipline," 17.

45. Yosef Lapid, "The Third Debate: On the Prospects of International Theory in the Post-Positivist Era," *International Studies Quarterly* 33, no. 3 (1989): 235–54.

46. Kofi Annan, "Preventing Conflict in the Next Century," in *The World in 2000*, special issue of the *Economist*, ed. Dudley Fishburn (London: Economist Newspaper Limited, 1999), 51.

47. Ibid., 51.

48. Ken Booth, "Dare Not to Know: International Relations Theory versus the Future," in Booth and Smith, *International Relations Theory Today*, 344.

49. Ibid., 344.

50. Ibid., 344.

QUANTITATIVE INTERNATIONAL POLITICS AND ITS CRITICS

Then and Now

Russell J. Leng

One way to provide an accounting of the state of quantitative international politics at the turn of the millennium is by evaluating its record against the skepticism of its early critics. Traditional international relations scholars, in fact, took a rather jaundiced view of the scientific study of world politics when the subfield was in its infancy at the beginning of the second half of the twentieth century. One of the most skeptical critiques came from the British classicist Hedley Bull who argued that the scientific approach was "likely to contribute very little to the theory of international relations, and in so far as it is intended to encroach upon and ultimately displace the classical approach, it is positively harmful."[1]

Bull based his dire predictions on the presumed intractability of the subject matter: an unmanageable number of variables and the impossibility of controlled experiments or even direct observation of key phenomena. Those adopting a scientific approach would be forced to work at the "marginalia of the subject that are susceptible of measurement and direct observation." The prospect of achieving any cumulative findings, Bull predicted, was "very bleak indeed."[2]

There was more than a hint of defensiveness in Bull's critique. One of his complaints was that scientists do not appreciate the quality of contributions from classical scholars. A fetish with scientific method, Bull feared, would lead to a neglect of philosophy and history in university teaching. We would be producing students and scholars well trained in statistical methods, game theory, or model building but ignorant of diplomatic history, lacking a feel for politics, and with scant understanding of the moral issues with which classical scholars have been wrestling over the centuries.

A couple of years passed before J. David Singer, who became the point man for advocacy of the scientific study of world politics, published a response.[3] Singer was willing to recognize the past contributions of the classicists, but he asserted that they "have gone almost as far as they can go in adding to social science knowledge in any appreciable way."[4] Singer held out an olive branch, but it was in the form of an offer to accept converts. The relationship between the two approaches resembled that of a new faith confronting an established religion, say Christianity claiming to supersede Judaism, or Islam claiming to supersede Christianity. The new faith is willing to accept some of the revelations of the old, while claiming to move beyond them, but the old religion cannot accept the revelations of the new without being rendered obsolete. The arguments of the participants may be based on theological or epistemological differences, but the passions with which they are expressed are fueled by political stakes. In the first two decades of what Karl Deutsch called the "fourth wave" of world politics research,[5] the only cross-fertilization between the two fields was in the form of mudslinging.

I return to the issue of the relationship between the classical and scientific traditions in the concluding section. But the first task is to consider the extent to which quantitative international politics research has been able to meet the challenges posed by its foremost early critic.

The Record

Bull had a laundry list of complaints about scientific research, but they can be reduced to three general categories: (1) triviality; (2) a failure to achieve cumulative knowledge; and (3) a harmful substitution of methodological training for an understanding of the content of the subject matter and appreciation of knowledge gained through centuries of classical scholarship. After considering each of these challenges, I will return to the issue of the contentiousness between the classicists and scientists.

Research Questions

Bull asserted that scientific research was doomed to remain on the margins of the central questions of world politics because he assumed that the research would be limited to phenomena that were easily measured. The big questions would be beyond the bounds of quantitative research.

Leaving aside statistical issues related to different levels of measurement, the problem to which Bull refers is that of obtaining valid and reliable descriptions of the phenomena of interest. That problem, however, is not limited to the scientific study of international politics. It has confronted every serious student of human affairs, beginning with the ancients. Consider, for example, the disclaimer offered by Thucydides at the beginning of his history of the Peloponnesian Wars as he described the problems he faced as he attempted to reconstruct speeches for which there was no written record:

> Some I heard myself, others I got from various quarters; it was in all cases difficult to carry them word for word in one's memory, so my habit has been to make the speakers say what was in my opinion demanded of them by the various occasions, of course, adhering as closely as possible to the general sense of what they really said.[6]

Thucydides faced a similar problem in his attempt to construct a narrative of events occurring during the war, and his comments illustrate his concern with reliability as well as validity: "I did not even trust my own impressions, but [my account] rests partly on what I saw myself, partly on what others saw for me, the accuracy of the report being always tried by the most severe and detailed tests."[7]

The most easily described political phenomena are those that are tangible and relatively static, such as the size of a country's armed forces, the number of diplomatic missions within a state, or its gross national product. The variables most difficult to operationalize are those that are less tangible and dynamic, for example, the rate at which a dispute escalates or the influence strategies employed by the contending states. Reporting is more complete in the modern age, but the validity and reliability problems faced by students of international conflict are essentially the same as those faced by Thucydides. The difference lies in the explicitness of the procedures for generating the descriptions. We have no way of knowing where Thucydides obtained his information, how many sources he consulted, or how much of the content of any of the great battles or speeches he described consists of reconstructions based on his perception of the context in which the event occurred. We have no way of knowing what constituted his "most severe and detailed tests" of the information. Issues of descriptive validity and reliability continue to be a problem in classical historical research. In fact, they provide the fuel for repeated cycles of revisionist history. A major advantage of the scientific approach is its methodological explicitness, its replicability.

Thucydides' history has attained its unparalleled greatness because it deals with the heart of interstate politics—great debates, decisions, and actions of states and their leaders. Bull's "triviality" challenge presumed that the scientific approach would never get that close to the stuff of international politics. It must be admitted that the evolution of scientific studies of world politics has been driven to some extent by data availability issues. Too often research agendas have been determined by the availability of data, or the relative ease with which new data could be generated, rather than by the most interesting questions. The problem, however, has been less that of subject matter intractability than a lack of adequate funding, imagination, and energy, as has been demonstrated by the success of those who have been willing to undertake ambitious data generation enterprises.

Notable of these efforts is Singer's own Correlates of War Project,[8] which was beginning to get off the ground as Bull wrote his critique. Within a decade, Singer was publishing studies dealing with questions that Bull claimed to be beyond the reach of scientific investigations, such as the relationship between the structure of the interstate system and war. Other major projects that have come to fruition more recently are Brecher and Wilkenfeld's work on the attributes of crises, Gurr's on intercommunal conflict, and Bercovitch's on mediation to name a few.[9] My own research on interstate crisis behavior has generated a data set designed to obtain the fullest possible descriptions of the behavior of states in evolving crises.[10]

There are, to be sure, some areas that remain beyond the bounds of a solely empirical approach. Normative and legal questions cannot be answered completely by scientific investigations. But even when dealing with normative issues, scientific findings can clarify our choices. They can tell us what means are necessary to achieve certain ends, and they can inform us of the consequences of employing those means.

My research on learning during enduring rivalries encountered questions, particularly those related to the perceptions of national leaders, that required qualitative judgment.[11] But the qualitative judgments were aided by empirical findings. Having an accurate account of what states were doing provided insights into what state decision makers were thinking. Conversely, the accounts of national leaders provided greater insight into empirically generated patterns of state behavior. The most interesting research questions often are those that require the integration of quantitative and qualitative methods.

Before leaving this section, something should be said about the recent postmodernist challenge to scientific claims to objectivity. At a fundamental level, postmodernists claim that there is no objective reality; there are only the experiences and perceptions of individuals who relate stories based on those perceptions. How we describe the world and the actions of states, it is argued, is an unavoidable function of our experiences, biases, and perceptions. Without entering into the larger debate over the application of postmodernism to social science research, it would be remiss to fail to acknowledge the important warning imbedded in its sometimes obscure arguments.[12]

During the beginning phase of our research on the behavior of states in militarized crises, David Singer and I set out to construct an "atheoretical" typology of state actions. After some reflection, we realized that such an enterprise was impossible. We both were too grounded in presuppositions about the working of international politics to create anything that was truly atheoretical, so we settled on an attempt to develop a typology that was sufficiently "multitheoretical" to allow the greatest amount of flexibility as the research progressed.[13] Even then we recognized that the typology rested on a realist theoretical foundation that was an inescapable part of our thinking about interstate conflict. That foundation, which postmodernists would call the "subtext" of the constructed typology, is evidence that descriptions of reality can never be entirely free of preconceptions. But this is not an "either-or" issue. If it is true that we ultimately approach a limit, in the mathematical sense, in the attempt to be completely objective, the degree to which we succeed matters. It is the conscious effort to narrow the gap between objectivity and accounts based on preconceptions that distinguishes scientific research from pamphleteering. As Weber argued, the first presupposition of science is that the scientific method itself is valid.[14]

Cumulative Knowledge

The issue of how to obtain cumulative knowledge has been a part of the discourse among scientific researchers ever since James Rosenau brought together a group of "first generation IR scientists" in Ojai, California, in 1973 to discuss the state of the subfield.[15] The debate over how to achieve accumulation continues with Starr's arguments in his chapter in this collection. The discussion here focuses on the progress to date.

During the Ojai meetings, Harold Guetzkow referred to the subfield as having achieved no more than "islands of theories."[16] Three decades later we have progressed to where there are islands of findings.

The findings are not trivial. Consider the paramount problem of world politics, war. We now know a great deal about war per se: when it has occurred; the magnitude, intensity, and severity of interstate and civil wars; war's evolution over time;[17] and the relationship between war and changes in the structure of the interstate system.[18] We also know that most modern wars have occurred between contiguous states;[19] that democracies have rarely, if ever, fought wars with each other;[20] that a relatively small number of states account for an inordinately high proportion of militarized disputes and wars;[21] and that states with high recidivism rates tend to fight each other.[22] We also know that the locus of crises in the past century has shifted from Europe to the Third World, to Africa in particular, as has the locus of most ethnopolitical conflict.[23]

There is strong evidence that wars are most likely to grow out of disputes over territory;[24] that contiguity is a strong predictor of violence in militarized crises;[25] that the most effective influence strategy in a militarized crises is a "firm-but-flexible" variant of tit for tat;[26] that the lesson most commonly drawn by rival states from their crisis experiences is to adopt a more coercive influence strategy in their next crisis;[27] and that state power transitions—not civilizational clashes—have been the best predictors of ethnopolitical warfare.[28]

Several things stand out when one considers these findings. First, they are by no means marginal to the central questions of world politics. Second, none of them could have been obtained with confidence without employing scientific methods of inquiry. Third, in their present state they remain islands of findings in the sense that none qualifies as an explanatory theory of state or substate behavior; they exist as unfitted pieces of a much larger, multivariate puzzle.

Elsewhere I have compared our findings regarding war to the much more heavily funded research on the relationship between diet and coronary artery disease (CAD).[29] There, too, there have been starts and stops; correlational findings that resulted in runs on grocery supplies of items like oat bran have been refuted by later studies. But the frontier of science always looks uncertain and contentious as findings are replicated or refuted, and theories contend for acceptance. Behind the frontier of CAD research there is a base of accepted core knowledge, established theory regarding the relationship between serum cholesterol and the buildup of plaque on artery walls. The trend line of CAD research is wavy, but it is cumulative.

Accumulation in CAD research has occurred through the integration of laboratory research with correlational population studies. The integration of the two approaches provides stronger explanatory power than is possible with just one of the tools, and sometimes the results are surprising. For example, a basic preventive strategy for CAD is to lower the blood serum levels of low-density lipoproteins (LDL), the bad cholesterol, while raising those of high-density lipoproteins (HDL), the good cholesterol. Laboratory research indicated that estrogen produces both of the desired effects. Population studies demonstrated that the risk of CAD in women rises after menopause, when women stop producing estrogen. Consequently, hormone replacement therapy, that is, adding estrogen, was presumed to aid in reducing the incidence of CAD in postmenopausal women. In fact, women who took estrogen did live longer and have less heart disease than those who did not take estrogen.

It appeared to be a perfectly straightforward, easily explained relationship until a team of scientists conducted a blind study of at-risk postmenopausal women in which estrogen was matched against a placebo.[30] Over a three-year period, the study found no significant difference in the incidence of CAD within the group of women taking estrogen and the group taking a placebo. The most plausible biological explanation for the null finding is not that estrogen has no effect, but that it has *several different* effects that cancel out each other. Besides the beneficial effect of lowering serum levels of LDL and raising those of HDL cholesterol, estrogen promotes clotting and contributes to the inflammation of arteries, factors that *increase* the risk of heart disease.[31] There also is a plausible societal explanation for the earlier positive correlational findings, which is that women who choose the hormone replacement therapy after menopause are likely to be more educated and more likely to take other steps to reduce the risk of heart disease. There is yet another contextual explanation. The participants in the Herrington study were all women who already had some evidence of CAD. It could be that estrogen does have predominantly beneficial effects, but only for women who have not yet accumulated any significant buildup of plaque in their arteries.[32]

The estrogen story illustrates the risk associated with relying on correlational evidence from uncontrolled population studies, an inescapable problem in most quantitative international politics research. But it also demonstrates the multiple effects that can be produced by a single variable. To turn to two examples closer to home, consider two impressive correlational findings regarding the war proneness of state dyads: the democratic peace and the positive association between contiguity and war.

The democratic peace thesis grows out of the finding that there have been no, or virtually no, wars between two democratic states. There is considerable debate over the significance of the statistical finding, as well as over contending explanations for its occurrence. The inability to conduct a controlled study renders the debate regarding the significance of the statistical evidence endless. Critics point out that democracies historically have been less likely to share borders, more likely to be wealthy, and thereby content with the status quo, and more likely to share memberships in international institutions.

When it comes to explaining *why* democracies would be less likely to go to war with each other, the two most prominent contending explanations (cultural and structural) covary to such a degree that it is impossible to conduct a comparative test. Thus, researchers are left with attempting to find indirect indicators suggestive of one or another explanation.[33]

But suppose it were possible to conduct a controlled experiment like the estrogen test described earlier. Is it possible that we would find that the potential effects of democracy on foreign policy are as mixed as those of estrogen on the body? The two explanations mentioned in the previous paragraph are based on beneficial cultural and structural attributes presumed to be present in all democracies. But, like estrogen, democracy is a variable with many attributes, and different attributes can have different effects on relations with other states, and, as some have suggested in the case of estrogen, it also may be that the potency of particular effects are contextually dependent. Mansfield and Snyder argue, for example, that the early phase of a democracy in transition from an authoritarian regime may lead to a nationalistic, contentious foreign policy under popularly elected demagogues.[34] It may be that statistically the more dangerous effects of majority rule and mass enthusiasm may be masked by a rapid transition to authoritarianism following the popular election of demagogues.

Besides the special case of democratic dyads, the best statistical predictor of whether a pair of states will find themselves at war with each other is whether or not they share a common border. Wars tend to be fought over territory, and contiguity provides more opportunities for territorial disputes. But preliminary findings from a study by Starr using geographic information systems imaging indicates that among contiguous states, disputes are significantly less frequent in those border areas in which there are greater opportunities for cross-border interactions and transactions, that is, higher population density, better transportation facilities, and more economic transactions.[35] Contiguity, it appears, can have contradictory effects. Depending on other variables, it can encourage border disputes or it can encourage community-building communication and transactions of the sort once described by Deutsch et al.[36] As in the estrogen story, what appears to be a straightforward explanation based on an observed association turns out to be an oversimplification of the predictor variable's effects on the phenomenon of interest.

When one considers the number of variables that are likely to exert a significant influence on complex social phenomena such as war, and the mixed effects of any one of the variables identified to date, it appears that we still are scratching at the surface of explanatory theory. We are all working at the frontier of scientific international politics research.

The scientific frontier is a contentious place. One writer has described the process of scientific cumulation as "Darwinian evolutionary epistemology."[37] No new finding is accepted without challenge, and only the most robust survive. But the expectation in a mature science is that new findings ultimately will lead to the acceptance of new theories that will expand upon or supplant their predecessors. Those theories that meet with long-term acceptance will lead to the expansion of the cumulative core of knowledge. The question in our own field is whether there is any theory to date that has achieved sufficient consensus to be accepted as core knowledge.

My own sense is that there is not. Consequently, we continue to work on the frontier of scientific research without the core knowledge that would provide irrefutable evidence of cumulative science.

Policy Relevance

Another difference between quantitative international politics research and that on CAD is that there has been nothing like the stampede to act upon findings in peace research that would be analogous to the explosion of sales of putative "heart-friendly" foods like oat bran or olive oil. People are most likely to act on those findings that are consistent with their existing beliefs, that serve their immediate interests, and that present few psychological or political costs and risks. Thus it is not surprising that American politicians have seized upon the democratic peace proposition. Conversely, as the war in Chechnya grinds to a close, it should come as no surprise that Huntington's "civilizational clash" hypothesis is viewed by Russian academicians as the most important new work in world politics, while Gurr's empirically based counterfindings are largely ignored.[38] The policy relevance of our work, at least in the minds of political leaders, is dependent on their political agenda.

Methodology versus Content

At the beginning of this essay, I noted how the intensity of the early debate between classicists and scientists was fueled by political stakes. Nowhere is that more evident than when curricular issues are considered. After all, which approaches graduate students, and even undergraduates, are taught will determine the future direction of world politics research. There is a limited amount of room in any curriculum, so when something new is added, something old must be removed. Bull's fear was that an emphasis on training in scientific methods would squeeze out more traditional subjects, such as diplomatic history, international law, and normative theory. His fears, insofar as the dominance of scientific approaches is concerned, have not been realized. Political science, and world politics in particular, lag behind their sister social science disciplines in the teaching of scientific approaches at the undergraduate level in all but a few, primarily Midwestern, universities. The pattern is more mixed at the graduate level, where at least some training in scientific method has become an established part of the world politics curriculum.

Nevertheless, Bull sounded two notes of caution that are worth considering. The first is that an overemphasis on methodological training could lead to a generation of scientists who know little about the political or historical content of the subject that they are researching. I recently attended a professional meeting where a graduate student from a major university presented an empirical study of the origins of the Franco-Prussian War of 1870. At one point, the author referred to Napoleon III of France as Napoleon Bonaparte's grandson, or, he added, "maybe great grandson."[39] The enormous chronological error demonstrated such a lack of knowledge of the historical period that one wondered about the propositions that propelled the study, the research design, and the interpretation of the findings. There is such a thing as gaining a "feel" for the subject matter to guide one's thinking about it. Without that feel, one is likely to wander down research dead ends, or produce findings that rediscover the obvious.

My experience in teaching undergraduates for more than thirty years has convinced me that we are best served by putting the content of world politics at the center of early undergraduate teaching, and supplementing it with training in method, with increased emphasis on theory and method, in upper-level courses. I do not underestimate the intellectual service that we provide to undergraduates by teaching scientific methods, but we should not do so at the expense of the joy of studying politics per se. We need to remember that students do not select courses in world politics because they want to learn more about mathematics.

Second, there is the danger of dogmatism regarding what qualifies as acceptable knowledge. A lack of knowledge of the normative and philosophical issues debated by classicists, Bull argued, can lead to an unconscious or uncritical acceptance of a particular philosophical position. One does not have to be a social constructivist to recognize the problem to which Bull referred. A decade after the Bull-Singer debate, Vasquez published a study showing how extant scientific investigations were guided, perhaps unconsciously, by the underlying assumptions of realism.[40] The problem is not only that realism may be outdated or incorrect in some contexts. When one works within the realist tradition there is a tendency to focus on conflict per se at the expense of the techniques for reducing, terminating, or avoiding it.

It should be noted, however, that the unconscious acceptance of the realist paradigm has grown out of the ubiquity of the realist tradition in classical studies of world politics. If there is a cure for chronic realism it is likely to lie in the acceptance within the scientific community of findings and theories that challenge simplistic realist assumptions. The findings on the democratic peace may be one example. I would offer my own findings on conflict bargaining, escalation, and learning as another.[41]

Summary

The final issue to consider is that of the relationship itself, that is, the current state of the cold war between the classicists and scientists. But before doing so, it may be useful to summarize the preceding points to provide some perspective on the evolution of quantitative world politics research.

Certainly, Bull's charge of triviality can be laid to rest. Recent quantitative studies have focused not on the margins of world politics but directly on the decisions of national leaders and the actions and interactions of states, the same events that represented the core of Thucydides' history. It should be noted, however, that an increasing number of those studies are augmented by qualitative case studies.

The issue of attaining a cumulative science of world politics is no longer that of attainability but of how long it will take to move from islands of findings to an established base of core knowledge. I can offer no prediction with regard to how long that will take, nor do I think that there is any magic formula for reaching closure. Agreement will occur only when a combination of theory and findings is sufficiently robust to withstand the ready challenges of all comers on the frontier of science.

There is some validity to Bull's third concern that the scientific study of world politics could lead to an emphasis on methods over content, particularly as we become more sophisticated in our methodology and more successful in our research. I am convinced that, as in so many other professional activities, meaningful empirical research requires a feel for the subject matter, which comes only through a deeper familiarity with the substance of politics. I am less worried about Bull's related concern, that a superficial understanding of classical theory could lead to a facile dogmatism. As I noted earlier, the rarified air of theoretical debate has not cured the classicists. The best antidote to theoretical dogmatism would appear to be robust counterfindings from scientific studies.

Moving from Competition to Integration

The last issue is that of the contentiousness between the classical and scientific communities that is so evident in the early exchange between Bull and Singer. During much of the 1970s and 1980s the relationship could best be described as peaceful coexistence in the Soviet sense of the term: ideological, political, and economic competition short of violent hostilities. But over the past decade some of the competitiveness has lost its edge, and there is a growing tendency to combine classical and scientific approaches. Those working within the classical tradition are more likely to buttress their arguments with data-based analyses; those adopting a scientific approach are more likely to add qualitative case studies to add depth to their investigations. Despite his earlier criticisms of classical methods, Singer recently coauthored a book-length study that includes a number of qualitative case studies.[42] I recently completed a study of learning in enduring rivalries that combines quantitative analyses of state behavior and qualitative descriptions of foreign policy-making in comparative case studies.[43] The cold war between the classical and scientific approaches is more likely to end through an unconscious integrative solution that serves the interests of both sides than through the triumph of one research paradigm over the other.

Notes

1. Hedley Bull, "International Theory: A Case for a Classical Approach," *World Politics* 18 (1966): 362. Bull's understanding of the classical approach is based on the methodologies of law, philosophy, and history, with particular emphasis on "the exercise of judgment." Ibid., 361.
2. Ibid., 363.
3. J. David Singer, "The Incomplete Theorist: Insight without Evidence," in *Contending Approaches to International Politics*, ed. Klaus Knorr and James N. Rosenau (Princeton, N.J.: Princeton University Press, 1969).
4. Ibid., 82.
5. See Harvey Starr, in this volume.
6. Thucydides, *A Comprehensive Guide to the Peloponnesian War*, ed. Robert Strassler (New York: Free Press, 1996), 15.
7. Ibid., 15.
8. Melvin Small and J. David Singer, *Resort to Arms: International and Civil Wars, 1816–1980* (Beverly Hills, Calif.: Sage, 1982).
9. Michael Brecher and Jonathan Wilkenfeld, *A Study of Crisis* (Ann Arbor: University of Michigan Press, 1997); Ted R. Gurr, *Minorities at Risk: A Global View of Ethnopolitical Conflict* (Washington, D.C.; U.S. Institute of Peace Press, 1993); Jacob Bercovitch and Allison Houston, "The Study of International Mediation: Theoretical Issues and Empirical Evidence,"

in *Resolving International Conflicts: The Theory and Practice of Mediation*, ed. Jacob Bercovitch (Boulder, Colo.: Lynne Rienner, 1996).

10. Russell J. Leng and J. David Singer, "Toward a Multitheoretical Typology of International Behavior" (paper presented at the Events Data Conference, East Lansing, Mich., April 15–16, 1970); Russell J. Leng and J. David Singer, "Militarized Interstate Crises: The BCOW Typology and Its Applications," *International Studies Quarterly* 32 (1987): 155–73.

11. Russell J. Leng, *Bargaining and Learning in Recurring Crises: The Soviet-American, Egyptian-Israeli, and Indo-Pakistani Rivalries* (Ann Arbor: University of Michigan Press, 2000).

12. See Pauline M. Rosenau, *Post-Modernism and the Social Sciences: Insights, Inroads, and Intrusions* (Princeton, N.J.: Princeton University Press, 1992); Michael J. Shapiro, "Textualizing International Politics," in *International/Intertextual Relations: Postmodern Reading of World Politics*, ed. James Der Derian and Michael J. Shapiro (New York: Lexington Books, 1989).

13. Leng and Singer, "Toward a Multitheoretical Typology of International Behavior."

14. Max Weber, "Science as a Vocation," in *From Max Weber: Essays in Sociology*, ed. H. H. Gerth and C. Wright Mills (1919; reprint, New York: Oxford University Press, 1946), 143.

15. James N. Rosenau, ed., *In Search of Global Patterns* (New York: Free Press, 1976).

16. Harold Guetzkow, "Sizing Up a Study in Simulated International Processes," in Rosenau, *In Search of Global Patterns*, 91. Guetzkow's assessment assumes a rather loose definition of theory. "Islands of hypotheses" would have been more accurate.

17. Small and Singer, *Resort to Arms*.

18. J. David Singer, Stuart Bremer, and John Stuckey, "Capability Distribution, Uncertainty, and Major Power War, 1820–1965," in *Peace, War, and Numbers*, ed. Bruce Russett (Beverly Hills, Calif.: Sage, 1972); Frank Wayman, "Bipolarity and War: The Role of Capability Concentration and Alliance Patterns among Major Powers, 1816–1965," *Journal of Peace Research* 21 (1984): 25–42; Daniel S. Geller and J. David Singer, *Nations at War: A Scientific Study of International Conflict* (Cambridge: Cambridge University Press, 1998), ch. 6.

19. Peter Wallensteen, "Incompatibility, Confrontation, and War: Four Models and Three Historical Systems, 1816–1976," *Journal of Peace Research* 18 (1981): 57–90; Stuart Bremer, "Dangerous Dyads: Conditions Affecting the Likelihood of Interstate War, 1816–1965," *Journal of Conflict Resolution* 36 (1992): 309–41.

20. Zeev Maoz and Bruce Russett, "Normative and Structural Causes of Democratic Peace, 1946–1986," *American Political Science Review* 87 (1993): 624–38; Michael Doyle, "Liberalism and World Politics," *American Political Science Review* 80 (1986): 1151–61.

21. Charles S. Gochman and Zeev Maoz, "Militarized Interstate Disputes, 1816–1976: Patterns, Procedures, Insights," *Journal of Conflict Resolution* 28 (1984): 585–615.

22. Zeev Maoz, "Pacifism, Dispute Proneness, and Addiction: Patterns and

Correlates of National and Dyadic Conflict History, 1816–1992" (paper presented at the annual meeting of the Peace Science Society [International], Yale University, New Haven, Conn., October 27–29, 2000).

23. Brecher and Wilkenfeld, *A Study of Crisis;* Ted R. Gurr, "Peoples against States: Ethnopolitical Conflict and the Changing World System," *International Studies Quarterly* 38 (1994): 347–77.

24. John A. Vasquez, *The War Puzzle* (Cambridge: Cambridge University Press, 1993).

25. Brecher and Wilkenfeld, *A Study of Crisis.*

26. Russell J. Leng, *Interstate Crisis Behavior, 1816–1980: Reciprocity versus Realpolitik* (Cambridge: Cambridge University Press, 1993); P. K. Huth, *Extended Deterrence and the Prevention of War* (New Haven, Conn.: Yale University Press, 1988).

27. Leng, *Interstate Crisis Behavior;* Leng, *Bargaining and Learning in Recurring Crises.*

28. Gurr, "Peoples against States." For more complete accounts of recent findings related to international conflict and war, see Geller and Singer, *Nations at War,* and Vasquez, *The War Puzzle.*

29. Russell J. Leng, "Cumulation in Q.I.P.: 25 Years after Ojai," *Conflict Management and Peace Science* 18 (2000): 133–47.

30. David M. Herrington et al., "Effects of Estrogen Replacement on the Progression of Coronary-Artery Atherosclerosis," *New England Journal of Medicine* 343 (2000): 522–29.

31. Ibid., 527.

32. See Elizabeth Nabel, "Coronary Heart Disease in Women: An Ounce of Prevention," *New England Journal of Medicine* 343 (2000): 572–73.

33. Bruce M. Russett, *Grasping the Democratic Peace: Principles for a Post–Cold War World* (Princeton, N.J.: Princeton University Press, 1993), 40–42.

34. Edward Mansfield and John Snyder, "Democratization and the Danger of War," *International Security* 20 (1995): 5–38.

35. Harvey Starr, "The 'Nature' of Contiguous Borders" (paper presented at the annual meeting of the Peace Science Society [International], Yale University, New Haven, Conn., October 27–29, 2000).

36. Karl W. Deutsch et al., *Political Community and the North Atlantic Area* (Princeton, N.J.: Princeton University Press, 1957).

37. Ernst Mayr, *This Is Biology: The Science of the Living World* (Cambridge, Mass.: Belknap Press, 1998).

38. Samuel P. Huntington, *The Clash of Civilizations: Remaking of World Order* (New York: Simon and Schuster, 1996); Gurr, *Minorities at Risk;* Gurr, "Peoples against States."

39. Napoleon III was Bonaparte's nephew.

40. John A. Vasquez, "Coloring It Morgenthau: New Evidence for an Old Thesis on Quantitative International Politics," *British Journal of International Studies* 5 (1979): 210–28.

41. Leng, *Interstate Crisis Behavior;* Leng, *Bargaining and Learning in Recurring Crises.*

42. Geller and Singer, *Nations at War.*

43. Leng, *Bargaining and Learning in Recurring Crises.*

Qualitative Methods
in International Relations

Jack S. Levy

Three decades ago, Sartori complained about the number of "un-conscious thinkers" in the field of comparative politics, and the same could be said of the study of international relations.[1] Most qualitative analyses were idiographic rather than nomothetic,[2] historically specific rather than theoretically driven, and too little concerned with the logic of inference and questions of generalizability. Scholars gave little attention to the problem of how to control for extraneous variables in situations in which the number of variables typically exceeded the number of cases, or to the question of whether there are alternative methods for validating causal inferences in a single case. Both critics and advocates of case study methods agreed that qualitative research in the 1950s and 1960s precluded the cumulation of knowledge across historical cases.[3] This lack of scientific rigor created an image of qualitative analysis as highly subjective, pliable in fitting facts to theoretical arguments, nonreplicable, and essentially nonfalsifiable.

Much has changed in the last two or three decades, both in terms of the growing body of literature on the methodology of qualitative analysis and the increasing social science orientation of most qualitative research in international relations. My aim in this essay is to survey the expanding literature on qualitative methods and to high-

This essay has benefited from the helpful comments of Andrew Bennett, Jack Snyder, and the editors of this volume.

light some of its major themes. Qualitative analysis includes everything from interpretive ethnographic studies to macrohistories spanning millennia to microanalyses of particular events, and individual cases have been analyzed by quantitative as well as qualitative methods. Thus we should not equate qualitative methods with the case study method. The core of the literature on the methodology of qualitative research in the international relations field focuses on comparative and case study methods from a positivistic perspective, however, and that is the focus of this essay. I give particular attention to the meaning of the case concept, the different kinds and purposes of case studies, the different types of case study designs for testing theories, and the distinctive contributions and limitations of comparative and case study methods.

A well-defined body of literature on comparative and case study methods was beginning to emerge just as Sartori lamented unconscious thinking in the field.[4] These efforts to develop a methodology of comparative analysis were informed by comparable work in sociology,[5] and were stimulated by the success of historical sociology.[6] By the early 1990s, the methodology of comparative and case study analysis had a well-defined place in the fields of comparative and international politics.[7]

The publication of King, Keohane, and Verba's *Designing Social Inquiry* triggered another surge of interest in the methodology of qualitative research.[8] This was in part a response to the "KKV" argument that there is a single logic of scientific inference, that qualitative analysis is not fundamentally different from large-N statistical analysis, and that the former needs to conform more closely to the latter. These arguments led to a major debate in the discipline. Symposia in the *American Political Science Review* (1995) and in the *APSA-CP Newsletter* (1998) and subsequent articles and books dealt with the "single logic" question, the advantages and limitations of case study approaches, the different types of case study approaches, and specific problems of case selection and other aspects of research design.[9] One indicator of the expanding interest in qualitative methodology is the increasing number of graduate courses offered in this area. Another is the organization of the Inter-University Consortium on Qualitative Research Methods (CQRM), which includes instructional workshops, collection of syllabi, and on-line discussion groups.[10]

Advances in the methodology of qualitative research have been paralleled by an increasing methodological self-consciousness and sophistication in applications of qualitative methods to empirical research. The current generation of qualitative international relations researchers are much more nomothetic in their general orientations, both in terms of their interest in using explicitly stated theories to guide historical interpretations and in their greater interest in developing theoretical generalizations valid across time and space. They are more attentive to the question of proper case selection and other aspects of research design, more sensitive to potential threats to valid inference, and generally more social scientific in orientation.[11]

Definitions

Although some define the case study method as distinct from the comparative method,[12] nearly all case studies involve comparisons, whether they be explicit or implicit, across cases or within cases. In addition, the literature has evolved in such a way that the comparative method has come to be associated with the analysis of a small number of cases,[13] further eroding any distinction between the case study and comparative methods. Some use the term *case study* to refer to a single case study and *comparative method* to refer to comparisons among a small number of cases, but the similar logic underlying both single and multiple case studies leads most scholars to use *case study method* to refer to both.[14]

Despite the pervasiveness of case study analysis in international and comparative politics, scholars are far from agreement on how to define either case or case study. Ragin and Becker have edited a book entitled *What Is a Case?* but provide no clear definition or answer.[15] Precisely how one defines "case" depends in part on the purposes of inquiry. Those who are primarily interested in understanding and interpreting a particular historical episode, with little interest in constructing or testing more general theoretical propositions, tend to define case in terms of a set of events bounded in time and space. For such scholars, World War I or the cold war may each be a "case" to be explained.

Given the shift toward a more theoretical orientation in the international relations field and an increasing interest in constructing and validating theoretical propositions, the vast majority of scholars conceive of a case as an *instance* of something else, of a theoretically defined class of events.[16] The question is always, What is this a case of? In this sense World War I itself is not a case, but certain theoretically defined aspects of World War I may be cases of some broader phenomenon, such as deterrence, balance of power, power transition, diversionary action, or war termination. This is explicit in George's conception of the method of "structured, focused comparison," which focuses on a particular analytically defined aspect of a set of events and uses a well-defined set of theoretical questions to structure empirical inquiry. This analytical orientation recognizes that observation is theory laden, and that researchers' theoretical preconceptions will lead them to decide which of the myriad of events constituting a historical episode are to be selected out, studied, and recast in terms of "variables."[17]

From this perspective, "cases come wrapped in theories" and do not exist independently of the analytic framework a scholar brings to a particular subject.[18] Cases are analytical constructions. They are made, not found; invented, not discovered.[19] This does not imply that there are multiple, equally valid answers to our questions about the world, only multiple questions that we might ask.

It is important to emphasize that a case generally includes many observations on the same variable. The July 1914 crisis, for example, includes a substantial number of observations of the use of coercive threats, domestic influences, and misperceptions, to name but a few variables. Indeed, one of the main strategies of case study analysis, just like large-N analysis, is to generate as many testable implications of one's hypotheses as possible in a given case.[20] This standard view of multiple observations per variable per case is more useful than Eckstein's definition of a case as "a phenomenon for which we report and interpret only a single measure on any pertinent variable,"[21] and most methodologists have moved away from Eckstein's definition.

Types of Case Studies

There are many types of case studies and numerous ways of classifying them. Most classifications focus on the purpose or function of case studies and build on Lijphart's typology of atheoretical, interpretive, hypothesis-generating, theory-confirming, theory-infirming, and deviant case studies.[22] Eckstein suggests a similar typology: configurative-idiographic, disciplined-configurative, heuristic, and crucial case studies based on most likely and least likely designs.[23] Eckstein suggests the additional category of plausibility probe. These are ideal types, and in practice many case studies combine several of these aims. The following classification represents a combination of the Lijphart and Eckstein categories.

Atheoretical or *configurative-idiographic* case studies are traditional single-case analyses often associated with area studies. They are highly descriptive and aim to understand and interpret a single case as an end in itself rather than to develop broader theoretical generalizations. Idiographic case studies are inductive; they involve a minimum of a priori theoretical preconceptions, and the interpretation emerges from the case itself. The analyst generally attempts to create a gestalt or holistic picture of a historical episode, explaining all aspects of the episode and all of their interconnections. This is "total history," which "cannot decide to leave out *any* aspect of human history *a priori.*"[24]

Interpretive or *disciplined-configurative* case studies also aim to explain/interpret a single case, but that interpretation is explicitly structured by a theory or well-developed theoretical framework that focuses attention on some theoretically specified aspects of reality and neglects others. This is analytic history rather than total history, but it is still idiographic in that it aims to explain a particular historical episode rather than develop or test theoretical generalizations.

Although such "case-explaining" case studies are common in the international relations field, they are less highly valued than work that generates or tests theories,[25] and many international relations theorists believe that historically specific research is best left to historians. This is understandable but unfortunate, because the explicit and structured use of theory to explain discrete cases often provides better explanations and understandings of those cases—or at least some aspects of those cases—than do less structured historical analyses. The more case interpretations are guided by theory, the more explicit their underlying analytic assumptions, normative biases, and causal propositions; the fewer their logical contradictions; and the easier they are to validate or invalidate empirically. Theoretically guided, interpretive case studies can significantly enhance our descriptive understanding of the world, and international relations scholars have much to contribute to this task.[26]

Whereas atheoretical and interpretive case studies are basically idiographic in their explanatory objectives, *hypothesis-generating* or *heuristic* case studies are more nomothetic in their aims. They examine a particular case or perhaps several cases for the purpose of developing more general theoretical propositions, which can then be tested through other methods, including large-N methods and perhaps alternative case study methods. Case selection is driven by theoretical considerations, not by the intrinsic interest or historical importance of the case itself, and only particular aspects of the case are investigated.

It would be more correct to say that case studies can contribute to the *process* of theory construction than to theory itself, for the latter—defined as a logically interconnected set of propositions about empirical phenomena—requires a more deductive orientation than case studies provide. Thus Achen and Snidal argue, "the logic of comparative case studies inherently provides too little logical constraint to generate dependable theory," and they complain that findings of case studies have "too often . . . been interpreted as bodies of theory."[27] The same can be said of statistical or experimental methods. The application of each of these methods can stimulate the imagination and suggest new hypotheses, but isolated hypotheses fall short of theory, and neither case study methods nor statistical methods can by themselves generate theory.

Case studies permit an intensive examination of particular historical sequences, and in doing so they can contribute to the process of theory development by helping to clarify the meaning of key variables and the validity of empirical indicators used to measure them, and by suggesting additional causal mechanisms, causal variables, and interaction effects. They can also help to identify the contextual variables that affect hypothesized causal processes and to identify the scope conditions under which particular theories are valid. These are all important steps in the theory-building process. Thus Achen and Snidal argue that "because they are simultaneously sensitive to data and theory, case studies are more useful for these purposes [of developing analytic theory] than any other methodological tool."[28]

The role of case studies in generating hypotheses, or at least in refining and sharpening them, is enhanced by the close interaction of theory and data in case study analysis. The analyst begins with a theory, uses it to interpret a case, and simultaneously utilizes the case to suggest important refinements in the theory, which can then be tested on other cases or perhaps even on other aspects of the same case.[29] George and Smoke's analysis of deterrence in American foreign policy, for example, is organized sequentially in terms of theory specification, application of the theory to historical cases, and reformulation of the theory based on the cases.[30] The interplay between theory and evidence is also explicit in "analytic narratives" in which formal rational choice theory guides analytic histories, the anomalies of which are then used to refine the theory.[31]

Although hypothesis-generating case studies can sometimes contribute to the development of entirely new hypotheses, through unexpected discoveries in the process of investigating other phenomena, case studies are often more useful in helping the researcher to refine existing hypotheses, as in George's method of structured, focused comparison.[32] The greater the theoretical structure guiding inquiry, and the better defined the researcher's hypotheses, the more efficient the hypothesis-generating process. But sometimes a full-fledged test of a hypothesis is premature. *Plausibility probes*, like pilot studies in experimental or survey research, are intermediate steps between hypothesis construction and hypothesis testing. They enable the researcher to refine the hypothesis or theory before engaging in a costly and time-consuming research effort, whether through the massive collection of quantitative data or through extensive fieldwork.

Deviant case studies, which focus on empirical anomalies in established theoretical generalizations in order to explain them and refine existing hypotheses, are a particularly powerful strategy for theory refinement, much like examining the residuals in a statistical analysis. Deviant case studies can help to validate the measurement of key variables; identify omitted variables, interaction effects, or alternative causal paths; or identify the scope conditions under which a particular theory is valid. Revised hypotheses can then be tested over a broader set of cases or unexplored aspects of the same case. The analysis of "borderline" cases in the hypothesized absence of war between democracies is a form of deviant case analysis.[33]

Another way case studies can contribute to theory development is through what Lazarsfeld described as the "analysis of the dependent variable."[34] The analyst examines cases that on the surface appear to be similar on the dependent variable, in order to identify its different subtypes. This facilitates the development of a more differentiated conception of the dependent variable and a more nuanced set of hypotheses. George and subsequently George and Bennett develop this idea in their discussion of "typological theory."[35] They emphasize that there may be a number of alternative causal paths to a given outcome (equifinality) and attempt to identify these alternative causal paths and, if possible, to specify the conditions under which each is most likely to occur. An example is George and Smoke's exploration of the various ways in which deterrence can fail and their elaboration of the different causal paths associated with each. Similar logic underlies Collier and Levitsky's effort to articulate various subtypes of democracy.[36]

Many scholars emphasize this role of comparative and case study methods in contributing to the process of theory building, in stimulating the imagination and generating hypotheses that can then be more rigorously tested. Stinchcombe suggests that "lots of facts" can be "good hard stones for honing ideas."[37] Lijphart argues that a comparative perspective (as distinct from the comparative method per se) can be a helpful element in discovery.[38] He quotes Stretton, who argues that "the function of comparison is less to stimulate experiment than to stimulate imagination. . . . Comparison is strongest as a choosing and provoking, not a proving, devise; a system for questioning, not for answering."[39]

In addition to playing an essential role in the explanation of individual historical episodes and a contributory role in the generation of hypotheses, case studies can also be used to test hypotheses and theories. This is Lijphart's *theory-confirming* and *theory-infirming* roles of case studies, which are best collapsed into a single theory-testing category.[40] As Lijphart recognizes, however, the use of case studies for testing hypotheses faces a very serious problem: the existence of many variables in conjunction with a relatively small number of cases. As a consequence, outcomes are overdetermined, and it is difficult if not impossible to be certain that changes in the dependent variable are due to changes in the hypothesized independent variables and not to the effects of extraneous variables. Much of the literature on the comparative method and on case study analysis deals with the problem of how to make causal inferences in small-N research, when the number of variables generally exceeds the number of cases.[41]

Lijphart recognized the many variables/small-N problem and offered a number of possible solutions.[42] Three try to directly influence the ratio of cases to variables: increase the number of cases by expanding the domain of the analysis both spatially and temporally; reduce the number of variables, either by collapsing conceptual categories or by data reduction techniques such as factor analysis; or focus on a relatively small number of key variables by constructing more parsimonious theories. Lijphart's fourth solution focused on "comparable cases"—cases similar in terms of the control variables but different in terms of hypothesized explanatory variables that one wants to investigate.

In emphasizing an increase in the ratio of cases to variables, Lijphart basically accepted the utility of large-N analysis and conceded that the comparative method was inferior to the experimental or statistical methods for the purposes of causal inference. He concluded that comparative analysis was a "first stage" devoted to the careful formulation of hypotheses, which are then tested in a "second stage" statistical analysis.[43] He also acknowledged a certain tension between the goals of increasing the number of cases and focusing on similar cases, because the latter narrows the range of possible cases.

In a subsequent article on the comparative method, Lijphart conceded that the maximizing-N strategy—which is based on controlling for extraneous variables through partial correlations—and the comparable-cases strategy—which is based on control through a carefully selected set of matched cases—involved different logics and were more fundamentally opposed than he had initially acknowledged.[44] He retracted his earlier argument that the comparative method works best with a larger number of cases, and defined the comparative method as equivalent to the small-N analysis of comparable cases. In this way Lijphart moved closer to Eckstein who stressed the advantages of small-N analysis, including single-case analysis.[45]

Following Lijphart, scholars now conceive of the comparative method and case study methods as strategies for dealing with a relatively small number of cases. The comparative method is often defined as a strategy for conducting research on naturally occurring phenomena in a way that aims to control for potential confounding variables through careful case selection and matching rather than through experimental manipulation or partial correlations.[46]

Varieties of Case Selection Strategies

The comparable-cases strategy is closely related to John Stuart Mill's *method of difference*, which focuses on cases that have different values on the dependent variable and similar values on all but one of the independent variables.[47] In terms of the logic of inference, this facilitates the identification of causal factors that vary with the dependent variable by eliminating all variables that are constant over the similar cases. Mill's *method of agreement* focuses on cases that are similar on the dependent variable and different on all but one of the independent variables, in order to eliminate all factors that vary across cases on the independent variable and that therefore cannot account for similar outcomes across cases on the dependent variable.

Mill's methods of agreement and difference are comparable to "most-different" and "most-similar" systems designs, respectively.[48] A *most-different systems* design identifies cases that are different on a wide range of explanatory variables but not on the dependent variable, while a *most-similar systems* design identifies cases that are similar on a wide range of explanatory variables but different on the value of the dependent variable.[49] The former eliminates extraneous causal variables that vary across cases, while the latter eliminates causal variables that do not vary across cases.

Mill argued that the method of difference was more powerful than the method of agreement in establishing causation. Similarly, Lijphart and Smelser each preferred most-similar systems designs.[50] Przeworski and Teune, on the other hand, preferred most-different systems designs, which maximize the number of extraneous variables that can be eliminated because they vary while the dependent variable does not.[51] The basic logic of the two designs is the same— to identify patterns of covariation and to eliminate independent variables that do not covary with the dependent variable.

It is rare that either strategy alone can fully eliminate extraneous variables, and the best strategy generally involves the combination of most-similar and most-different systems designs. Mill recognized this and argued for a method of "concomitant variation" involving a combination of the methods of agreement and difference.

One problem in the application of Mill's methods and of most-similar and most-different systems designs is the difficulty of identifying cases that are truly comparable—identical or different in all respects but one. In addition, because of the possibility that several different sets of conditions may lead to the same outcome—which Mill identified as the "plurality of causes" and which modern systems theorists refer to as "equifinality"—Mill's methods can lead to spurious inferences if they are used mechanically or not supplemented with the use of within-case methods like process tracing. Mill acknowledged this and concluded that for this reason the application of the methods of agreement and difference to political science was "completely out of the question."[52]

Proponents of comparative case methods argue that Mill was far too cautious, and that insisting on precise and absolute comparability imposes "a too exacting scientific standard."[53] Comparative researchers emphasize that experimental and statistical methods themselves are imperfect, and they focus on the question of how best to overcome the acknowledged limitations of the comparative method. They give particular emphasis to strategies of case selection and to process tracing to supplement basic controlled comparisons. I return to process tracing in the next section and focus here on case selection strategies.

Within-case comparisons of hypothesized relationships at different points in time within the same case are particularly powerful. Such longitudinal comparisons generally take the form of most-similar systems designs because they are able to hold so many variables constant: political history, culture, institutions, geography, and other variables that change only slowly (if at all) over time. This facilitates the identification of the small number of variables that vary with the dependent variable of interest. George, and George and Bennett, use the label of the "congruence method" for this kind of within-case comparison within the methodology of structured, focused comparison.[54] Rosen's analysis of Indian strategic doctrine over time and how it changed as a function of changing strategic culture within a relatively static geopolitical context is a good example of a longitudinal most-similar systems design.[55]

Another useful case study design, which facilitates the control over additional variables, involves a combination of across-case and within-case comparisons. A good example is Snyder's study of imperial overextension, which combines comparisons of the behaviors of different states, different individuals within the same state, and the same individuals within a given state over time.[56]

While comparative researchers argue about the relative merits of alternative case selection strategies, one thing they agree on is that the strategy of random selection of cases, so useful in large-N statistical analysis, will often generate serious biases in small-N research.[57] Scholars generally argue that the analysis of a limited number of cases is better served by a careful selection of nonrandom cases.

One of the most serious dangers in the deliberate selection of nonrandom cases involves overrepresenting cases from either end of the distribution of a key variable. This is particularly serious when it involves cases with extreme values on the dependent variable, because it results in a reduction in the slope estimates generated by regression analyses (assuming linear relationships) and thus underestimates the strength of causal effects.[58] Selecting cases with very high (or very low) values of the dependent variable are common as well as consequential. Precisely because of their historical significance and high salience, major wars and major revolutions are the kinds of cases that most attract scholarly attention.

The selection of cases with extreme values of the independent variable does not have a comparable effect, and this asymmetry is the basis for warnings of the dangers of "selecting on the dependent variable."[59] These problems apply to small-N as well as large-N research.[60] Research based on the selection of cases with no variation at all on the dependent variable ("no-variance" designs) are particularly problematic. In the study of the causes of war, for example, if the analyst were to examine only wars and observed a particular factor present in every case, she could not infer that this factor systematically contributes to the outbreak of war because there might be countless other cases not observed in which the same factor were present but in which war did not occur.

Although warnings to avoid selecting on the dependent variable have been useful in reminding students of wars, revolutions, and other phenomena to include cases in which wars or revolutions did not occur—to think about the "dogs that didn't bark"—the mechanical application of this basic rule obscures some important situations in which selection of observations on the dependent variable might be a useful strategy for research. One involves the strategy of studying deviant cases for the purpose of analyzing why they deviate from theoretical predictions. Another is situations in which the hypothesis posits necessary conditions for the occurrence of a particular outcome.

For testing hypotheses that posit necessary conditions, the basic logic of inference requires the selection of cases on a particular value of the dependent variable because the only observations that can falsify the hypothesis in question are those in which a particular outcome of the dependent variable occurs in the absence of a condition that is hypothesized to be necessary for that outcome.[61] If the hypothesis is deterministic in its assertion of necessary conditions, and if one is confident that no measurement error is present, the observation of a single case in which the posited condition is absent is in principle sufficient to falsify the hypothesis. If we allow for some measurement error, even a small number of anomalous cases in which the hypothesized causal factor is not present can significantly undermine our confidence in a hypothesis based on necessary conditions.[62]

Similarly, causal propositions positing sufficient conditions for a given outcome can usefully be tested through a case study research design, though here it is essential to select cases on a particular range of values of the independent variable posited to be sufficient for a given outcome.[63] If the prediction is strong and if measurement error is negligible, hypotheses positing sufficient conditions can be seriously undermined by identifying a very small number of cases in which the hypothesized sufficient condition is not followed by the predicted outcome.

The analysis gets more complicated if there is more than one necessary or sufficient condition, or if there are multiple causal paths that can lead to the same outcome. A particular condition might be necessary for one sequence to operate, and that sequence may be sufficient for a particular outcome to occur, but there may be other sequences that also lead to the same outcome but that do not involve the key condition in the first sequence. The impact of some variables may be contingent on the values of other variables, so that simple additive models will not work, and the analyst must examine the combinations or interaction effects of different sets of factors. Ragin refers to this general problem as "multiple conjunctural causation."[64] He argues that standard statistical methods cannot easily deal with this phenomenon,[65] and develops "qualitative comparative analysis" based on Boolean algebra to identify and test combinatorial hypotheses.[66]

Another strategy for case selection for the purposes of testing theories involves what Eckstein called *crucial case studies*, which are related to the concepts of *most-likely* or *least-likely* case research designs.[67] A most-likely case is one that almost certainly must be true if the theory is true, in the sense that all the assumptions of a theory are satisfied and all the conditions hypothesized to contribute to a particular outcome are present, so the theory makes very strong predictions regarding outcomes in that case. If a detailed analysis of a most-likely case demonstrates that the theory's predictions are not satisfied, then our confidence in the theory is seriously undermined. The logic of inference is Bayesian, in the sense that the marginal impact of the data on our confidence in the validity of a hypothesis depends on our a priori judgments of the validity of the hypothesis.[68] The greater the a priori likelihood of the hypothesis, the lower the impact of confirmatory data and the greater the impact of disconfirmatory data.

Similar logic applies to a least-likely case design, which selects "hard" cases in which the predictions of a theory are quite unlikely to be satisfied because few of its facilitating conditions are satisfied. If those predictions are nevertheless found to be valid, our confidence in the theory is increased, and we have good reasons to believe that the theory will hold in other situations that are even more favorable for the theory. Least-likely case research designs follow what I call the "Sinatra inference"—if I can make it there I can make it anywhere. Most-likely case designs follow the inverse Sinatra inference—if I cannot make it there I cannot make it anywhere.

Most-likely and least-likely case designs are often based on a strategy of selecting cases with extreme values on the independent variables, which should produce extreme outcomes on the dependent variable, at least for hypotheses positing monotonically increasing or decreasing functional relationships. Alternatively, a most-likely case design can involve selecting cases where the scope conditions for a theory are fully satisfied, while a least-likely case design identifies cases in which the theory's scope conditions are satisfied weakly if at all.

A good example of a most-likely case design is Lijphart's study of political cleavages and stability in the Netherlands.[69] Pluralist theory, which was widely accepted in the discipline, argued that cleavages that cut across various social groups promoted social peace and political stability, while cleavages that were mutually reinforcing across various social groups contributed to social conflict and political instability.[70] Because there were very few cross-cutting cleavages in the Netherlands, pluralist theory predicted high levels of social conflict and low levels of political stability. By demonstrating that the opposite was true, Lijphart's analysis contradicted the unconditional statement of the theory and went a long way toward refuting it. This is a good example of the power of a well-selected individual case study to seriously undercut a widely accepted theory.[71]

The power of most-likely and least-likely case analysis is further strengthened by defining most likely and least likely not only in terms of the predictions of a particular theory but also in terms of the predictions of leading alternative theories. This builds on the idea that a theory is falsified not by the data alone but by a "three-cornered test" involving the theory, the data, and a rival theory.[72] The strongest support for a theory comes when a case is least likely for a particular theory and most likely for the rival theory, and when observations are consistent with the predictions of the theory but not those of its competitor.

A good example here is Allison's application of three models of foreign policy decision making to the Cuban missile crisis.[73] Allison argued that the missile crisis was a least-likely case for the organizational and bureaucratic models of decision making and a most-likely case for the rational-unitary model. We might expect organizational routines and bureaucratic politics to affect decision making on budgetary issues and on issues of low politics, but not in cases involving the most severe threats to national security, where rational calculations to maximize the national interest should dominate and where politics should stop "at the water's edge." If Allison could show that bureaucratic and organizational factors had a significant impact on key decisions in the Cuban missile crisis, we would have good reasons to expect that these factors would be important in a wide range of other situations.[74]

Process Tracing

The preceding discussion of case selection strategies suggests that certain kinds of individual case studies can contribute to hypothesis testing as well as to hypothesis construction. Most between-case and within-case comparisons are correlational in nature and examine whether a particular set of conditions is associated with hypothesized outcomes, while holding constant as many other factors as possible. Thus George, and George and Bennett, refer to within-case comparisons of hypothesized relationships at different points in time within the same case as the "congruence method" and include it within the methodology of structured, focused comparison.[75]

There is another approach to within-case analysis, one that is quite common in the practice of case study research but that is often neglected in attempts to formally describe case study methodology, and that is *process tracing*.[76] Process tracing follows a different logic and tries to uncover the intervening causal mechanisms between conditions and outcomes through an intensive analysis of the evolution of a sequence of events within a case. The logic of inference is much more similar to what philosophers of history call *genetic explanation*[77] than to explanations based on covering laws and deductive nomological logic.[78]

Process tracing provides several comparative advantages for testing many kinds of intervening causal mechanisms, particularly those involving propositions about what goes on inside the "black box" of decision making and about the perceptions of actors.[79] One of the implications of the democratic peace proposition, for example, is that democracies are perceived differently than autocracies and that these differences have a significant impact on behavior. These perceptions are often better explored through small-N case study methods than through large-N statistical methods.

Case study process-tracing methods can also be extremely useful in the empirical analysis of nonlinear propositions involving critical inflection points. The testing of such propositions is extremely sensitive to the accurate identification of these inflection points. In order to avoid circular inferences, this must be done with indicators measured independently of the behavior predicted by the theory. It may be difficult to identify empirical indicators of these inflection points that are valid across a large number of cases for the purposes of a large-N analysis, and case study methods can be used to help identify these tipping points and why they occur.[80] Similarly, process tracing can be extremely useful in the exploration of path-dependent macrohistorical processes that are extremely sensitive to patterns of timing and sequence.[81]

Many proponents of case study analysis argue that process tracing has a comparative advantage over large-N statistical methods in validating intervening causal mechanisms, because statistical methods are limited to establishing correlations while case studies can trace the steps in a causal chain.[82] While there may be some truth to this argument—particularly for propositions that involve equifinality, complex and contingent interaction effects, or path dependencies— this argument goes too far and needs to be qualified. There is a tendency among some case study researchers both to underestimate the possible utility of statistical analysis for empirically differentiating among hypothesized causal mechanisms[83] and to exaggerate the utility of process tracing for this purpose.[84]

Those engaged in a close process tracing of a causal chain still face the problem identified by Hume, the impossibility of establishing causality from empirical observation. We cannot know for certain that a particular outcome y is the causal result of a set of factors x rather than another set of factors z that have been omitted from the formal analysis. Our confidence in such an inference is greatest, however, if each link in the causal chain is based on a well-established empirical regularity (probabilistic or otherwise) that has been confirmed by large-N studies or possibly comparative case studies in other comparable empirical domains.[85] It is true that we have few strong regularities in international relations, and that this limits our ability to infer causality based on covering laws. But this is a general problem of any approach that attempts to infer causality from a sequence of empirical observations, not just a problem with the covering law model.

It is more useful to think of causality as an analytical construct, a component of our theories rather than something that can be inferred directly from empirical observation.[86] All theories about the empirical world have testable implications.[87] Many of these implications concern the relative frequencies or magnitudes of readily observable events and can be best validated by large-N statistical studies. Other implications deal with hypotheses that posit necessary or sufficient conditions, that fall within the rather opaque black box of decision making, or that are for various reasons difficult to measure with validity and accuracy over large numbers of cases in different historical and cultural contexts. These implications can often be effectively analyzed through process tracing. The greater the empirical validation of the testable implications of a theory, by whatever method, the more confidence we can have in a theory, and hence in the causal mechanisms posited by the theory.

Limitations of Case Study Methods

I have argued that case studies are essential for the description, explanation, and understanding of particular historical episodes, and that they can also be useful in the development and refinement of more general theoretical propositions. Case studies can demonstrate that certain constellations of variables generate predictions with nonempty cells, even if they cannot establish the relative frequency with which the predicted event occurs. Case studies can also play a role in theory testing, particularly if the theory is very strong and makes point predictions or posits necessary or sufficient conditions. Few of our theories of international relations satisfy these criteria, however, and for the purposes of testing most theories case study methods have a number of rather serious limitations.[88]

One is the large number of variables relative to the small number of cases, which is probably the central issue in the literature on the comparative method and case studies over the past three decades. In attempting to demonstrate that her hypothesized causal variables, and not other variables, explain various outcomes, the case study researcher can achieve some degree of control through careful case selection based on most-similar or most-different systems designs, or preferably a combination of both. The researcher can gain additional leverage over her theory through most-likely and least-likely designs, defined both in terms of the theory and the leading rival theories. If a theory's scope conditions are fully satisfied, if its testable implications are precise, if measurement is valid and accurate, and if cases are carefully selected, the case study researcher can often make a plausible argument that the theory is either supported or disconfirmed for the cases under investigation.[89] It is much less likely, however, that she will be able to convincingly demonstrate that her findings are valid for comparable instances of the same phenomenon beyond her immediate study. The case study researcher gains leverage on internal validity, but only at the expense of external validity.[90]

A related problem is that case study methods cannot easily get at "probabilistic" theories, whether those theories involve probabilistic causal mechanisms or whether the operationalization of more deterministic theories involves substantial measurement error. Both kinds of theories lead to probability distributions of predicted outcomes rather than to point predictions and can be falsified with confidence only with a fairly large number of cases. This is a major strength of statistical analysis and a serious limitation of small-N research.[91]

Many case study researchers acknowledge the limitations of their method for the analysis of probabilistic relationships. Unlike large-N researchers, case study researchers want to explain *all* variation and leave to chance no variation or anomalous results, whether because of omitted variables or measurement error. Ragin and Zaret, for example, argue that comparative methods "are logical and not statistical in nature because they are used to identify *invariant* relationships, not statistical or probabilistic relationships . . . to identify patterns of constant association, not to explain variation."[92] Ragin argues that "the comparative method does not work with samples or populations but with all relevant instances of the phenomenon of interest. . . . [Explanations] are not conceived in probabilistic terms because every instance of a phenomenon is examined and accounted for if possible. . . . The comparative method is relatively insensitive to the relative frequency of different types of cases."[93] Similarly, Becker argues that "narrative analysts . . . are not happy unless they have a completely deterministic result. Every negative case becomes an opportunity to refine the result, to rework the explanation so that it includes the seemingly anomalous case."[94]

This emphasis on refinement and reworking is the key. Rather than stopping with a probabilistic relationship that explains a certain amount of the variation in outcomes, with omitted variables and measurement error captured by an error term, case study researchers continue to probe in an attempt to reduce further both sources of error and explain additional variation. In doing so they can generate more complete explanations, but of a smaller number of cases and with a loss of parsimony and generalizability.

It may be possible to explain nearly all variation in a handful of variables of interest in a modest number of cases, and some phenomena we want to explain might involve a relatively small number of cases (hegemonic decline, for example), but most phenomena of interest to international relations theorists occur too frequently to conduct detailed case studies of all of them. We need some means of generalizing beyond our sample of cases. Statistical methods do this through a combination of control through partial correlations and randomization of other extraneous influences, but the latter works only if N is large. Although case study methods based on least-likely or most-likely system designs permit generalization, these generalizations are based more on deductive logic (the Sinatra inferences) than empirical demonstration and must be tested on other cases.

Case study researchers face another problem: they have difficulty in assessing the relative causal weights of the various factors influencing a particular outcome, unless those factors are either necessary or sufficient for certain outcomes to result. Case study methods can be useful in determining the presence or the absence of a particular variable and its impact on the presence or absence of outcomes. They might also be able to establish empirically the *direction* of a variable's impact, and perhaps provide a very rough approximation of its impact in terms of categories of high and low. Case studies are much more limited in their ability to determine empirically the relative magnitude of various causal influences when those factors are neither necessary nor sufficient for a given outcome.[95] Because necessary or sufficient conditions are rare, this is another important limitation of case study methods.

The ability to estimate different causal effects empirically is a major strength of statistical analyses of larger numbers of cases (assuming the functional relationship is correctly specified and the key variables are measurable across cases, which can be quite problematic). Regression analyses can estimate the amount of variance explained by each variable, the additional amount of variance explained when another variable is added to the model, and the proportional effects on the dependent variable of comparable changes in each of the independent variables.

Combining Case Study and Statistical Methods

Statistical methods have their own limitations, of course, particularly concerning the validity of concepts and the operational indicators used to measure them across a large number of cases (the "unit homogeneity" assumption). Proponents of comparative case studies also worry about this problem. They talk at length about balancing the need for "conceptual traveling" (using concepts that are valid across time and space, which facilitates generalization) with the dangers of "conceptual stretching" (applying concepts in historical and cultural contexts in which they have a different meaning or are otherwise not appropriate).[96] This is not the place for a detailed comparative evaluation of the advantages and disadvantages of statistical and comparative methods, but many analysts from each methodological perspective have increasingly come to the conclusion that by combining both statistical and case study methods, researchers can use the advantages of each to partially offset the limitations of the other.

These methods can be combined in a single study or sequentially as part of a "research cycle" in a larger research program.[97] Work that integrates statistical and case study methods in a single study includes Huth's analysis of the success and failure of extended deterrence, Ray's study of the democratic peace, Martin's analysis of the role of international institutions in multilateral economic sanctions, and Simmons's study of the politics of adjustment to international economic pressures of the 1920s and 1930s.[98] Examples of the sequential integration of statistical and case study methods in a larger research program include the International Crisis Behavior Project,[99] Doyle's research program on the democratic peace,[100] and the Mansfield and Snyder project on democratization and war.[101] Although scholars agree on the utility of mixed-method approaches, and although we have begun to see more efforts of this kind, scholars have made few efforts to elaborate on exactly how different methods can be combined or the proper sequence for combining them.

While Russett, Lijphart, and others suggest a sequence involving comparative methods for refining hypotheses followed by statistical methods to test them, reversing this sequence can also be useful.[102] In the democratic peace research program, for example, statistical methods were first used to establish the extraordinarily strong empirical relationship between democratic dyads and the absence of war. Case study methods were then used to validate whether states were properly classified as democracies or nondemocracies; to explore the intervening causal mechanisms linking peaceful outcomes to the characteristics of democracies or possibly to alternative causal mechanisms; and to explore additional testable implications of the democratic peace hypothesis, including differences in leaders' perceptions of democratic and nondemocratic adversaries.[103]

Case study methods can also be usefully combined with formal rational choice theories, in part because of the difficulty of systematically measuring some of the key concepts in rational choice theory (preferences, utilities, probabilities, and informational environments, for example) across a large number of cases. In his study of the July 1914 crisis, for example, Levy empirically examined how political leaders perceived the set of feasible outcomes of the crisis and rank-ordered their preferences over those outcomes, and used this framework to anchor an analytic case study of the outbreak of World War I.[104] Examples of a more deductively structured use of rational choice theory to guide case study analysis include the "analytic narratives" research program[105] and Bueno de Mesquita's analysis of church-state relations in medieval Europe.[106]

Conclusions

In a volume on quantitative and qualitative methods it is natural to focus on questions of method. The utility of particular methods cannot be separated from questions of theory, however, and in many respects the greatest potential for advances in our knowledge about international relations remains theoretical. Developing better theories is particularly important for those who wish to test theories with qualitative methods, because the number of observations needed to test a theory is inversely related to the precision of a theory's predictions. The stronger the theory, the more specific its predictions, and the greater the divergence in predictions from those of a rival theory, the fewer the number of observations that are necessary to provide a satisfactory test of the theory, and thus the more valuable case study methods. This is why case study methods are so useful for testing theories that posit necessary or sufficient conditions. If theories are weaker, and if divergence between the predictions of competing theories is smaller, a greater number of observations are required for a meaningful empirical test, and case study methods are at a disadvantage.

Building better theories is not the only solution here. Another is to think more carefully about the testable implications of existing theories, in terms of quality as well as quantity. Competing theories generate both overlapping and divergent testable implications. The former are irrelevant for testing competing theories, but the latter are critical. As a field we have probably done a better job building theories and developing methods for testing them than thinking creatively about identifying those testable implications of competing theories that are most divergent and consequently most conducive to providing definitive tests between rival theories. The application of all methods would benefit from more imaginative and clever thinking at this critical stage of research, at the juncture of theory and research design, but qualitative case study researchers have particularly strong incentive to do this.

Notes

1. Giovanni Sartori, "Concept Misinformation in Comparative Politics," *American Political Science Review* 64, no. 4 (1970): 1033–53.
2. Idiographic inquiry aims to describe, understand, and interpret individual events or a temporally and spatially bounded series of events, whereas nomothetic inquiry aims to generalize about the relationships between variables and, to the extent possible, construct lawlike propositions about social behavior. See Jack S. Levy, "Explaining Events and Testing Theories: History, Political Science, and the Analysis of International Relations," in *Bridges and Boundaries*, ed. Colin Elman and Miriam Fendius Elman (Cambridge: MIT Press, 2001), 39–83.
3. For example, Brecher, Steinberg, and Stein argued that most empirically oriented foreign policy analyses were single country in orientation and "usually devoid of theoretical value." Michael Brecher, Blema Steinberg, and Janice Stein, "A Framework for Research on Foreign Policy Behavior," *Journal of Conflict Resolution* 13, no. 1 (1969): 75.
4. Sidney Verba, "Some Dilemmas in Comparative Research," *World Politics* 20, no. 1 (1967): 111–27; Adam Przeworski and Henry Teune, *The Logic of Comparative Social Inquiry* (New York: Wiley, 1970); Arend Lijphart, "Comparative Politics and the Comparative Method," *American Political Science Review* 65, no. 3 (1971): 682–93; Arend Lijphart, "The Comparable Cases Strategy in Comparative Research,"

Comparative Political Studies 8, no. 2 (1975): 133–77; Harry Eckstein, "Case Study and Theory in Political Science," in *Handbook of Political Science,* vol. 7, ed. Fred I. Greenstein and Nelson W. Polsby (Reading, Mass.: Addison-Wesley, 1975), 79–138; Alexander L. George, "Case Studies and Theory Development," in *Diplomacy: New Approaches in Theory, History, and Policy,* ed. Paul Lauren (New York: Free Press, 1979), 43–68.

5. Arthur Stinchcombe, *Constructing Social Theories* (New York: Harcourt, Brace and World, 1968); Neil Smelser, "The Methodology of Comparative Analysis," in *Comparative Research Methods,* ed. Donald P. Warwick and Samuel Osherson (Englewood Cliffs, N.J.: Prentice Hall, 1973), 42–86; Theda Skocpol and Margaret Somers, "The Uses of Comparative History in Macrosocial Inquiry," *Comparative Studies in Society and History* 22, no. 2 (1980): 156–73.

6. Barrington Moore Jr., *Social Origins of Dictatorship and Democracy: Lord and Peasant in the Making of the Modern World* (Boston: Beacon Press, 1966); Charles Tilly, ed., *The Formation of National States in Western Europe* (Princeton, N.J.: Princeton University Press, 1975); Theda M. Skocpol, *States and Social Revolutions* (New York: Cambridge University Press, 1979).

7. Charles Tilly, *Big Structures, Large Processes, Huge Comparisons* (New York: Russell Sage Foundation, 1984); Alexander George and Timothy McKeown, "Case Studies and Theories of Organizational Decision Making," in *Advances in Information Processing in Organizations,* ed. Robert Coulam and Richard Smith (Greenwich, Conn.: JAI Press, 1985), 43–68; Charles C. Ragin, *The Comparative Method* (Berkeley: University of California Press, 1987); Charles C. Ragin, "Introduction to Qualitative Comparative Analysis," in *The Comparative Economy of the Welfare State,* ed. Thomas Janoski and Alexander M. Hicks (New York: Cambridge University Press, 1994), 299–319; Barbara Geddes, "How the Cases You Choose Affect the Answers You Get: Selection Bias in Comparative Politics," in *Political Analysis,* vol. 2, ed. James A. Stimson (Ann Arbor: University of Michigan Press, 1990), 131–50; Charles C. Ragin and Howard Becker, eds., *What Is a Case?* (New York: Cambridge University Press, 1992); David Collier, "The Comparative Method," in *Political Science: The State of the Discipline II,* ed. Ada Finifter (Washington, D.C.: American Political Science Association, 1993), 105–19; David Collier and James Mahoney, "Conceptual Stretching Revisited: Adapting Categories in Comparative Analysis," *American Political Science Review* 87, no. 4 (1993): 845–55.

8. Gary King, Robert Keohane, and Sidney Verba, *Designing Social Inquiry* (Princeton, N.J.: Princeton University Press, 1994).

9. David Collier and James Mahoney, "Insights and Pitfalls: Selection Bias in Qualitative Research," *World Politics* 49, no. 1 (1996): 56–91; Douglas Dion, "Evidence and Inference in the Comparative Case Study," *Comparative Politics* 30, no. 2 (1998): 127–46; Timothy J. McKeown, "Case Studies and the Statistical World View," *International Organization* 53, no. 1 (1999): 161–90; Charles C. Ragin, *Fuzzy-Set Social*

Science (Chicago: University of Chicago Press, 2000); Alexander L. George and Andrew Bennett, *Case Studies and Theory Development* (Cambridge: MIT Press, forthcoming).

10. For further information about the consortium, and for syllabi on qualitative methods, see http://www.asu.edu/clas/polisci/cqrm.

11. There has been an interesting reversal in the "balance" between the literature on qualitative methodology and applications of qualitative methods over the last three decades. In the early 1970s, the methodological literature on comparative and case study methods failed to adequately reflect the theoretical and methodological sophistication of some of the best applied research in the field, including work by George and Brecher. Today, applied qualitative research probably lags behind developments in the literature on the methodology of qualitative analysis. Alexander L. George and Richard Smoke, *Deterrence in American Foreign Policy* (New York: Columbia University Press, 1974); Michael Brecher, *The Foreign Policy System of Israel: Setting, Images, Process* (New Haven, Conn.: Yale University Press, 1972).

12. Lijphart, "Comparative Politics and the Comparative Method," 682.

13. Collier, "The Comparative Method," 105.

14. Andrew Bennett, "Case Study: Methods and Analysis," in *International Encyclopedia of the Social and Behavioral Sciences,* ed. Neil J. Smelser and Paul B. Baltes (New York: Pergamon, forthcoming).

15. Ragin and Becker, *What Is a Case?*

16. See George, "Case Studies and Theory Development."

17. If we think of cases as instances of broader theoretical categories, and if we acknowledge that historians are more idiographic in orientation than are political scientists, it should not be surprising that historians rarely use the term *case.* Levy, "Explaining Events and Testing Theories."

18. John Walton, "Making the Theoretical Case," in Ragin and Becker, *What Is a Case?* 122.

19. For further discussion of whether cases are made or found see Ragin and Becker, *What Is a Case?*

20. See King, Keohane, and Verba, *Designing Social Inquiry.*

21. Eckstein, "Case Study and Theory in Political Science," 85.

22. Lijphart, "Comparative Politics and the Comparative Method," 691.

23. Eckstein, "Case Study and Theory in Political Science," 96–123. The first two in the list come from Verba, "Some Dilemmas in Comparative Research."

24. Eric Hobsbawm, *On History* (New York: New Press, 1997), 109. Because of their "total" orientation toward the subject matter, atheoretical case studies do not fit the definition of a "case" as an *instance* of a broader class of phenomena.

25. Stephen Van Evera, *Guide to Methods for Students of Political Science* (Ithaca, N.Y.: Cornell University Press, 1997); Levy, "Explaining Events and Testing Theories."

26. One example is Allison's use of three alternative theoretical frameworks to interpret the Cuban missile crisis (though this study had theo-

retical aims as well). Graham Allison, *Essence of Decision: Explaining the Cuban Missile Crisis* (New York: Little, Brown, 1971).

27. Christopher Achen and Duncan Snidal, "Rational Deterrence Theory and Comparative Case Studies," *World Politics* 41, no. 2 (1989): 145.

28. Ibid., 169.

29. The widely accepted injunction against testing a theory or hypothesis against the same *data* from which it was generated does not preclude us from testing hypotheses generated in a case study against different data from the same case. If a case study of the origins of the cold war leads a researcher to formulate hypotheses about enduring rivalries, and if those hypotheses have implications for the termination of enduring or militarized rivalries, then those same hypotheses can be tested against evidence from the end of the cold war. Indeed, one of the most useful ways of validating a historical interpretation is to derive additional implications of that interpretation for other aspects of that particular historical episode.

30. George and Smoke, *Deterrence in American Foreign Policy.*

31. Robert Bates, Avner Greif, Margaret Levi, Jean-Laurent Rosenthal, and Barry Weingast, *Analytic Narratives* (Princeton, N.J.: Princeton University Press, 1998).

32. George, "Case Studies and Theory Development."

33. See James Lee Ray, *Democracies and International Conflict* (Columbia: University of South Carolina Press, 1995); John Owen IV, *Liberal Peace, Liberal War: American Politics and International Security* (Ithaca, N.Y.: Cornell University Press, 1997).

34. Noted in Howard S. Becker, "Cases, Causes, Conjunctures, Stories, and Imagery," in Ragin and Becker, *What Is a Case?* 209.

35. George, "Case Studies and Theory Development"; George and Bennett, *Case Studies and Theory Development.*

36. David Collier and Steven Levitsky, "Democracy with Adjectives: Conceptual Innovation in Comparative Research," *World Politics* 49, no. 3 (1997): 430–51. One caveat is worth noting. If the proliferation of subtypes and of the number of causal paths leading to them is taken to an extreme, the theory might explain all the anomalies but only at the cost of a loss of analytic power and parsimony. This problem is minimized if the variety of causal paths is linked to the conditions under which each is most likely to occur.

37. Arthur L. Stinchcombe, *Theoretical Methods in Social History* (New York: Academic Press, 1978), 5.

38. Lijphart, "The Comparable Cases Strategy in Comparative Research," 159.

39. Hugh Stretton, *The Political Sciences* (London: Routledge and Kegan Paul, 1969), 245–47.

40. Lijphart, "Comparative Politics and the Comparative Method," 692.

41. The many variables/small-*N* problem affects the use of case studies for theory testing but not for describing and explaining individual historical episodes or for generating or refining hypotheses to be tested by other means. If the universe of cases is relatively small (hegemonic

wars, for example), and if the aim of case study analysis is to generate hypotheses, there may be advantages of using a small number of cases. This leaves a maximum number of cases for hypothesis testing, given the need to test hypotheses on data that are independent of the data from which the hypotheses are generated.

42. See also King, Keohane, and Verba, *Designing Social Inquiry*, 217–18.

43. Lijphart, "Comparative Politics and the Comparative Method," 685.

44. Lijphart, "The Comparable Cases Strategy in Comparative Research," 163.

45. Campbell also emphasized the utility of a single case, but only after retracting his earlier argument to the contrary. Donald Campbell, "Degrees of Freedom and the Case Study," *Comparative Political Studies* 8, no. 2 (1975): 178–93. See also McKeown, "Case Studies and the Statistical World View."

46. John Frendreis, "Explanation of Variation and Detection of Covariation: The Purpose and Logic of Comparative Analysis," *Comparative Political Studies* 16, no. 2 (1983): 255.

47. John Stuart Mill, *A System of Logic* (1875; reprint, London: Longman, 1970).

48. Przeworski and Teune, *The Logic of Comparative Social Inquiry*; Theodore Meckstroth, "'Most Different Systems' and 'Most Similar Systems': A Study in the Logic of Comparative Inquiry," *Comparative Political Studies* 8, no. 2 (1975): 133–77.

49. This terminology has generated some confusion. Mill defines agreement or difference in terms of the *dependent* variable, whereas most similar and most different are defined in terms of *explanatory* variables. Thus Mill's method of agreement is equivalent to a most-different systems design, and Mill's method of difference is equivalent to a most-similar systems design.

50. Lijphart, "The Comparable Cases Strategy in Comparative Research"; Smelser, "The Methodology of Comparative Analysis."

51. Przeworski and Teune, *The Logic of Comparative Social Inquiry*.

52. Mill, *A System of Logic*, bk. 6, ch. 7.

53. Lijphart, "Comparative Politics and the Comparative Method," 688.

54. George, "Case Studies and Theory Development"; George and Bennett, *Case Studies and Theory Development*.

55. Stephen Peter Rosen, *Societies and Military Power: India and Its Armies* (Ithaca, N.Y.: Cornell University Press, 1996).

56. Jack Snyder, *Myths of Empire: Domestic Politics and International Ambition* (Ithaca, N.Y.: Cornell University Press, 1991).

57. See King, Keohane, and Verba, *Designing Social Inquiry*, 126; Collier and Mahoney, "Insights and Pitfalls."

58. King, Keohane, and Verba, *Designing Social Inquiry*, ch. 4.

59. Ibid., ch. 4.

60. Collier and Mahoney, "Insights and Pitfalls."

61. An example involving large-*N* designs is Bueno de Mesquita's empirical analysis of his core hypothesis that a positive expected utility for war is a necessary condition for a state to initiate war. Bruce Bueno de

Mesquita, *The War Trap* (New Haven, Conn.: Yale University Press, 1981).

62. Dion, "Evidence and Inference in the Comparative Case Study."

63. The proposition that democracies rarely if ever go to war with each other posits that joint democracy is a sufficient condition for peace, and for the analysis of this proposition scholars focus exclusively on cases of democratic dyads.

64. Ragin, *The Comparative Method.*

65. Ragin argues that because the number of interaction effects necessary to capture combinatorial effects increases rapidly with the number of variables, serious degrees-of-freedom problems result. Ibid. For a new statistical approach to modeling multiple causal paths see Bear F. Braumoeller, "Modeling Multiple Causal Paths: Logic, Derivation, and Implementation" (manuscript, Harvard University, 2000).

66. For an application of Boolean models to the study of deterrence see Frank P. Harvey, "Practicing Coercion: Revisiting Successes and Failures Using Boolean Logic and Comparative Methods," *Journal of Conflict Resolution* 43, no. 6 (1999): 840–71.

67. Eckstein, "Case Study and Theory in Political Science," 113–23.

68. This assumes that measurement error is low.

69. Arend Lijphart, *The Politics of Accommodation* (Berkeley: University of California Press, 1968).

70. See David Bicknell Truman, *The Governmental Process* (New York: Knopf, 1951).

71. Ronald Rogowski, "The Role of Theory and Anomaly in Social-Scientific Inference," *American Political Science Review* 89, no. 2 (1995): 467–70. Lijphart also contributed to theory construction by suggesting hypotheses on why the theory of cross-cutting cleavages broke down in the Netherlands. See Lijphart, *The Politics of Accommodation.*

72. Imre Lakatos, "Falsification and the Methodology of Scientific Research Programmes," in *Criticism and the Growth of Knowledge,* ed. Imre Lakatos and Alan Musgrave (Cambridge: Cambridge University Press, 1970), 91–196.

73. Allison, *Essence of Decision.*

74. Similarly, if the rational-unitary model cannot explain state behavior in an international crisis as acute as the one in 1962, we would have little confidence that it could explain behavior in situations of noncrisis decision making.

75. George, "Case Studies and Theory Development"; George and Bennett, *Case Studies and Theory Development.*

76. Ibid.

77. Ernest Nagel, *The Structure of Science* (Indianapolis: Hackett, 1979), 564–68; W. B. Gallie, "The Historical Understanding," *History and Theory* 3, no. 2 (1963): 149–202.

78. Carl G. Hempel, "The Function of General Laws in History," *Journal of Philosophy* 39 (1942): 35–48.

79. Experimental methods may be superior for testing many of these hypotheses because of their ability to control for extraneous variables. It

is often difficult, however, to generalize from laboratory settings that do not incorporate the relevant political variables and that cannot fully replicate the stakes and emotions inherent in the contexts of foreign policy decision making.

80. Sidney Tarrow, "Bridging the Quantitative-Qualitative Divide in Political Science," *American Political Science Review* 89, no. 2 (1995): 474.

81. Paul Pierson, "Increasing Returns, Path Dependence, and the Study of Politics," *American Political Science Review* 94, no. 2 (2000): 251–67; Ira Katznelson, "Periodization and Preferences: Contributions of Comparative Historical Social Science" (manuscript, Columbia University, 2000).

82. Andrew Bennett and Alexander L. George, "The Alliance of Statistical and Case Study Methods: Research on the Interdemocratic Peace," *APSA-CP Newsletter* 9, no. 1 (1998): 6–9.

83. A good example of a large-N study that empirically distinguishes between alternative causal mechanisms within the black box of decision making is Schultz's statistical test of competing institutional constraint and informational signaling models of the democratic peace proposition. Kenneth A. Schultz, "Do Democratic Institutions Constrain or Inform? Contrasting Two Perspectives on Democracy and War," *International Organization* 53, no. 2 (1999): 233–66.

84. Many of those committed to large-N analysis exaggerate in the opposite directions.

85. Clayton Roberts, *The Logic of Historical Explanation* (University Park: Pennsylvania State University Press, 1996).

86. Thomas D. Cook and Donald T. Campbell, *Quasi-Experimentation* (Chicago: Rand McNally, 1979), ch. 1.

87. If theories have no observable consequences, they cannot explain the variation in outcomes that is the primary task of social science, and hence those theories have no explanatory power. This does not imply that all theories are easy to test.

88. For an argument that hypotheses involving necessary conditions are more common, see Gary Goertz and Harvey Starr, eds., *Necessary Conditions: Theory, Methodology, and Applications* (Lanham, Md.: Rowman and Littlefield, forthcoming).

89. These are very demanding criteria. They lead Lieberson to conclude that Mill's methods cannot be applied if the number of cases is small because they do "not allow for probabilistic theories, interaction effects, measurement errors, or even the presence of more than one cause." Stanley Lieberson, "Small N's and Big Conclusions," in Ragin and Becker, *What Is a Case?* 105–18; Stanley Lieberson, "More on the Uneasy Case for Using Mill-Type Methods in Small-N Comparative Studies," *Social Forces* 72 (June 1994): 1225–37. Multiple causes and interaction effects can probably be dealt with, but only by increasing the number of cases in order to encompass all possible interaction effects. This creates a practical problem for intensive case study methods. Some case study researchers acknowledge this problem and supplement Mill's methods with process tracing (George and Bennett,

Case Studies and Theory Development), while others have adopted a Boolean-based "qualitative comparative analysis" (Ragin, *The Comparative Method*).

90. The large-N researcher makes the opposite trade-off.
91. Whether social science theories can have causal mechanisms that are truly probabilistic—as opposed to those that reflect measurement error, the misspecification of functional forms, or omitted variables that have yet to be understood and specified—is quite problematic. See Wesley C. Salmon, *Four Decades of Scientific Explanation* (Minneapolis: University of Minnesota Press, 1990), and George and Bennett, *Case Studies and Theory Development*. I prefer to speak of a theory's probabilistic testable implications rather than probabilistic causal mechanisms. My thinking (admittedly provisional) on this complex issue has benefited from conversations with Andrew Bennett.
92. Ragin and Zaret, 1983, 744.
93. Ragin, *The Comparative Method*, 15. Ragin's exploration of the relevance of the logic of fuzzy sets for social science analysis is an attempt to deal with the problem of measurement error and probabilistic testable implications. Ragin, *Fuzzy-Set Social Science*.
94. Becker, "Cases, Causes, Conjunctures, Stories, and Imagery," 212.
95. Dorothy Vaughan, "Theory Elaboration: The Heuristics of Case Analysis," in Ragin and Becker, *What Is a Case?* 184. Proponents of "offense/defense theory," for example, theorize about whether military technology favors the offense or defense but fail to establish the magnitude of this effect relative to that of the balance of material capabilities and related variables. Sean M. Lynn-Jones, "Offense-Defense Theory and Its Critics," *Security Studies* 4, no. 4 (1995): 660–91.
96. Sartori, "Concept Misinformation in Comparative Politics"; Collier and Mahoney, "Conceptual Stretching Revisited."
97. Skocpol and Somers, "The Uses of Comparative History in Macrosocial Inquiry."
98. Paul Huth, *Extended Deterrence and the Prevention of War* (New Haven, Conn.: Yale University Press, 1988); Ray, *Democracies and International Conflict*; Lisa L. Martin, *Coercive Cooperation* (Princeton, N.J.: Princeton University Press, 1992); Beth A. Simmons, *Who Adjusts?* (Princeton, N.J.: Princeton University Press, 1994).
99. Brecher, *The Foreign Policy System of Israel*; Michael Brecher, with Benjamin Geist, *Decisions in Crisis: Israel, 1967 and 1973* (Berkeley: University of California Press, 1980); Michael Brecher and Jonathan Wilkenfeld, *A Study of Crisis* (Ann Arbor: University of Michigan Press, 1997).
100. Michael Doyle, "Liberalism and World Politics," *American Political Science Review* 80, no. 4 (1986): 1151–70; Michael Doyle, *Ways of War and Peace* (New York: Norton, 1997).
101. Edward D. Mansfield and Jack Snyder, "Democratization and the Danger of War," *International Security* 20, no. 1 (1995): 5–38; Jack Snyder, *From Voting to Violence: Democratization and Nationalist Conflict* (New York: Norton, 2000).

102. Bruce M. Russett, "International Behavior Research: Case Studies and Cumulation," in *Approaches to the Study of Political Science,* ed. Michael Haas and Henry S. Kariel (Scranton, Penn.: Chandler, 1970), 425–43; Lijphart, "Comparative Politics and the Comparative Method."

103. Bennett and George, "The Alliance of Statistical and Case Study Methods."

104. Jack S. Levy, "Preferences, Constraints, and Choices in July 1914," *International Security* 15, no. 3 (1990–91): 151–86.

105. Bates et al., *Analytic Narratives.*

106. Bruce Bueno de Mesquita, "Popes, Kings, and Endogenous Institutions: The Concordat of Worms and the Origins of Sovereignty," *International Studies Review* 2, no. 2 (2000): 93–118.

CASE STUDY METHODOLOGY IN INTERNATIONAL STUDIES

From Storytelling to Hypothesis Testing

Zeev Maoz

Introduction

Case study is arguably the most common methodology in international studies—including both international relations and comparative politics. It is also the most widely used across subfields of the discipline. Whereas other methodologies are more likely to be associated with certain substantive subfields than others, the case study methodology appears to be sufficiently flexible so as to apply to almost all subfields. For example, it is difficult to imagine the application of game theory or rational choice models to a constructivist analysis of change in international politics, but a case study employing the concepts and tools of constructivism can be easily imagined.[1] Likewise, the analysis of singular events—such as the collapse of the Soviet Union—through the use of quantitative studies using a large number of cases is difficult to apply. Yet an in-depth case study of such events is easily conceivable.[2]

It is ironic that—compared with other disciplines where case studies have been used extensively, for example, psychiatry and clinical psychology, social work, social anthropology, ethnography, and history—the discussion of the foundations and considerations of this approach in political science is relatively sparse and surprisingly unsophisticated. This is reflected not only in the methodological discussions of political case studies. It is evident even more in the practice—or malpractice—of case study methodologies in empirical research.

The present paper offers a general criticism of the way case study methodology has been used in research on international studies. I do not suggest that case study is an improper or somehow inferior methodology in such research. On the contrary, from several perspectives, case study research is not only a proper methodology in such research but offers several advantages that other methodologies do not. The problem is not in the method; it is in the way it was used. Consequently, I attempt to offer some elements of a general strategy that can serve the systematic use of case study research—mostly, but not exclusively—for confirmatory purposes.[3]

I focus on three aspects of the case study methodology that are symptomatic of the misuse of this methodology and suggest some principles and considerations for a more proper use of this approach: case selection, case design, and cross-case comparison. All three aspects of case study methodology have a major impact on the ability to make inferences from the study. This paper is designed as follows. First, I discuss some of the important properties of case study methodology for confirmatory purposes. I argue that case study may in many ways have significant advantages over other methods used in political research. However, to capitalize on those advantages, systematic considerations of selection, design, and comparative analysis must be built into the research projects. Second, I discuss the problems of case selection, case design, and cross-case comparison using examples of two projects that have relied on case study research: projects on deterrence theory[4] and the case study examination of the democratic peace proposition.[5] Finally, I discuss the implications of these issues for theory development and theory testing in international relations.

Some Advantages of Case Study Research Methodologies

The literature on case study in political science,[6] as well as more general treatment of this approach,[7] suggests that case study approaches have some important properties that make them useful as a research methodology. Some of these points are important not only in justifying case study research, in general, but also in preferring this approach to other research methodologies in some cases.

Cost-Effective Exploratory Research Methodology

Case studies enable exploratory analyses at relatively low cost of resources. Conducting surveys or data collection projects on large populations just to discover that the variables used in the study are not the central ones in the process under study may be an exercise in futility. Even the cost of a pilot study on these issues may be exorbitant.

Process Tracing

Good theories are more than a set of hypotheses each positing a bivariate relationship between variables. Good theories—especially in a social context—outline a process that tells a story; the more dynamic the story, the more aesthetically attractive the theory.[8] However, capturing a story in a set of quantitative analyses is often a very complex operation (for example, requiring multiple equation models, dealing with endogeneity problems, and so forth). Due to both methodological and practical problems, quantitative analyses often break theories into sets of bivariate or multivariate hypotheses that do not capture the dynamic aspects of the stories. For that reason, the actual ability to match a hypothetical story that contains an explicit process derived from the theory with an actual story is a unique feature of the case study method.

Just as the ability to match a theory-derived story with the actual case is important, so is the potential of uncovering deviations between the actual story and the theory. By uncovering differences between the expected story and the actual story, a researcher could identify factors that are outside of the theory but that account for important facts in the historical case.

Unveiling Causal Processes in Nonevents: Dogs That Don't Bark and Dogs That Don't Growl

An important attribute of in-depth case study research is the ability to uncover nonevents and their characteristics. Unfortunately, this attribute has received little attention in the literature, and—until quite recently—was underexplored in actual research. Briefly, certain theoretical approaches attempt to account for nonbehavior (alienation-related explanations of nonturnout in voting, democracy and peace, deterrence success, and so forth). In such cases, process tracing can attempt to uncover the dynamics of the propositions not only by examination of deviant cases but also by examining whether the proposition offers a viable explanation in "typical" cases that seemingly "match" the hypothesized nonbehavior. I will elaborate on this property later.

Systematic Comparison of Processes

A given variable x might be related to another variable y across a large number of cases, but the process by which these variables may be related can differ across cases. For example, education may be related to income across a large number of individuals, but the relationship may be different for different individuals. For example, a subset of the cases (people) fitting the rich-educated bracket may be actually old-money people, that is, people who were born into affluent families and whose education was determined by their family origins. Another subset of rich people may well be people who come from lower-income families and, due to their drive to obtain high education, acquire education-related wealth. Likewise, some poor people may be born into poor families who were unable to support their education, thus making for second-generation poverty. On the other hand, another subset of poor people may be people who come from affluent families who failed to adjust to structural changes in the economy (for example, rural families who lost their wealth as prices for agricultural products declined).

Systematic comparison of processes may reveal unspecified features of the theory, even theories that were supported by quantitative evidence. As such, the ability of mixing exploratory and confirmatory analysis in the same design is an important feature of case study research.

In light of these advantages, it is evident why case study approaches have been so commonly used in political research. Yet it is ironic that little cumulation has been accomplished in international studies due to the use of case studies. In the following sections, I discuss some basic features of case study use and misuse in international relations in order to suggest a more coherent general strategy for the use of such research in the future.

Case Selection

There is a nearly complete lack of documentation of the approach to data collection, data management, and data analysis and inference in case study research. In contrast to other research strategies in political research where authors devote considerable time and effort to document the technical aspects of their research, one often gets the impression that the use of case study absolves the author from any kind of methodological considerations. Case studies have become in many cases a synonym for freeform research where everything goes and the author does not feel compelled to spell out how he or she intends to do the research, why a specific case or set of cases has been selected, which data are used and which are omitted, how data are processed and analyzed, and how inferences were derived from the story presented. Yet, at the end of the story, we often find sweeping generalizations and "lessons" derived from this case. We are also confronted by policy prescriptions from time to time. In other instances authors pay lip service to the methodology, citing typically outdated methodological discussions of case study approaches in political science, and jump straight into the story. The studies in which authors make a conscious effort to spell out what exactly they attempt to do and why they are doing what they are doing are extremely few.

Consider the inferential leaps in the discussion of methodology in one of the—admittedly more insightful—studies of the cold war:

> We examine the impact of deterrence and compellence in detailed studies of the two most acute Soviet-American confrontations of the last quarter century: the Cuban missile crisis of 1962 and the crisis in the Middle East in 1973. *We demonstrate the largely pernicious consequences of threat-based strategies in most cases. . . .* In our reconstruction of both crises, we explore the contradictory consequences of nuclear threats and nuclear weapons.
>
> *These two crises provide a window on the broader relationship between the United States and the Soviet Union during the Cold War. . . . We contend that the strategy of deterrence prolonged the Cold War and helped to extend the life of communism in Eastern Europe and the Soviet Union.* We agree with George Kennan that the primacy of military over political policy in the United States during the Cold War delayed rather than hastened the great changes that finally overtook the Soviet Union. *By looking through the window of these two crises at the broader superpower relationship, we can learn lessons that will be applicable to the prevention, management, and resolution of international conflict beyond the Cold War.*[9]
>
> *The choice of the Cuban missile crisis needs little justification.* It is universally recognized as the most acute confrontation of the Cold War. . . .
>
> *We analyze a second Soviet-American crisis to control for the idiosyncrasies of Cuba.* The most serious superpower crises

of the postwar period were over Berlin in 1948–49 and 1959–62, and the crisis that erupted in the Middle East in 1973. . . . *A comparative analysis of the missile crisis and Berlin would have been unrepresentative of Soviet-American interaction in crisis during the Cold War.* The crisis in 1973 seemed a more appropriate choice. *It reflects a different style of crisis management in Moscow and in Washington, but includes a strong nuclear threat, and in contrast to the Cuban missile crisis, took place in an era of strategic parity and superpower detente.*[10]

As noted in the italicized portions of this text, a lot of heroic inferences are made from this study that uses two cases. Not only do the authors suggest important insights about the conduct and consequences of the cold war, but they also offer "insights" about crisis management and conflict resolution in more general domains. How credible are these insights?

When authors discuss methodological considerations prior to the case study, they typically focus on case selection. The selection of cases is admittedly a very important element of a more systematic approach to case study research.

Case selection must be based on a basic understanding of the properties of the population from which the cases are drawn. This understanding requires—first and foremost—a clear and unbiased definition of the general population. In the examples discussed herein, authors in many cases make a sincere effort to define the population of cases; however, this definition is often biased. Therefore, the actual choice of cases—no matter how carefully done—tends also to be biased.

Both qualitative deterrence literature and the qualitative democratic peace literature focus on crises. They offer elaborate explanations of why crises are important laboratories for testing propositions about deterrence or about the democratic peace. In both bodies of literature, however, crises represent only a small subset of the relevant cases for most types of investigation.

The key problem in biased case selection lies in improper logical definition of the research problem. Often, it emerges out of a truncated specification of the problem. Consider a typical research problem posed by deterrence theory: do deterrence threats work, and if so, under what conditions are these threats effective? We expect, as do most deterrence theorists, that states resort to this strategy in situations where two parties confront each other in a conflict of interests. At least one party (the challenger) is perceived to want to change a certain political, territorial, or economic status quo. The other party (the defender) wishes to defend it. The deterrence situation consists of the defender making a series of threats that promise to impose an excessively high cost on the challenger should it act forcefully to change the status quo. We typically consider deterrence effective if it results in the peaceful (or nonviolent) preservation of that status quo. So, let us lay out the problem in terms of the relationship between deterrence and status quo preservation. Suppose we studied two hundred crises. In each crisis we identified the challenger and the defender. We examined whether or not threats were made by the defender, whether they were credible (conveying both capability and intent), whether they were clearly communicated and clearly understood by the challenger, and so forth.

Table 1 seemingly suggests that if we coded two hundred crises, using systematic case studies or other data collection methods, we would conclude that there is fairly good evidence that deterrence is an effective war-prevention strategy.

But the context in which deterrence operates is not *crises* but *conflict,* of which crises are but one—fairly extreme—manifestation. Testing the effectiveness of threats in crisis is akin to studying determinants of election outcomes on the basis of exit polls; the information about nonvoters may be as important or more important in many respects as the information about voters' choices. Therefore a truncated definition of the population is apt to lead to biased inferences. Consider the example discussed previously. Suppose that

Table 1. Deterrence and Status Quo Preservation

Effectiveness of Threats	Status Quo Preservation		Total Row
	Preserved (crisis resolved)	Not Preserved (war)	
Effective threat	60	40	100
	(45)	(55)	
Ineffective/no threat	30	70	100
	(45)	(55)	
Total column	90	110	200

Note: $\chi^2 = 18.2$, $df = 1$, $p < .01$, Yule's Q $= 0.556$.

the actual crises constitute a small proportion of all *crisis opportunities,* that is, situations that could potentially erupt into crises. Suppose, also, that once we examined those opportunities, we got the distribution shown in table 2.

Now, the positive relationship between effective deterrence threats and status quo preservation turned into a negative one. This inferential fallacy stems from selection bias. It can arise out of quantitative research as well as from case studies. However, because case studies by definition represent a much smaller—and typically nonrandom—subset of all cases, the likelihood of inferential bias is substantially higher than in quantitative analysis.

The same logic applies to the democratic peace case study literature. Simply replace the labels of the independent variable by Joint Democracy/No Joint Democracy, and one gets the same type of problem.

How do we deal with these problems? First and most important, we must recognize that case selection entails the risk of selection bias and thus of resultant inferential bias. Second, it is important to recognize the context in which case selection—under any type of systematic confirmatory method—is conducted. This context defines to a large extent the range of solutions available to the researcher. The elements of the context are twofold: the logic of experimental design and the concept of sampling. A step toward proper case selection process requires considering both elements.

Without going into the logic of experimental design in great detail, the basic notion is that two processes operate simultaneously, one

Table 2.

Effectiveness of Threats	Status Quo			
	Preserved— No Crisis	Preserved— Crisis Resolved	Not Preserved— War	Total Row
Effective threat	200 (250)	60 (22)	40 (28)	300
Ineffective/ no threat	800 (750)	30 (68)	70 (82)	900
Total column	1,000	90	110	1,200

Note: $\chi^2 = 107.1$, *df* = 2, gamma = -0.541, $p < .01$.

with an experimental treatment and one without. However, assignment of subjects to groups is based on systematic establishment of similarity among subjects. Specifically, the control and experimental groups should be identical (or similar) in terms of their distribution on a number of variables that are considered confounding (that is, likely to affect the outcome of the process). Where the two groups differ is in the type of experimental treatment they receive. Thus, selection of subjects is done on the basis of confounding variables, and assignment to groups determines the value of independent variable (no treatment, treatment Type I, Type II, etc.). The purpose of these features is to ensure control and variability in independent variables. Once the distribution of the overall population of subjects has been determined in terms of the potential confounding variables, the assignment of subjects to control/experimental groups is based on randomizing within strata. The implication is that cases are not selected on the basis of the distribution of the dependent variable but rather in terms of variability in a set of potentially confounding variables. More important, if a systematic selection of cases is conducted, it should be on the basis of the distribution of independent variables rather than on the basis of the dependent variable.

Sampling requires a similar process. A certain part of the process must allow for systematic stratification of the population in terms of confounding variables, and in terms of the independent variables. If we wish to examine hypotheses about the relationship between foreign policy positions and presidential candidate preferences, and we have reason to believe that candidate preference is also affected by race and region, we want to make sure that the racial and regional makeup of the sample is proportional to the distribution of these variables in the general population. This requires systematic—or stratified—sampling. Another part of the process, however, requires randomization.

Sampling and experimental design provide some clues for a rational case selection strategy in case study design. The following principles may be applicable:

1. Understand your theory. Lay out the hypotheses and spell out their status. Do your hypotheses state that X is a necessary condition for Y, a sufficient condition, or both?
2. Define what kind of variability is required to test your theory. In general, the greater variability you allow for in your design, the more credible your conclusions are likely to be.

3. Identify potentially confounding variables—that is, factors that are likely to affect the dependent variable/s that are not explicitly included in your theory.
4. Explicitly define your population, and assess the consequences of the criteria of inclusion and exclusion in your population.
5. Attempt, as far as possible, to determine how the population is distributed on the confounding variables.

Case Study Design

The key difference between exploratory and confirmatory case studies lies in case design. An analogy might help explain this point. Consider a detective trying to solve a murder case. By the time the detective gets to the crime scene, the basic contours of the situation have been worked out by the crime scene police teams (forensics, pathology, etc.). The identity of the victim (if available) is known, the murder weapon (if available) is identified, and the proximate time of death is established. Other basic information is gleaned just at the outset, and this information forms the basis of the detective's investigation. The first stage of the investigation entails identifying suspects. If several suspects are identified, the detective tries to narrow the range of suspects by matching details about each of them with the characteristics and clues from the murder scene and other background material. Alibis are checked by matching the suspects' whereabouts with the proximate time of murder. Motives are investigated, and physical evidence from the murder scene or related material (e.g., fingerprints, DNA, blood stains, etc.) is matched with suspects and their belongings. A process of elimination ensues until one person emerges as the prime suspect.

At that point, a case for the prosecution is prepared. At this stage, the process consists of integrating the evidence into one coherent story that contains a logical and consistent explanation of the motive and the process leading up to the murder (as well as postmurder events that are connected to the crime scene, such as cover-up attempts—hiding the body, the murder weapon, destroying physical evidence, and so forth). A hypothetical reconstruction of the murder is conducted (assuming that the suspect does not confess). That reconstruction, then, is the case that the prosecutor presents in court.

Just as in the analogy, by the time we start our case study, the basic contours of the case are known. We know the outcome (we have a body). We know the background of the case (we know something about the victim). And in the typical case study, we know the basic details of the story. Given this starting point, exploratory case study is equivalent to the first stage wherein the detective attempts to narrow down the range of suspects to one suspect. Confirmatory case study consists of preparing the case for prosecution in court once a prime suspect has been identified.

The confirmatory advantages of the case study approach over other methods lie—as we have pointed out—in the ability to contrast the actual facts with an *expected process.* The case study can reveal the *why*—the causal mechanism—underlying a relationship of the type *x is related to y* specified in a hypothesis. However, if we are to take full advantage of this feature, we must specify a priori what kind of process we expect to unveil.

The design problem in case studies consists of a backward-reasoning process—from an outcome to an antecedent explanation. This is especially the case with respect to those studies dealing with "familiar" cases, the general elements of which are known. The art of case study design is—to a large extent—the art of reconstruction. In exploratory design we typically work with a kind of "protocol" about the general class of problems within which the case falls. Just like the detective looking for suspects, the search is based on a general strategy, derived from cumulative past experience of the detective herself and of the general discipline of police investigation. But the general "protocol-based" search must gradually adapt to the specific case in point.

In confirmatory research, the design of the case is theory driven. The theory lays out a hypothetical story. The researcher's role is to operationalize the story in the particular case. Specifically, the confirmatory case study design requires the a priori specification of a story that contains traceable elements, each of which is derived from the theory. Because research in the positivist tradition assigns greater significance to refutation than to confirmation, two types of elements are required, confirmatory and disconfirmatory. A prosecutor preparing a case for court must work on the assumption that she must prove guilt beyond reasonable doubt, whereas the defense's task is just to invoke reasonable doubt. Thus, physical evidence connecting the suspect to the murder scene (e.g., DNA from a hair sample found on the murder victim) is important confirmatory evidence. However, if the suspect has a firm alibi, this counts more in the final judgment. For that reason, the fact that there exists a plausible story and that the expected facts derived from that hypothetical story match the actual case is not sufficient to support the theory. The case study must be able to disconfirm other plausible explanations or to eliminate possible evidence that generates reasonable doubt about the theory in the case. Very often, the facts that match the story are not necessarily the opposite of the facts that invoke a reasonable doubt. Therefore, the design of the case must be based on both a priori specification of evidence *for* the theory and evidence *against* the theory.

This requirement is especially important if what is under investigation is not one explanation but two competing ones, which is often the case in political research. In this case, the design requires not only specifying the evidence *supporting* each theory individually but also identifying the areas of converging expectations of both theories and—most important—the *area of competing expectations*. It is only in this area of competing expectations that evidence consistent with one of the theories is inconsistent with the other. The assumption that whenever two theories compete with one another all the expectations derived from them must also compete with each other often drops even the most experienced researcher into an inferential trap.[11]

Finally, as previously mentioned, one of the underused attributes of the case study methodology is the ability to overcome the problem of "the dog that didn't bark" (or even "the dog that didn't growl").[12] Consider the case of deterrence theory. One of the common complaints of scholars who use case studies to study deterrence theory is that we can only study deterrence failures, because such instances are easily identifiable. Since successful deterrence induces inaction, it is impossible to actually test cases of deterrence success. This is analogous to claims that whereas the failure of legal sanctions in preventing criminal behavior is clearly detectable, the success of such sanctions cannot be fully and reliably established.

But deterrence theory lays out a fairly straightforward process of war prevention. We first establish an initial condition of the presence of a conflict of interest. One side is said to harbor operational plans or general intentions to forcefully change a territorial and/or political status quo. The other side views that status quo as highly desirable and wants to preserve it. The defender then chooses to base its plan to preserve the status quo on deterrence, that is, on a set of credible threats promising to inflict disproportionate punishment on the challenger if it attempts to change the status quo by force. The threat is then communicated to the would-be challenger and, if effective, is supposed to alter the challenger's calculus of conflict initiation. What a good case study of deterrence success can do is define observable traces of such a process. Specifically:

1. Specify evidence for an intention by the challenger to upset the prevailing status quo by force (e.g., documentary or other indications of operational plans, political discussions, mobilization efforts, force design and deployment, and so forth).

2. Identify the deterrence effort and its operational manifestations. Specify what would constitute evidence that the defender identified either specific or general risk to the status quo emanating from the challenger: a decision process by the defender resulting in a deliberate policy of deterrence; a policy that communicates the deterrence threat and backs it up by concrete steps that are designed to establish or foster its credibility (e.g., military force-building and deployment, civilian mobilization, trip-wiring policies, boosting public support for the policy, etc.).

3. Identify evidence suggesting that the challenger has received and digested the deterrent threat and has incorporated the implications of the threat (the probability that the defender would carry it out, the cost of implementing the action subject to retaliation, and so forth).

4. Identify evidence suggesting that the decision-making process entailed specific consideration of the threat and its implications. In other words, evidence should suggest that there were references by the decision makers to the deterrent threat and to the intentions and capabilities of the defender.

5. Identify evidence suggesting that the calculus of the decision was altered due to the deterrent threat, so that the decision taken may well have been different from the one actually made either without the challenger's awareness of a deterrent threat or if the threat had been seen as less credible than it actually was. One approach to demonstrating the effect of the deterrent threat on the challenger's decision process is to conduct sensitivity analysis on elements of the credibility of the threat. For example, if decision makers referred to a certain level of probability that the defender would carry out the threat, assess how crucial this assessment was in determining decisional outcomes. Alternatively, if decision makers indicated that they might incur a certain cost as a result of the defender's imple-

mentation of its threatened response, consider what might have been the effect on the final outcome had the cost not been incorporated into the decision calculus, or if the extent of loss would have been lower.[13]

6. If the decision making of the challenger ends with a decision to refrain from violating the status quo or to delay decision on violation of the status quo, then we have a "candidate" for deterrence success. Otherwise, this is a fairly clear case of deterrence failure.

7. In a candidate case for deterrence success, we must make sure that our case is valid beyond a reasonable doubt.[14] How do we do that? As noted earlier, two related operations must take place. First, we must make sure that the evidence for our theory is consistent with the theory's expectations as well as inherently logical. For example, we must show a correspondence between the nature of the threat issued by the defender and the way the threat was perceived by the challenger. We must be able to identify the impact of the deterrent threat on the challenger's calculus in prespecified terms, and so forth.

   Second, we must be able to identify potential evidence that may be consistent with alternative explanations and eliminate it. For example, if it is argued that public opinion or competing elites in the challenger's state opposed foreign policy adventurism, we must be able to identify how domestic considerations might have affected the challenger's calculus and examine how pivotal such evidence was in accounting for the final decisional outcome.[15] This could be done by employing a similar test to the one applied in order to determine how pivotal were deterrence-related considerations in the challenger's decision.

8. If possible, it is advisable to develop "crucial experiments" or discriminating tests, where competing theories offer contradictory predictions about a set of observable facts. This is a difficult operation, and not always feasible. Yet it is worth the effort because—if successfully conducted—it removes analytical ambiguities of the sort discussed previously.

The significance of testing evidence for a theory against competing explanations cannot be overemphasized. Severe headaches are associated with migraines and hypertension, which are treated by painkillers, but such headaches are also associated with aneurysms or brain tumors that require high-risk surgery to treat. If neurosurgeons or general practitioners were to design their diagnostic processes as many of us design our case studies, the courts would have been overflowed with malpractice suits, and the number of unnecessary surgical operations would have been extremely high.

Some examples from the case studies on the democratic peace can serve to demonstrate both the problem and avenues for dealing with it. Layne examines the Fashoda Crisis of 1895–98 between France and Britain.[16] Layne also examines a series of crises that pitted France against Great Britain between 1830 and 1848.[17] Rock examines U.S.-Anglo relations over the 1845–1930 era.[18] These studies examine why crises between democracies did not escalate into war in an effort to test the normative and institutional explanation of the democratic peace proposition. In these studies, the authors lay out a set of hypotheses emerging, *in their view*, from the democratic peace and the political realist paradigms in order to examine whether democratic norms and institutions or *Realpolitik* considerations averted war in these crises.[19]

Because in none of these studies is there an a priori outline of a process that should follow from these sets of hypotheses, facts are presented in a manner suggesting that their selection and presentation were chosen deliberately to refute one theory and support another. For example, Layne's discussion of the 1830–32 "crises" between France and Britain over the Belgian question seems to ignore the seemingly negligible fact that in reality both France and Great Britain were on the same side of the issue: both supported Belgian independence from Holland, and both resisted Prussian attempts to reannex Belgium to Holland (and to involve Russia in the process). The debate between France and Great Britain in these crises was in fact over a British fear that a highly assertive action by France against Holland would provoke a combined Prussian-Austrian-Russian attack. Because of domestic reasons, the British feared that they would be drawn into such a war on France's side but against their own personal wishes. Examining the crises of 1830–32 strictly in a French-British context, without examining the broader context— wherein France used force successfully against the Dutch and both Britain and France joined forces to deter Prussia and Russia from aiding the king of Holland—suggests sloppy historical work apart from a weakly designed case study.[20]

But beyond creating the impression that history has become a victim of a certain theoretical inclination, the principal problem of these case studies is that none of the facts presented by the authors suggests that if one explanation is meaningful, the other is not. In fact, both domestic politics, institutional constraints, and hardcore realpolitik calculations may have played a role in each and every instance discussed by the authors. Because the two sets of hypotheses are spelled out such that they could both be additively valid (or additively false), they in fact support the findings of previous studies on the democratic peace that both *realpolitik and normative or structural factors* account for changes in the probability of dyadic conflict.[21] Both case studies that attempt to study the phenomenon of peaceful termination of crises between democracies failed to specify a critical test, thus inhibiting any meaningful inferences about the validity or limitations of the democratic peace proposition.

Cross-Case Comparison

Just as one must carefully design the research of an individual case, it is imperative to design a priori the comparison of cases. All those who have written about the use and strategy of case study research in political science have pointed out that case studies are useful confirmatory methods only if the results could be generalized beyond the cases. Let us return to our murder case analogy to illustrate this point. Each murder case is unique and must be treated as such by an investigator. It has its individual victim, its specific circumstances, and of course, its murderer/s. As such it is seemingly ungeneralizable. However, if this were the case, either anybody could solve murder cases or nobody could. The fact that some people specialize in murder investigations implies that cumulative experience matters. The underlying assumption must be that no matter how unique each case may be, there are underlying characteristics of many murder cases that are similar across individual victims, circumstances, and perpetrators. The structure of such investigations is, in general, quite similar, and so is the structure of the prosecution's work once a suspect is identified. That cumulative experience may matter is a significant point in police work. But experience can make a difference only if an investigator is capable of inferring meaning from both similar and dissimilar features of a given case with respect to other cases. To be able to infer such meaning, a person must have in mind a "typical" structure of murder cases—so that each case can be matched against this structure.[22]

Thus, in comparative case study design, a necessary condition for generalization is a systematic design of individual cases and the execution of case studies in a manner that allows a fair comparison. There needs to be an underlying hypothetical story that guides the collection of data and the account of each case so that the final results of individual cases can be meaningfully compared with each other. The purpose of this underlying story is to enable the researcher to both match facts and detect mismatches. For example, in the outline of the deterrence process, we required that the challenger understand the deterrent threat in the terms intended by the defender. If the facts of an individual case suggest that this was not what happened in reality, we have a problem of communication. How this problem affects the challenger's decision process is something that becomes very significant as an indicator of the theory's propositions.

An important part of the difficulty of drawing meaningful inferences from the case study literature on deterrence and the democratic peace stems from the fact that different case studies are based on different hypothetical stories (when such stories are given by the authors to begin with). This is typically the case when edited volumes seek to "test" a set of hypotheses derived from a given theory or research program. An examination of the Jervis, Lebow, and Stein volume on deterrence and the Fendius-Ellman volume on the democratic peace suggests that each author went pretty much on his or her own in terms of the methodology of individual cases.[23] Without denying that many of these case studies offer important insights into the workings of deterrence theory, it is clear that any general inferences from these cases as a whole are virtually impossible. This is, first and foremost, because it is impossible to tell whether the inferences derived from an individual case—even if intrinsically valid in terms of the case itself—are due to the inherent characteristics of the case, the decision makers involved, the specifics of the dyadic or regional context, or the different design of the study by the author.[24]

Suppose we were to design an experiment on the effect of a certain drug on the rate of recovery of patients from pneumonia. Suppose we decided to replicate this experiment several times and assigned each experiment to another person. Suppose each person was instructed to divide the subjects into experimental and control groups, but we did not provide the experimenters with details of the experimental design. Now, suppose that once we collect the data from the experiments we notice that the age groups of the subjects varied across experiments: one experimenter used young subjects, whereas another experimenter used adults, and still another experimenter used older subjects. The experimental and control groups differed also in terms of the timing of the intervention: in one case the drug was given to subjects at an early stage of the disease, whereas in another it was administered at an advanced stage of the disease. Also, the dosages of the drug given to subjects varied substantially across experiments. Now, how are we to interpret variations in results across experiments? Are they due to the unstable effects of the drug or to the variations in the design in the experiment? Given the large number of factors that distinguished the experimental designs, it is impossible even to start assessing these questions. What is obvious is that this project can hardly constitute any type of evidence regarding the potential effect of the drug on the rate of recovery from pneumonia.

When single authors develop comparative case studies, there is clearly more structure in the design than one can expect in an edited volume or a series of books, each written by a different person. The work of George and Smoke on deterrence suggests that there is an underlying theoretical structure that guides the cases studied therein.[25] In that case, the specific design of the case study is rather loose and couched in a series of questions the authors ask about the given case. Nevertheless, the ability to compare the cases of deterrence failure in this study is far more reliable than in the other examples cited herein.

Comparative case study takes us into the realm of replication. For that reason we must bear in mind the principles guiding replicative research while designing such a project. Replication is not necessarily duplication. Rather it is a process where the principal characteristics of the original design are preserved, but in most cases, at least one characteristic is altered, so that the original experiment can be generalized under controlled conditions. To use our pneumonia drug example, if the original experiment was administered to patients in the 15-to-45-year-old age group, we may want to replicate the original experiment (using identical dosages, on subjects at the same stage of the disease, with a similar male-female mix) now employing subjects in the 46-to-70-year-old age group. The next replication may vary the dosage while keeping other characteristics constant, and so forth. This implies that unless we control some fundamental elements of the case study design, we may not be able to compare across cases. This brings us to some basic principles of comparative case design:

1. Case design must assume that all cases contain some fundamental similarities as well as fundamental differences. The purpose of a common design is to sort out, as much as possible, which elements of the process in each case match the hypothetical story that underlies the theory being tested, and which are unique to the case.

2. The most important principle of cross-case comparative design is transparency. Let the reader know the criteria by which the comparison is conducted and by which inference is derived in cross-case comparison.

3. Develop a cross-case comparative design. Specify what features of the process in each case are crucial for the ability to make inferences from the case with respect to the theory tested in the study. Identify at the outset which cross-case variabilities are not necessarily detrimental to your theory. (For example, in the case of deterrence theory, one may argue that a fairly accurate perception of the deterrent threat by the challenger is a pretty crucial element of the ability to test the effect of deterrence on the preservation or change of the status quo. On the other hand, the structure of the decision-making body in the challenger—small group, individual, or large cabinet—may be of less importance as long as all or most participants in that body knew that they were contemplating violation of a status quo against a deterrent threat.)

4. Define standards of inference from multiple cases in light of possible variability in results across cases. Note that a perfect fit between all cases and the theory arouses suspicion because history is seldom fully accountable by a single theory, no matter how good the theory. The typical situation is that some cases support the theory while others do not. More likely, the typical situation is that some cases fit a subset of the elements of a theory, while other cases fit another subset of the theory.

   For example, suppose that in our hypothetical study of deterrence, we have three cases that are fully consistent with a relationship between effective deterrence and preservation of the status quo. (Two were cases where deterrent threats were credible, were properly communicated, and were shown to have prevented the challenger from violating the status quo, and one was a case where the deterrent threat was not credible and the challenger ended up acting to change the status quo by force.) Suppose that two more cases were cases that provide rather clear evidence against the theory. (In both cases deterrent threats were credible and perceived as such by the challenger, but the latter nevertheless went ahead and launched an attack.) Finally, in three additional cases, evidence was mixed. (In one case the defender had the will and capacity to carry out the threat, but the challenger was not fully aware of the nature of the red line [or trigger] of the deterrent threat. In two other cases, the challenger's decision makers who had been aware of the threat and the consequences of violating the status quo were nonetheless forced into action by domestic public opinion or by the pressure of allies.)

How are we to interpret deterrence theory in light of this kind of mixed evidence? Statistical tests have clear standards to determine whether a hypothesis is supported or refuted (e.g., the probability of Type I error). What are the standards for case study? Clearly, it is impossible to apply the rules of inference used in statistical analysis to case study research. No matter how many cases are compared, they probably do not make for a minimum number enabling statistical analysis–like inference.[26] It is difficult to establish rules of thumb for such situations. Yet two principles are crucial. First, list the evidence— for, against, and mixed—explicitly in the comparison. Second, whatever the final verdict, clearly the qualifications need to be stated explicitly and be consistent with the strength of evidence.

5. State the possibly confounding factors that your case studies revealed. If these factors reappear in different cases, they suggest possible omitted variable bias. Such bias requires redefinition or refinement of the theory.

Principles of cross-case comparison are no less important than principles of case selection and case design, and more effort should be put into developing systematic processes of comparison in case study research than exists currently in the methodological work on qualitative research in general and case study research in particular.

Conclusion

As noted, in recent years there have been some methodological improvements that are available to scholars who wish to use case study methodology to test theories. Unfortunately, these advances have gone largely unnoticed by most practitioners of this methodology in international studies. More often than not, readers of case studies get the impression that case selection and case design issues are presented as lip service to methodology and that cross-case comparison criteria are almost always left unspecified. This paper suggests some elements of a strategy that may help make case study research a more scientifically meaningful methodology than it has been in the past. By treating explicitly considerations of case selection, case design, and cross-case comparison, we may be able to capitalize on the many and important properties of case study research in the context of testing political theories systematically.

Several general principles should guide the use of a given methodology for confirmatory purposes.

Transparency

For a case study to have any confirmatory value, the design must be transparent. Readers must understand what was studied in the case, what was included and what was excluded, how evidence was collected, and how it was processed. Finally, the considerations of the analysis and weighting the evidence in the process of making substantive inference must be explicit. Transparency serves several purposes. First, it allows detection of the underlying assumptions of the various decisions made in the research. Second, it allows replication. Third, it enables meaningful criticism. All these elements are crucial for scientific progress.

Adequacy

A methodology must fit the nature of the problem to be examined. This is less of a problem for case study research than for other methodologies because of the flexibility of the method, but it is important to understand that not all methods can be applied to all problems. On the other hand, a more common problem in science is that there are multiple methods that can adequately treat a certain problem. In such cases the researcher's choice of the method may be based on which one is the most effective in terms of the theory tested, in terms of the nature of the data, and in terms of practical considerations such as time, budget, and so forth.

Limitations and Evolution of Methodologies

There is no perfect methodology. In science we often think of experimental design as being the most "scientific" methodology because of the ability to achieve control in everything but the specific variable that is being manipulated. We tend to treat all other methodologies as somewhat inferior to an experimental design. It is important to note, however, two things about experimentation that are even truer about less "reliable" methodologies. First, experimentation is useful only if and when it is replicated. Replication establishes not only whether the findings in any given experiment hold up when repeated. Rather, replication allows identification of the limits of generalizability of a given set of experiments. That is, replication allows researchers to establish up to what level of variability in experimental conditions the effect of the independent variable holds up. In contrast to a growing tendency to replicate findings in quantitative research on international problems, case study research shows little or no effort to replicate findings and approaches of previous research. Typically, the variability across sets of case studies testing given theories is so large that any comparison is meaningless. Standardization of case study research using more systematic and transparent criteria of case selection, case design, and cross-case comparison may move us a great distance toward replication in case-based research.

Second, the experimental method itself is dynamic and constantly undergoing improvement. If we were to compare methodology textbooks in social psychology of the 1990s to their predecessors of the 1970s and 1960s, we would observe major changes in the methodology of experimental design. The same applies to the evolution of quantitative methodologies—even in the context of international relations research.[27] The same applies to case study methodology. There are important innovations in case study research. Some of these innovations take place in other substantive domains that use case studies. It is important to be aware of them and see whether they could be incorporated into our studies.

Openness to Multimethod Research

Each methodology has some liabilities and weaknesses. Also, generalizing about a theory or making theoretical inferences requires testing for the theory's robustness. We have noted the importance of replication in establishing robustness of a given theory. However, it is important to note that robustness can and should be tested across methods. If inferences are based on a given methodology, then the theory's propositions should be more suspect than if those inferences hold across studies using different methodologies. For that reason, we must be open to using multiple and varied methodologies to test our theories.

The significant advances in international studies over the years reflect constantly growing theoretical, substantive, and methodological pluralism in the field. In the process, we often make mistakes. Science learns both from the mistakes and from the accomplishments of previous research. This was an effort to reflect upon the use of case studies in international relations in order to help improve future research.

Notes

1. Alexander Wendt, *Social Theory of International Politics* (Cambridge: Cambridge University Press, 1999).
2. The notion that single events cannot be used to confirm or refute general theoretical arguments has long been rejected. See Gary King, Robert O. Keohane, and Sidney Verba, *Designing Social Research: Scientific Inference in Qualitative Research* (Princeton, N.J.: Princeton University Press, 1994), 11–12.
3. The present paper does not attempt to replace the extensive literature on case studies in general or in international studies in particular. There are several good texts on the subject. (King, Keohane, and Verba, *Designing Social Research*, is by far the best book on the subject.) Rather, it attempts to highlight some issues in case study research that have received relatively little attention in the methodological literature and almost no attention in actual research using case studies.
4. Alexander L. George and Richard Smoke, *Deterrence in American Foreign Policy: Theory and Practice* (New York: Columbia University Press, 1974); Robert Jervis, Richard Ned Lebow, and Janice Gross Stein, *Psychology and Deterrence* (Baltimore: Johns Hopkins University Press, 1985).
5. Miriam Fendius-Ellman, ed., *Paths to Peace: Is Democracy the Answer?* (Cambridge: MIT Press, 1997).
6. Arend Lijphart, "Comparative Politics and the Comparative Method," *Comparative Politics* 65, no. 3 (1971): 682–98; Harry S. Eckstein, "Case Study and Theory in Political Science," in *Handbook of Political Science*, vol. 1, *Political Science: Scope and Theory*, ed. Fred Greenstein and Nelson W. Polsby (Menlo Park, Calif.: Addison-Wesley, 1975); Alexander George, "Case Studies and Theory Development," in *Diplomacy*, ed. Paul G. Lauren (New York: Free Press, 1979); Alexander George and Timothy J. McKeown, "Case Studies and Theories of Organizational Decision Making," *Advances in Information Processing in*

Organizations 2, no. 1 (1985): 21–58; King, Keohane, and Verba, *Designing Social Research*, 43–46; Stephen Van Evera, *Guide to Methodology of Students of Political Science* (Ithaca, N.Y.: Cornell University Press, 1997); Andrew Bennett, "Causal Inference in Case Studies" (paper presented at the annual meeting of the American Political Science Association, Atlanta, 1999).

7. For example, John W. Creswell, *Qualitative Inquiry and Research Design: Choosing among Five Traditions* (Beverly Hills, Calif.: Sage, 1998); Jacques Hamel, *Case Study Methods* (Thousand Oaks, Calif.: Sage, 1993); Robert Stake, *The Art of Case Study Research* (Thousand Oaks, Calif.: Sage, 1995).

8. Charles Lave and James G. March, *Introduction to Models in Social Science* (New York: Wiley, 1974).

9. Richard N. Lebow and Janice Gross Stein, *How We All Lost the Cold War* (Princeton, N.J.: Princeton University Press, 1993), 4–5. Italics added.

10. Ibid., 7. Italics added.

11. See for example the interesting study of diagnosis of breast cancer in David M. Eddy, "Probabilistic Reasoning in Clinical Medicine," in *Judgment under Uncertainty: Heuristics and Biases*, ed. Daniel Kahneman, Paul Slovic, and Amos Tversky (Cambridge: Cambridge University Press, 1982).

12. Fendius-Ellman, *Paths to Peace*, 48.

13. For example, for probability-based sensitivity analysis in case studies see the following: Janice Stein and Raymond Tanter, *Rational Decision Making: Israel's Security Choices, 1967* (Columbus: Ohio State University Press, 1980); Zeev Maoz, "The Decision to Raid Entebbe," *Journal of Conflict Resolution* 25, no. 4 (1981): 677–707. The application of a similar logic with respect to the relative effects of certain value dimensions is given in Astorino-Courtois. Astorino-Courtois conducts a value-based sensitivity analysis by sequentially removing dimensions of values that were present in a decision process to examine their effect on the stability of actual decisions. Beyond the usefulness of the technique in testing for effects of a given threat on decisions, it is a nice approach for dealing with counterfactuals in foreign policy research. Allison Astorino-Courtois, "Clarifying Decisions: Assessing the Impact of Decision Structures on Foreign Policy Choices during the 1970 Jordanian Civil War," *International Studies Quarterly* 42, no. 4 (1998): 733–54.

14. The significance of going to extra lengths to "prove" deterrence success (or failure) is due to the risk of committing a "Type I" error, that is, of rejecting the null hypothesis when it is valid. This is considered a more severe violation than committing a "Type II" error (accepting the null hypothesis when it is false). On this issue as it relates to case study research, see a later part of this section.

15. In many cases both types of evidence may be present. For example, if we were to eliminate the domestic value dimension or the "deterrence" from the challenger's decision calculus, the decision may have changed. In such cases, the evidence *for* deterrence does not outweigh the evi-

dence for alternative explanations. This suggests the need to develop more discriminatory tests.

16. Christopher Layne, "Kant or Cant: The Myth of the Democratic Peace," *International Security* 19, no. 2 (1994): 87–125.

17. Christopher Layne, "Lord Palmerston and the Triumph of Realism," in Fendius-Ellman, *Paths to Peace,* 61–100.

18. Stephen R. Rock, "Anglo-U.S. Relations, 1845–1930," in Fendius-Ellman, *Paths to Peace,* 101–50.

19. I say *in their view* because most of the hypotheses attributed to the normative or structural explanations of the democratic peace propositions are *in my view* clearly unrelated to these explanations as outlined by democratic peace scholars. See Zeev Maoz and Bruce Russett, "Normative and Structural Causes of Democratic Peace," *American Political Science Review* 87, no. 3 (1993): 624–38; Bruce Russett, *Grasping the Democratic Peace: Principles for a Postwar World* (Princeton, N.J.: Princeton University Press, 1993); and Zeev Maoz, "Realist and Cultural Critiques of the Democratic Peace," *International Interactions* 24, no. 1 (1998): 3–89, for discussion of these explanations and their misrepresentations by critics of the democratic peace propositions.

20. For a more detailed analysis of this crisis both in the French-Prussian and French-Dutch context, see the case summaries in the Web site that accompanies the book by Zeev Maoz and Ben D. Mor: *Bound by Struggle: The Strategic Evolution of Enduring International Rivalries* (Ann Arbor: University of Michigan Press, 2002). The Web site is located at http://spirit.tau.ac.il/poli/faculty/maoz/iha.html.

21. Zeev Maoz, "The Renewed Controversy over the Democratic Peace," *International Security* 23, no. 1 (1997): 193.

22. Of course, a risk entailed in such logic is that people would attempt to fit a specific case to a standard "structure," thereby downplaying or ignoring its unique features. This touches upon a long-standing debate in the literature on individual or social inference between those who claim that people typically use base rates to discount individual indicators and those who argue that people usually overestimate the significance of individual indicators at the expense of base rates. On this kind of debate as it applies to foreign policy decision making, see Zeev Maoz, *National Choices and International Processes* (Cambridge: Cambridge University Press, 1990), 201–2.

23. See Jervis, Lebow, and Stein, *Psychology and Deterrence;* Fendius-Ellman, *Paths to Peace.*

24. A similar problem characterizes the case studies conducted on crisis behavior by the International Crisis Behavior (ICB) Project, although the theoretical framework there is more developed than in the examples of deterrence studies or democratic peace studies. This is even more regrettable because most of the ICB case histories are full-volume studies. This affords the authors the opportunity to both recount in detail the specific events in the case as well as provide a more analytic account of the crisis behavior process in terms of the project's framework. The summary of the case study results provides important insights into crisis

behavior, but these are questionable in places due to differences in specific case designs. (See Michael Brecher and Jonathan Wilkenfeld, *A Study of Crisis* [Ann Arbor: University of Michigan Press, 1997]). In many cases, the authors of the individual case studies upon which this project is based do not offer any noticeable design. Some of the full-volume studies of the ICB Project include Michael Brecher with Benjamin Geist, *Decisions in Crisis: Israel in 1967 and 1973* (Berkeley: University of California Press, 1980), Alan Dowty, *Middle East Crisis* (Berkeley: University of California Press, 1984); Adeeb Dawisha, *Syria and the Lebanese Crisis* (New York: St. Martin's Press, 1980); and Avi Shlaim, *The U.S. and the Berlin Blockade 1948–1949* (Berkeley: University of California Press, 1983). Despite these problems, it must be stated that Brecher and Wilkenfeld's study is actually an outstanding and unique example of carefully conducted cross-case comparison in international studies research.

25. George and Smoke, *Deterrence in American Foreign Policy.*

26. King, Keohane, and Verba, *Designing Social Research*, 213–17. King, Keohane, and Verba assert that the minimal number of cases to make any kind of meaningful inferences in qualitative research is probably more than five, but there is no need for a comparative case design that exceeds twenty cases. Ibid., 216.

27. One of the interesting side effects of the democratic peace research program is that it invoked a lively methodological debate among quantitative scholars and a number of major innovations in testing issues related to democracy and peace and more general issues concerning international conflict. See, for example, Nathaniel Beck, J. N. Katz, and Richard M. Tucker, "Taking Time Seriously," *American Journal of Political Science* 42, no. 4 (1998): 1260–88; and Bruce Russett and John Oneal, *Triangulating Peace* (New York: Basic Books, 2000).

ABOUT THE CONTRIBUTORS

Steven J. Brams

Steven J. Brams is a professor of politics at New York University. He is the author or coauthor of fourteen books that involve applications of game theory and social choice theory to voting and elections, bargaining and fairness, international relations, and the Bible and theology. His most recent books are *Theory of Moves* (1994); *Fair Division: From Cake-Cutting to Dispute Resolution* (1996, with Alan D. Taylor); and *The Win-Win Solution: Guaranteeing Fair Shares to Everybody* (1999). He is a fellow of the American Association for the Advancement of Science and the Public Choice Society, a Guggenheim fellow, a past president of the Peace Science Society (International), and in 1998–99 was a visiting scholar at the Russell Sage Foundation.

Michael Brecher

Michael Brecher is the R. B. Angus Professor of Political Science at McGill University. Educated at McGill and Yale (Ph.D., 1953), he is the author or coauthor of eighteen books and eighty-five articles on India–South Asia, international systems, foreign policy theory and analysis, international crises, conflict and war, and the Indo-Pakistani and Arab-Israel protracted conflicts. Since 1975, he has been director of the International Crisis Behavior Project.

His most recent books are *Crises in World Politics* (1993) and *A Study of Crisis* (1997, 2000, with Jonathan Wilkenfeld). He has received two book awards: the Watumull Prize of the American Historical Association in 1960 for *Nehru: A Political Biography* (1959) and the Woodrow Wilson Award of the American Political Science Association in 1973 for *The Foreign Policy System of Israel: Setting, Images, Process* (1972). Among his other awards are the Fieldhouse Award for Distinguished Teaching, McGill (1986); the Distinguished Scholar Award of the International Studies Association (1995); the Leon-Gerin Prix du Québec for the human sciences (2000); and the Award for High Distinction in Research, McGill (2000). He has been a fellow of the Royal Society of Canada since 1976 and has held fellowships from the Nuffield, Rockefeller, and John Simon Guggenheim foundations. He has been a visiting professor at the University of Chicago, the Hebrew University of Jerusalem, University of California, Berkeley, and Stanford University. In 1999–2000 he served as president of the International Studies Association.

Bruce Bueno de Mesquita

Bruce Bueno de Mesquita is a senior fellow at the Hoover Institution at Stanford University and visiting professor of politics at New York University. Bueno de Mesquita holds a Ph.D. in political science from the University of Michigan and an honorary doctorate from the University of Groningen. He is president of the International Studies Association for 2001. His most recent books include *Principles of International Politics* (1999); *Governing for Prosperity* (2000); and the novel *The Trial of Ebenezer Scrooge* (2001).

Frank P. Harvey

Frank P. Harvey is director of the Centre for Foreign Policy Studies at Dalhousie University. He is also a professor of political science at Dalhousie. His current research interests include ethnic conflict in the former Yugoslavia, NATO military strategy and peacekeeping, and national missile defense.

His books include *The Future's Back: Nuclear Rivalry, Deterrence Theory, and Crisis Stability after the Cold War* (1997); *Conflict in World Politics: Advances in the Study of Crisis, War, and Peace* (1998, coedited with Ben Mor); and *Using Force to Prevent Ethnic Violence: An Evaluation of Theory and Evidence* (2000, with David Carment). He has published widely on nuclear and conventional deterrence, coercive diplomacy, crisis decision making, and protracted ethnic conflict in such periodicals as *International Studies Quar-*

terly, Journal of Conflict Resolution, Journal of Politics, International Journal, Security Studies, International Political Science Review, Conflict Management and Peace Science, Canadian Journal of Political Science, and several others. Professor Harvey is currently working on his next book, *Coercive Diplomacy and the Management of Intrastate Ethnic Conflict.*

Russell J. Leng

Russell J. Leng is the James Jermain Professor of Political Economy and International Law at Middlebury College. His recent works include *Bargaining and Learning in Recurring Crises: The Soviet-American, Egyptian-Israeli, and Indo-Pakistani Rivalries* (2000) and *Interstate Crisis Behavior, 1816–1980: Realism vs. Reciprocity* (1993).

Jack S. Levy

Jack S. Levy is a Board of Governors Professor of Political Science at Rutgers University. He is the author of *War in the Modern Great Power System, 1495–1975* and numerous articles on the causes of war and on foreign policy decision making. His current research projects include preventive war, great-power balancing behavior, the relationship between economic interdependence and international conflict, the militarization of commercial rivalries, diversionary theory and politically motivated opposition to war, prospect theory and international relations, and the methodology of qualitative research.

Zeev Maoz

Zeev Maoz is a professor of political science at Tel Aviv University. He is the author of several books, including *National Choices and International Processes* (1990); *Paradoxes of War: On the Art of National Self-Entrapment* (1990); *Domestic Sources of Global Change* (1996); and *Bound by Struggle: The Strategic Evolution of Enduring International Rivalries* (2002, with Ben D. Mor). His articles on international conflict, decision making, and international bargaining have been published in *American Political Science Review, World Politics, Journal of Conflict Resolution, International Studies Quarterly,* and other journals.

Michael Nicholson

Editors note: It is with sincere regret that the editors acknowledge the passing of Professor Michael Nicholson. A biography of Dr. Nicholson's work was compiled for this volume, but the editors felt it would be a fitting, and certainly more permanent, reminder of Professor Nicholson's contributions to international studies to include the following obituary written by lifelong friend and colleague Professor Amartya Sen. The obituary was published in *The Independent* newspaper October 17, 2001, and is reprinted here with their kind permission.

When the European Consortium of Political Research awarded to Michael Nicholson the first Lewis Fry Richardson Award for Lifetime Achievement (Fall, 2001), he was already very ill; he died on 4 October (2001). The date of the award, 11 September 2001, would have appeared to Nicholson to be oddly significant, as he had worked all his life on conflicts and wars, and on the possibility of peaceful resolution of disputes. From his first book, *Conflict Analysis* (1971), through his classic monograph, *Rationality and the Analysis of International Conflict* (1992), to his more recent writings on international relations, he made wonderful use of his skills and expertise as a social scientist to explore how conflicts can be avoided or defused, without resorting to violence and bloodshed.

The events of 11 September would have depressed him (as would the developments that followed), but, despite his great belief in the power of rationality, he would not have been altogether surprised by them. He had written about the limited use of reasoning and communication both in practical lives and in the theory of rational choice. Indeed, in a joint paper published earlier in 2001, Nicholson discussed the limitations from which the widely used instrumental view of rationality suffered.

Choosing the format of a self-deprecating illustration (a style of reasoning that used to be more common in England than it is now), he argued, "Given a belief that I shall go to Paradise if I kill the enemies of England, the act of killing can be construed as rational when otherwise it would not be." He went on to discuss other ways of seeing rationality, and how their relevance can be made more widely appreciated and pursued, and how rationality can be used to promote peace rather than war. Nicholson's ideas were becoming even more relevant to the contemporary world just as he was physically leaving us.

He was born in Yorkshire in 1933, son of Ernest and Irene Nicholson, and educated at Beverley Grammar School. I first met him in the autumn of 1953 shortly after we had both arrived as undergraduates at Trinity College, Cambridge, to do Economics. I came to know him very well only in my second year. By then, not only had he established himself as a brilliant student, but also his long-run interests (including rationality and conflict resolution) were already beginning to take shape. He was particularly interested in rational decision-making under uncertainty—a subject in which he would, later on, do his Ph.D. thesis and publish his earliest papers.

Apart from his warmth and kindness as a friend, I was struck by his combination of extraordinary intelligence, healthy scepticism of received doctrines, and humane commitment to use his professional training to make a positive difference to the world. I got a clearer idea of the origin of that commitment when I went with him to his home, in Beverley, near York, and met his parents. It was wonderful to hear the unalloyed voice of Christian humanism (aside from discovering how delicious Yorkshire pudding can be).

Nicholson absorbed and developed that humanism, shorn of religion (he remained an atheist throughout his adult life). Indeed, over the years he came to contrast reliance on reason with dependence on religious faith. "Once something is confined to being an Act of God," he wrote five years ago, "then there is nothing much one can do about it except pray."

"As I am sceptical of the power of prayer," he went on to say, "I put my hopes for some improvement in the human condition on the rigorous development of social scientific theory, and its testing by statistical methods, as a means of illuminating and hence perhaps influencing the future of society." That exacting programme summarises Nicholson's basic commitment rather better than any other description I can provide.

After Cambridge, he went to teach at Manchester University and then abroad—to Massachusetts Institute of Technology, Carnegie Institute of Technology (now called Carnegie-Mellon University) and the University of Stockholm. On his return to England, he took up a post at Lancaster University, and then one at University College London, before becoming in 1970 the Director of the Richardson Institute for Conflict and Peace Research, based in London and later in Lancaster. This was an excellent fit, given his strong commitment to this area of research. Aside from developing a fine institution, Nicholson also published several of his major works during his 12 years at the institute.

Then he went abroad again, to the University of Texas at Austin, to Carleton University in Canada, to the Netherlands Institute for Advanced Study (NIAS) in Holland, and to Yale University. In 1990, he became Professor of International Relations at the University of Kent at Canterbury, and finally joined Sussex University as its Professor of International Relations in 1993, and remained attached to that university until his death.

Nicholson married Christine Love in 1958. Christine, who too was a brilliant student, did English and Philosophy at Bristol University, and then did a master's degree on Kantian philosophy at Cambridge. She became involved in adult education and had a long academic career at the City Lit in London, until 1996; she died two years later. Although not particularly homebound, she was fascinated by the idea, against the current, of being a housewife, perhaps a "philosopher-housewife." In the author description that went with one of her papers in Philosophy, she insisted on being described, rather spectacularly, simply as "a Housewife." (Michael wrote in his obituarial note on her that, "though 'housewife' was never much of a theme for Christine in practice," she "bought many books on the subject.") Christine and Michael had a wonderfully close and intellectually interactive married life.

Having known Michael Nicholson closely from his undergraduate days, I am struck by the extent to which he managed to combine his intellectual discipline with his moral and political commitments. His was a life dedicated to humanity, but also lit by intelligence and guided by analysis. He remained actively engaged in his work till his death. In a joint paper with Karin Fierke (with whom he developed a personal relationship after Christine's death), published this year, he outlined an ambitious programme of integrating the formal demands of rationality with "the larger argument about rules, language and context."

A poet from Nicholson's college, John Dryden, has talked about the man who "trudged along unknowing what he sought, /And whistled as he went, for want of thought." Michael Nicholson's life is a lasting invitation to stop whistling and start thinking.

Amartya Sen

James Lee Ray

James Lee Ray is a professor of political science at Vanderbilt University. He is the author of *Democracy and International Conflict* (1995, 1998) and *Global Politics*, 7th ed. (1998). He is also the author of articles in such periodicals as *Annual Review of Political Science, British Journal of Political Science, Conflict Management and Peace Science, Journal of Conflict Resolution, Journal of Democracy, Journal of Peace Research, International Interactions, International Organization, International Studies Quarterly,* and *Political Research Quarterly,* and in numerous edited volumes. He currently serves as the editor of the journal *International Interactions.*

Harvey Starr

Harvey Starr received a Ph.D. from Yale University in 1971. His research and teaching interests include theories and methods in the study of international relations, international conflict and war, geopolitics and diffusion analyses, and domestic influences on foreign policy (revolution; democracy). His current research activities involve the two-level analysis of security management, various approaches to the democratic peace and democratic diffusion, geopolitics and the use of geographic information systems for the study of proximity and contiguity.

In 1991 he became editor of *International Interactions,* and he has served on numerous editorial boards. He has served as president of the Conflict Processes section of the American Political Science Association (1992–95) and as vice president of the American Political Science Association (1995–96). He also served on the National Science Foundation Advisory Panel for Political Science (1992–93). He previously taught at Indiana University, serving as chairman of the Department of Political Science from 1984 to 1989. In addition, he has been a visiting fellow in politics at the University of Aberdeen, Scotland (1971–72, 1978–79), as well as visiting lecturer (1985) and visiting researcher (1990) at the Centre for Defence Studies at the

University of Aberdeen. In 1996 he was a visiting fellow in the Department of International Relations, Research School of Pacific and Asian Studies, Australian National University. He is currently interim chair of the Department of Government and International Studies and Dag Hammarskjöld Professor in International Affairs at the University of South Carolina.

He is author or coauthor of eleven books and monographs and more than sixty journal articles or book chapters. His most recent books are *Anarchy, Order, and Integration: How to Manage Interdependence* (1997); *Agency, Structure, and International Politics* (1997, with Gil Friedman); *The Understanding and Management of Global Violence: New Approaches to Theory and Research on Protracted Conflict* (1999, edited volume); and *World Politics: The Menu for Choice,* 6th ed. (2000, with Bruce Russett and David Kinsella). In 1998 he won the University of South Carolina Russell Award for Research in Humanities and Social Sciences in recognition of outstanding research and scholarship.

Dina A. Zinnes

Dina A. Zinnes teaches at the University of Illinois at Urbana-Champaign. She received a Ph.D. from Stanford University in 1963. Professor Zinnes joined the department in 1980. She has received grants from the National Science and Ford foundations and the Advanced Research Projects Agency. She has been vice president and president of the International Studies Association, vice president of the American Political Science Association, president of the Midwest Political Science Association, and president of the Peace Science Society. She was a member of the council of the Inter-University Consortium for Political and Social Research. She is past editor of the *American Political Science Review* and has served on the editorial boards of the *American Journal of Conflict Resolution, International Studies Quarterly, World Politics,* and *Political Methodology.* She has also served as a member or chair of numerous professional organization committees.